Enemies Within

How the Church was Invaded by Unbelievers Vol.2

FIRST PRINTING

Billy Crone

Cover Design:
CHRIS TAYLOR

To Rhett Falkner.

Thank you for being
one of the first people
to ever reach out to me
and pull me out of
the world of illusion
I was living in.

Unknowingly
I was once a slave to lies
But you showed me
the Way the Truth & the Life
Through Jesus Christ.
And now I am not only set free
but for all eternity.

Thank you for caring
and loving me enough
to tell me the truth.
For this I am
eternally grateful.
I love you.

Contents

Preface

I never thought I'd become a Christian, let alone a Pastor. Prior to getting saved, I'd be the first one to call out Christians and label them as nothing but a bunch of hypocrites. I would also state that Pastors were just great conmen who existed not only to brainwash people but to rip them off of their cash. Then I would mock God and Jesus and the Bible with my demonic occult mentality and warped New Age thinking denigrating God's Word as a mere book whooped up by man. All I can say today is, praise God for His great lovingkindness and mercy upon me. Therefore, as a former skeptic, scoffer and persecutor of the Church and Christianity, when I entered the Church and started attending Bible College and later Seminary eight weeks after being born again, I just kept my mouth shut. I soaked in as much of God's truth as I could because I felt as a brand new Christian, who am I to say anything. I wasn't raised in the Church. I hardly knew anything about the Bible because I was the real hypocrite. I'd be the first one to tell Christians they were reading a book full of errors, yet I never even read it myself to see if that statement was true or not. Of course, upon later examination I discovered it wasn't true. But there I sat, week after week, just being a sponge, soaking it all in. However, it didn't take long to see, there was something strange going on in the Church. Lots of worldliness, tons of it. People professing to be Christians were acting like the world, speaking like the world, loving this world, promoting the things including the wickedness of this world. Now, I may not have been raised in the Church, but I could spot this deadly invasion a mile away as a former creature of the world. Unfortunately, this worldly invasion of the Church hasn't stopped right on up to this day. And now it has led to what God warned us about in the Bible nearly 2,000 years ago. The Great Apostasy. One last piece of advice; when you are through reading this book, will you please READ YOUR BIBLE? I mean that in the nicest possible way. Enjoy, and I'm looking forward to seeing you someday!

Billy Crone
Las Vegas, Nevada
2023

Chapter Nine

God's Judgment with a Relativistic Mind

As we have seen in our previous chapters, there are fakers in the church, unfortunately, doing what non-Christians do. And that is because we have allowed it to happen, and they are twisting God's truth. They say it's eros instead of agapao. They are twisting the definition of love. So that's why they say we should allow any and all sinful behavior. Then that led us next to the twisting of Biblical relations. This sick perverted version of love is now being used to try to justify how they twisted the rainbow and the Biblical view of the relationship that is marriage between a man and a woman. Now that's opened Pandora's Box. Now this twisting has led to twisted relationships of not only homosexuality and lesbianism, but now to polygamy, gender fluidity, pedophilia, and bestiality.

Why? Because as God has warned, when you go down this route, He will hand you over to a depraved mind and you will start doing things that you ought not to do. When you take a deeper look at what this depraved mind looks like, you see …

Depraved Interview
Depraved Ken Doll

Depraved Cartoons
Depraved Threat – Hate Crime – Gay Manifesto
Depraved Hypocrisy – Don't go after Muslims – Don't bake straight cakes
Depraved Threat – Want to kick us out of our country

The sad thing is that we are actually in the majority, people who have this mindset of a Biblical relationship, a man, and a woman in a marriage. But they have done their homework. They knew where to invade. They've invaded our government, they've invaded the media, they've invaded Hollywood, they've got lots of money, and they've invaded the school system. So, it looks like they have the biggest, loudest majority because they have a big, loud voice. That's not true. They just have a big, loud voice. We are the ones in the majority. We just have to keep that in mind. We just need to speak up and if revival is ever going to happen, then we the church need to get rid of our own hypocrisy!

In the last chapter we dealt with all the skeptical questions like, "Homosexuality isn't even mentioned in the Bible," or "You're interpreting that wrong," or "Love is love, what's the big deal," etc.? Now I want to revisit the depraved mind issue and see what causes that mindset to prevail. How did we go from the Judeo-Christian mindset to where we don't even know what a woman is today? We do, but our world, those with a loud voice, are saying they don't. And this is the current administration. The current administration is loading people up with this mindset, including the lady on the Supreme Court. She couldn't give a definition of what a woman was. Really? And you're on the Supreme Court? The administration is appointing these people now.

Not saying, thus sayeth the Lord, and I can't provide actual written proof of this, but I had an appointment with somebody who had an appointment with a person back in the Obama years. They were sitting on a plane next to another person professing to be a Christian. They started having a conversation with them. They were the head of the human resources department in the government. They were in charge of the health of all the government employees. So, this person began to spill the beans and say, I'm in a quandary. Here I am as a Christian and I have to sign off and give approval of this. What this person admitted was, while Trump was in office, one of the things he was doing behind the scenes, was he was appointing conservative judges, as fast as he could. I think some of that payoff has happened with the recent Roe v. Wade decision.

But what they exposed was that Obama, during his whole eight years, as fast as he could, he was flooding as many people that were pro-homosexual, pro-transvestites into every position in the government as he could. So, there is a deliberate takeover. But again, they don't go into small town USA, other than the schools and the media, but they go into positions of power and influence, the government, the media, and of course, the schools as well. This is what's going on. But how did we get to where people are lackadaisical with this? You have the conversation of, "What is a Woman?" and you're like, well, this is crazy.

How did we get to that mindset? Believe it or not, Israel suffered from the same behavior. For 450 years, longer than we have been in existence as a nation, this mindset crept into Israel and it led to non-stop cyclical, rotten, horrible behavior. That was the mindset that brought them 450 years of absolute misery. This is going to give you a state of the moral slide. They have been told that Israel at this point is completely veered off track. I mean massively off track. Let's take a look at where they're at on an average day, an average scenario of how bad it is.

Judges 17:1-6: "Now a man named Micah from the hill country of Ephraim said to his mother, 'The eleven hundred shekels of silver that were taken from you and about which I heard you utter a curse – I have that silver with me; I took it.' Then his mother said, 'The Lord bless you, my son!' When he returned the eleven hundred shekels of silver to his mother, she said, 'I solemnly consecrate my silver to the Lord for my son to make a carved image and cast an idol. I will give it back to you.' So, he returned the silver to his mother, and she took two hundred shekels of silver and gave them to a silversmith, who made them into the image and the idol. And they were put in Micah's house. Now this man Micah had a shrine, and he made an ephod and some idols and installed one of his sons as his priest. In those days Israel had no king; everyone did as he saw fit."

Judges 21:25: "In those days Israel had no king; everyone did as he saw fit."

That is exactly where we are at, and we have been running with that mindset for many decades now and basically, in a nutshell, it's what? Whatever you believe is true to you, whatever I believe is true to me. One guy says this:

"The Book of Judges describes one of the longest, bleakest epochs in Old Testament history. It covers a 450-year time frame extending from Joshua's conquest of the Promised Land until the time of Samuel—more years than America has been a nation. That entire era is riddled with horrific acts of evil, bloody conflicts and tales of human misery. It was an age of absolute moral chaos. Why? Because 'Everyone did what was right in his own eyes.'"

What is the mindset today? The people who profess to be Christians, in the church, not the world, just over half do not believe that the Bible is without error. It's about the same number, 52 – 52 percent say there is no absolute truth. That's this mindset. You're doing whatever's right in your own eyes. You make up the truth as you go. There's no absolute, whatever's true to you may not be true to me but whatever's true to me, it doesn't matter, it's all relative. You do whatever is right in your own eyes.

"The idea that everyone should get to define for himself what is right and true is a recipe for disorder and disaster."

That statement would be a fitting estimation of the moral state of our generation, too. In this increasingly secular culture, most people no longer believe there is any fixed, inviolable moral standard they need to obey. People regularly prompt one another with phrases like, "Find your own truth" and "Follow your heart"—as if that were a purely noble and upright way to live. But that, according to Scripture, is the essence of sinful foolishness.

Proverbs 12:15: "The way of a fool is right in his own eyes."

Proverbs 26:12: "Do you see a man who is wise in his own eyes? There is more hope for a fool than for him."

God condemns: **Jeremiah 13:10:** "Evil people, who refuse to hear [His] words, who stubbornly follow their own heart"

In short, **Proverbs 28:26:** "Whoever trusts in his own mind is a fool."

Why would the Bible say that? Where does truth come from? God is the truth. Jesus is the way, the truth and the life. No one comes to the Father but by Jesus. This book, the Bible, is the one thing you could stand on. A man's going to go up and down, backwards, this way, sideways, but the Bible stays the same yesterday, the same forever. This is the truth. God's the one who makes up the truth, right and wrong. And that's what caused the fall of man. **Genesis 3**, when satan got Adam and Eve to rebel against God. He says that you will be like God, knowing good from evil, you can decide what's right and wrong. That's what caused the fall of mankind. This is the mindset that crept in, not just to this individual household with Micah and his mother, but to the whole nation of Israel, it had become flooded with this.

It wasn't until God rose up the first judge, Saul. Unfortunately, what was Saul's problem? He didn't do what God said to do. Saul was more afraid of what people thought than what God said to do. Paul says in the New Testament, you don't need to be a people pleaser. He even got into the position that he went to a witch for advice. He disobeyed God and then said, "Well it wasn't that bad. I did part of what you said." Half obedience is still disobedience. He didn't follow the truth and then here comes David. 450 years and that period of Saul, when did you really start to see the heyday of Israel? David came, and he wasn't perfect, but David was a man after God's own heart. And that is what we need to get back to. Not necessarily in a political fashion, it starts with you and I. We need to get back to being that righteous judge in my house and my family, in my church and my community.

Deuteronomy 12:8: When Moses gave the law to the people of Israel, one of the chief principles he underscored for them was, "You shall not do according to all that we are doing here today, everyone doing whatever is right in his own eyes."

The idea that everyone should get to define for himself what is right and true is a recipe for disorder and disaster. It is the very definition of moral anarchy. That, of course, is the main theme in **Romans Chapter 1**. Paul goes on to chronicle the same steps of decline that are in the **Book of Judges**. It is a familiar pattern throughout human history. It is a descent into sin and depravity that has brought down every one of history's most powerful empires and currently threatens our civilization. It is a path that goes from unbelief to complete intellectual futility, and it drags whole societies through idolatry, uncontrolled lusts, degrading passions and every conceivable expression of unrighteousness. And it happens whenever people decide that everyone should do whatever is right in their own minds. The end result is "a depraved mind." **Romans 1:28:** a soul utterly given over to wickedness, irrationality, and contempt for everything that is truly righteous.

In an act of divine judgment, God withdraws His grace and allows an individual (or an entire culture) to reach that point of moral and spiritual insanity. And that is what we're dealing with today! So, as you read the transcription of this next video you are going to see the exact same mindset. It is, they did what was right in their own eyes. It's what I want to do, it's what my definition of what I think is true.

This video called "What is a Woman," opens with a beautiful birthday cake that says "Happy Birthday Twins. Two kids are blowing out the candles. There is a boy and a girl. The girl starts to open her gifts and puts a tiara on her head. She gets a miniature tea set.

Matt Walsh: *"Being a dad is one of the great privileges of my life. Give my son a BB gun and that's just about all the emotional support he needs. My daughter on the other hand ... I've heard people say there are no differences between male and female. Those people are idiots. I'm a* *husband, a father of four, I host a talk show, I give speeches, I write books, I like to make sense of things. Making sense of females is a whole other matter. Even astrophysicist Stephen Hawking who could come up with a theory on black holes was completely dumbfounded by women."*

Stephen Hawking: *"Women, they are a complete mystery."*

Matt Walsh: *"Now our culture is telling us that the differences between girls and boys don't matter. If you identify as something, then you are that thing. How do we help our kids make sense of this when they are bombarded with conflicting messages about gender and identity? Forget trying to figure out women, the real question is 'What is a Woman?'"*

The Daily Wire Presents: *"As you grow, your body changes from that of a young girl to that of a woman. Soon Molly will be a young woman having dates, going to dances in lovely romantic dresses."*

"The boy's shoulders are broad and his body muscular, while the girl's body is more curved."

Student: *"I'd like to know more about different kinds of hormones."*

The Daily Wire Presents: *"The presence of these hormones in the blood brings about many changes in the bodies of both boys and girls."*

A woman being interviewed: *"Being a woman is one of the things I like best about myself. I think you'll like it too.*

Matt Walsh: *"I like to come out here to think. Nature seems to always tell the truth. Even when we don't want to hear it. The truth is, I'm not very good at fishing. But what is truth? Is there a truth? Is this what progress looks like? Can my boys really become girls? Do I have four daughters? Do I now have to pay for four weddings? Is there a son trapped in my daughter's body? If so, how do I get him out? Are any of my kids who they claim to be? Who are these people? Who am I? I better see a therapist."*

Gert Comfrey, Gender Affirming Therapist: *"In the state of Tennessee, I'm a licensed marital and family therapist which basically means I've been trained up to think about family systems, how we were raised, how that shapes who we are today."*

Matt Walsh: *"So, on your website, if you'll bear with me quoting, you say, 'I use a combination of approaches in my therapeutic work including anti-oppression, feminist and narrative frameworks. I rely deeply on systems theory and understanding that individuals are products of, and in dialogue with, our surroundings including our families broader culture workplaces, nature, and political climates.' What does that mean?*

Gert Comfrey: *"So, thinking about the modalities that I use, I'm definitely informed by like a feminist, family therapy, and the idea is that we lived in gendered worlds where there are certain imperatives that are placed on us about who we are and what we do based on how we've been gendered. From the minute I was assigned female, I was told these are the kinds of clothing that you are going to wear, these are the types of play you're going to engage in as a child, the path that maybe your life will take because of social expectations."*

Matt Walsh: *"What do you mean by assigned female? Who assigns?"*

Gert Comfrey: *"So, most people when they are born, they are assigned to gender by the doctors.*

Matt Walsh: *"What do they base that assignment on?"*

Gert Comfrey: *"So, basically, it's based on genitalia. People looking at genitalia and deciding, this is a girl or a boy, we know now that sex and gender are so much more than just this binary. Some women have penises, some men have vaginas. That's not how gender works."*

Matt Walsh: *"How do we know that that's not true. Where do we learn that from?"*

Gert Comfrey: *"Well, I learned that from hearing from transgender people who've said, 'Oh, I'm a trans woman and just because I happen to have a penis that doesn't mean that is who I am as a person or that genitalia doesn't equal gender. Who they are is their gender expression, a trans woman, is a woman."*

Matt Walsh: *"The fluidity of these things, how do I know if I'm a woman?"*

Gert Comfrey: *"That's a great question."*

Matt Walsh: *"I like scented candles. I've watched Sex in the City. So, how do I know?"*

Gert Comfrey: *"Yeah. That question right there, is like when it's asked with a lot of curiosity. That's the beginning of a lot of people's gender identity development journeys."*

Matt Walsh: *"If my mom, who gave birth to me, is a woman, and my wife is a woman, though I haven't asked her, maybe I should. But if they are all women and also the boy who sits down with you and says, 'I think I'm a girl, actually is one, then what is a woman?"*

Gert Comfrey: *"Great question. I'm not a woman, so I can't really answer that."*

While standing outside the building after the interview…

Matt Walsh: *"I thought therapy would make me less confused. Am I the only one feeling this way? I need to hit the road and find out."*

He flies out to New York City to be the 'Man on the Street' asking passerby's questions.

Matt Walsh: *"We're talking about gender in society. Let me start with a real basic question. What is a woman?"*

1st passerby: *"A woman." (laughter)*

Matt Walsh: *"I don't want to assume, but you guys are all women?"*

1st passerby: *"Yeah, women."*

Matt Walsh: *"How would you define it, like in the simplest terms?*

1st passerby: *"That is hard. It's a stumper."*

2nd passerby: *"A woman is someone that likes to be pretty and thinks of himself as a delicate creature."*

Matt Walsh: *"I'm pretty and delicate. I could be a woman too."*

2nd passerby: *"Yes, you could."*

3rd passerby: *"Defining womanhood is just a project of someone who identifies as a woman."*

Matt Walsh: *"Yeah, but what do they identify as, they identify as a woman, but what is that?"*

3rd passerby: *"I honestly don't know."*

As he is walking down the street…

Matt Walsh: *"It's a simple question, so why is it so hard to answer? This is going to take some serious investigation. For all of human existence, women were understood to be a certain thing. So, what changed? No one can seem to answer the question now. Over 2,000 surgeries and counting, Dr. Marci Bowers is the nation's preeminent sex change surgeon. Surely, someone who does sex change surgeries can answer what a woman is."*

Now he flies to San Francisco to interview Dr. Bowers.

Matt Walsh: *"Dr. Marci Bowers, first of all, thanks for talking to us."*

Dr. Bowers: *"My pleasure."*

Matt Walsh: *"You're a world-renowned gynecologist and surgeon. You're also a transgender woman."*

Dr. Bowers: *"No, I identify as a woman."*

Matt Walsh: *"You're a woman?"*

Dr. Bowers: *"Right, I'm a woman. I mean that's my life day-to-day, but I have a transgender history."*

Matt Walsh: *"One thing on your website says, 'Gender firm GAV, gender affirming vaginoplasty. What is that exactly?"*

Dr. Bowers: *"A vaginoplasty is creation of a female vagina and vulva, we're altering the physical characteristics of the individual to fit better with a gender identity that is female."*

Matt Walsh: *"This is all constructed from the penis?"*

Dr. Bowers: *"Yes, that's right. The surgeries are quite refined in the sense that they not only do they look like female anatomy, but they also function that way. For the most part. I mean certainly it's a bit of a Faustian bargain. You know, it's not perfect."*

Matt Walsh: *"Does anyone ever regret their surgeries, or we know they do, but how often do people regret their surgeries?"*

Dr. Bowers: *"Well, actually we don't know that they do. There are legitimate detransitioners and there are people who truly feel that in their journey they may have made a mistake. Now fortunately, this is a really uncommon phenomenon.*

Matt Walsh: *"I don't know if you've ever heard of people going to the trans-abled community. These are people who are physically able-bodied but feel like they should be disabled or identify as such. For example, a man who has two arms but feels like he should have one. If a man in this kind of marginalized community went to the doctor and said I want to have my arm cut off. Do you think that ...?"*

Dr. Bowers: *"That doesn't have anything to do with gender identity."*

Matt Walsh: *"Well, if it's someone's self-identity."*

Dr. Bowers: *"Well, I'll accept it as a mental diagnosis, a psychiatric condition. I don't pretend to know what abdomenophilia is all about, but somehow it's the idea that when you know you're fascinated or charmed by having a limb or part of a limb missing, I would say that's, pardon my non-medical language, kookie."*

Matt Walsh: *"You don't see any, do you think this is totally irrelevant?"*

Dr. Bowers: *"Yep."*

Matt Walsh: *"So, the biggest, broadest question is what is a woman?"*

Dr. Bowers: *"A woman is a combination of your physical attributes and then what you're showing to the world and the gender clues that you give and hopefully those match your gender identity."*

Matt Walsh: *"The critics on the other side of this issue."*

Dr. Bowers: *"There aren't many but go ahead."*

Matt Walsh: *"There aren't many who would disagree with what you're saying?"*

Dr. Bowers: *"Well, you know the dinosaurs of the world are certainly out there."*

Now he has traveled to Aberdeen, Washington.

Matt Walsh: *"How long have you been running this shop here?"*

Don Sucher, owner Sucher & Sons Star Wars: *"Twenty-five years."*

Matt Walsh: *"Now you had an incident here a little while ago that went really viral online. Lots of reaction in the public."*

Newscaster: *"Aberdeen councilwoman, Tiesa Meskis, confronted owner Don Sucher about a sign he posted in his store."*

Don Sucher: *"One day I just put the sign up over here and he came around the corner and I thought, I recognize him. I said, 'Oh I recognize you, you're our new city councilman.' He said, 'No, I'm your new city councilwoman.' So, it was kind of on from there."*

Tiesa Meskis: *"No, it's not trans, women are women."*

Don Sucher: *"I've been doing this for 25 years. I've never had a problem with anybody, whether they're gay, trans sex, anything."*

Matt Walsh: *"You're saying councilman, he, this individual is saying, 'I'm a woman.'"*

Don Sucher: *"Right."*

Matt Walsh: *"And you said you're not a woman. How do you know that that person is not a woman?"*

Don Sucher: *"How do I know? It's common sense."*

Matt Walsh: *"Doesn't the science say that if someone identifies as a woman, then they are?"*

Don Sucher: *"No! That's completely bogus. I don't care if you think you are a sheep dog and you come into my store, it doesn't matter to me. Just don't come in and try to shove that down my throat."*

Matt Walsh: *"If it makes someone feel better, what about their feelings?"*

Don Sucher: *"I don't care about their feelings. I'm old."*

Matt Walsh: *"What about the Star Wars Universe. Jar Jar Binks, pansexual do you think? Transgender?"*

Don Sucher: *"Why would I even care?"*

Matt Walsh: *"It's his truth."*

Don Sucher: *"Well, it ain't true."*

Matt Walsh: *"You're not a scientist, you're not a gender studies major, or are you?"*

Don Sucher: *"No."*

Matt Walsh: *"How do you know that you're a man?"*

Don Sucher: *"How do I know? Because I have a (Bleep)."*

As he is leaving the store.

Matt Walsh: *"Well, I guess Don isn't overthinking it. He admits he's not a gender studies major or at the very least, a doctor. Maybe I should go talk to one."*

So, he flies to Providence, Rhode Island.

Michelle Forcier, MD: *"My name is Michelle Forcier, and I have a medical degree from University of Connecticut, residency, University of*

Utah, Pediatrics and I've worked for a number of different Planned Parenthoods for twenty-years. I do advanced contraception and abortion, as well as gender hormones, and sort of looking at the whole sort of schema of gender sex and reproductive justice."

Matt Walsh: *"So you've done a lot of work in this field. Can you just start by telling us at what age can a child first transition into another gender? Or identify themselves as a gender different from how they were born?"*

Michelle Forcier: *"There's research and data that show that babies and infants understand differences in gender. Some children figure out their gender really early, and the reason why we are saying, 'that's interesting or important' is because they're figuring out their gender identity is not necessarily congruent with their sex assigned at birth."*

Matt Walsh: *"When the doctor sees the penis and says that this is a male, has a sex of a male, that's an arbitrary distinction?"*

Michelle Forcier: *"Telling that family, based on that little penis, that your child is absolutely, a hundred percent, male identified, no matter what else occurs in their life, that's not correct."*

Matt Walsh: *"So what is gender affirmation care? You're a big proponent of if we walk through a child who's sitting down with you, is questioning their gender, what's the gender affirmation process?"*

Michelle Forcier: *"Affirmation means that as a pediatrician, as someone who says my job is to provide the best medical care for you. I need to listen really carefully and how I put it in words for kids so that they can understand it, is tell me your story. Where have you been in terms of your gender and your gender identity? Where are you right now? And more excitingly, where would you like to be in the future?"*

Matt Walsh: *"Have you ever met a four-year-old who believes in Santa Claus? This is someone who believes that a fat man is traveling through* *the sky with a flying reindeer at lightning speed, coming down his chimney with presents?"*

Michelle Forcier: *"Yeah."*

Matt Walsh: *"Would you say this is someone who has a tenuous grasp on reality?"*

Michelle Forcier: *"They have an appropriate four-year-old handle in the reality that's very real for them."*

Matt Walsh: *"I agree. But Santa Claus is real for them, but Santa Claus is not actually real."*

Michelle Forcier: *"Yeah, but Santa Claus does deliver their Christmas presents."*

Matt Walsh: *"Yeah, but he's not real though."*

Michelle Forcier: *"To that child, they are."*

Matt Walsh: *"When I see a child who believes in Santa Claus, and then let's say this is a boy, and he says, 'I'm a girl.' This is someone who can't distinguish between fantasy and reality so how could you take that as a reality?"*

Michelle Forcier: *"I would say as a pediatrician, and as a parent, I would say how wonderful my four-year-old and their imagination is."*

In a playground we are watching some kids playing.

Matt Walsh: *"Aren't kids famous for their active imaginations? Should we really let our children define reality?"*

Back in Hollywood, California, talking on the street to the people on the street:

Matt Walsh: *"If I say that I feel a certain way, then obviously you can't tell me I don't feel that way. But just because I feel that way does that mean that it's true?"*

1st passerby: *"If it's your reality, yeah, it's yours. Truly like none of my business."*

Matt Walsh: *"We all have our own identity realities? What if I said I want you to say that it's true that I'm a woman?"*

2nd passerby: *"Would you say that you're a woman?"*

3rd passerby: *"I would also say that if you want."*

2nd passerby: *"I honestly don't care, like whatever makes you happy."*

4th passerby: *"What's true to you can be false to me."*

Matt Walsh: *"What if I said that it's true. My truth is that you don't exist. Does that mean you no longer exist?"*

4th passerby: *"If that's your truth, sure. I don't."*

Matt Walsh: *"Because it's what you do."*

4th passerby: *"I mean if you're saying that I do, then I do."*

Matt Walsh: *"But even though I say that you don't, you still do because we're having this conversation."*

4th passerby: *"I mean, are we?"*

Matt Walsh: *"I think so, I mean I thought that's what you think."*

Walking down the walkway of the stars.

Matt Walsh: *"I should have known it would be hard to define reality in Hollywood. I should probably look to the place where truth is the foremost pursuit, the American University.*

Now he is inside the University to start his next interview.

Dr. Patrick Grzanka, Professor, Women Gender, and Sexuality Studies: *"What we do in gender studies is not just reduce gender to what psychologists might call individual differences, but rather thinking about gender - and that's not women and men - but gender as a social form. Something that kind of infuses itself into virtually all aspects of social life."*

Matt Walsh: *"Let's talk about that then. I guess we should start with, we've got gender and sex. Right? What's the difference? Is there a difference?"*

Dr. Grzanka: *"I saw that in your questions, and I thought my goodness, this is what we spend an entire semester kind of thinking through but what we tend to think about in the social sciences today, is that sex refers to a set of biological characteristics and gender is a social constructor category. What I think is often misleading about that characteristic is allowed to be sort of messy and complicated. But in that framing when you split them up into these holy discrete constructs. Scholars, and really more specifically, people who study gender and sex, we're not talking about sexuality, right? The academic universe that I travel is that we see how deeply gendered ideas, cultural ideas, about masculinity, feminine; maleness and femaleness both in humans and in lots of other animals."*

Matt Walsh: *"So are gender and sex two different things?"*

Dr. Grzanka: *"Well, I think that they both are, and they aren't. I'm comfortable saying that gender and sex are two different constructs, but they're deeply intertwined with each other."*

Matt Walsh: *"We are talking about gender and sex and there's a lot of controversies there if we're talking about a trans woman who has all of the male's physical characteristics, would that not be a male then? Couldn't we plainly say this person is a male?"*

Dr. Grzanka: *"Well, I guess it's like... Why are you asking me the question? I want to understand sort of why that's so important. So, if someone tells you...?"*

Matt Walsh: *"I want to sort of understand reality, you know?"*

Dr. Grzanka: *"I mean, I think when someone tells you who they are you should believe them. So, if a person says that they're a woman or they're a man, then that's them telling you their gender. I'm not sure what social interactions would have to do with maleness or femaleness that we've ..."*

Matt Walsh: *"I'm not even talking about the context. I'm just trying to start by getting to the truth. You know.*

Dr. Grzanka: *"Yeah, I mean I'm really uncomfortable with that language of like getting to the truth."*

Matt Walsh: *"Why is that uncomfortable?"*

Dr. Grzanka: *"Because that sounds deeply transphobic to me. And if you keep probing, we're going to stop the interview."*

Matt Walsh: *"If I probe about what the truth is?"*

Dr. Grzanka: *"You keep invoking the word truth, which is condescending and rude. I'm saying..."*

Matt Walsh: *"How is the word truth condescending and rude?"*

Dr. Grzanka: *"Why don't you tell me what your truth is and you're walking on 30 seconds more of tonight's before I get up."*

Matt Walsh: *"What my truth is? I don't think I really have a truth. I think there's just the truth, the reality. So, we should begin by trying to figure out what the reality is."*

Dr. Grzanka: *"And why are you concerned with when someone else tells you that they're a man or if they use the word male, why are you concerned with not believing them?"*

Matt Walsh: *"Well you keep bringing it back to how do you respond in a social situation."*

Dr. Grzanka: *"That's what I do. I'm a social scientist."*

Matt Walsh: *"Well, right, but we're in a university and this is the place of understanding truth, isn't it?"*

Dr. Grzanka: *"Absolutely, we pursue the truth and I'm a social scientist. And that's what I do."*

Matt Walsh: *"You just said truth is transphobic."*

Dr. Grzanka*:* *"If you're saying the truth is that, then I get to say you're not a man, show me your gentitalia. That's transphobia."*

Matt Walsh*:* *"No, I don't want to see anybody's genitalia. I just mean that someone can make a statement about themselves that could be untrue. For example, if I were to say that I'm a black man, would you accept that or would you be skeptical?"*

Dr. Grzanka: *"Are you black, are you African American, are you bi-racial?"*

Matt Walsh: *"I don't think so."*

Dr. Grzanka: *"Well, you don't look that, and I don't think that's, it doesn't sound like that's a genuine statement of who you are."*

Matt Walsh: *"So, that's my point. I could make a statement about who I am that's incorrect."*

Dr. Grzanka: *"Of course, I think it's well established that human beings can lie. Yes."*

Matt Walsh: *"Or not even lie, I mean I could just be mistaken."*

Dr. Grzanka: *"Yeah."*

Matt Walsh: *"I guess this all comes back, just it all comes down to really one question. Especially, women, gender, and sexuality studies. So, what is a woman?"*

Dr. Grzanka: *"Why do you ask that question?"*

Matt Walsh: *"Because I would really like to know."*

Dr. Grzanka; *"What do you think the answer to that question is?"*

Matt Walsh: *"I'm asking. That is why I came to a college professor. This is what you do."*

Dr. Grzanka: *"What other kinds of answers have you gotten?"*

Matt Walsh: *"A lot of like this, where you're not answering. I've gotten a lot of that."*

Dr. Grzanka: *"I think it's interesting that you say that some of the people you've interviewed have been reluctant to answer it and I think that has a lot to do with the way the questions that preceded it and the way you have conducted yourself in the interview."*

Matt Walsh: *"How have I conducted myself?"*

Dr. Grzanka: *"How do you think you've conducted yourself?"*

Matt Walsh: *"You really don't want to answer the questions, do you?"*

Dr. Grzanka: *"I came today very willing and enthusiastic about answering questions about women's gender and sexuality studies which is what you wanted to do."*

Matt Walsh: *"You wanted to answer questions about women's studies, so shouldn't the first answer you should be able to provide is what exactly is a woman?"*

Dr. Grzanka: *"Well, for me it's actually a really simple answer and that's a person who identifies as a woman."*

Matt Walsh: *"But what are they identifying as?"*

Dr. Grzanka: *"A woman."*

Matt Walsh: *"What is that?"*

Dr. Grzanka: *"As a woman."*

Matt Walsh: *"Do you know what a circular definition is?"*

Dr. Grzanka: *"I do."*

Matt Walsh: *"It's sort of like what you're doing right now. Where a woman is a woman."*

Dr. Grzanka: *"Because you're seeking what we would call in my field of work, an essentialist definition of gender. I think it sounds like what you would like me to give you. A set of biological or cultural characteristics that are associated with one gender or the other."*

Matt Walsh: *"I'm not seeking any kind of definition; I'm just seeking a definition."*

Dr. Grzanka: *"I gave you one."*

Well, that interview is over, and he has left the University.

Matt Walsh: *"Well, now I can say I've been to college. Glad I didn't pay for it. Is there anyone willing to give me a straight answer? Ideally somebody with a bunch of medical degrees on the wall.*

Matt Walsh: *"Dr. Grossman, thanks for talking to us. You're a psychiatrist, medical doctor and you've done a lot of work with child psychiatry. What is transgenderism from a psychiatric standpoint?"*

Miriam Grossman, MD: *"The best way to approach it, is by speaking about gender dysphoria. Which is an intense loathing and discomfort with one's biological sex. They exist anywhere between one in thirty thousand people and one in one hundred ten thousand. It's important to distinguish those people from what's happening much more recently, which is kids that never had any discomfort or dysphoria as it's now called with their biological sex, and then quite suddenly, as preteens or as adolescents, they come out and announce that they are gender fluid, or they start to question their sex.*

So, first let's define the terms. Sex and gender. Sex is biology. Sex is unchanging. It's based on chromosomes. 99.999 percent of the cells in the body are marked either male or female. Gender on the other hand is a perception. It's a feeling. It's a way of identifying. It's an experience that's subjective."

Matt Walsh: *"It sounds like what you're saying is that if a man is male but thinks of himself as a woman, he's not actually a woman?"*

Dr. Grossman: *"That is correct."*

Now he is back to the interview with Dr. Forcier.

Matt Walsh: *"Male gametes, that's what makes me male."*

Dr. Forcier: *"No, your sperm doesn't make you male."*

Matt Walsh: *"Then what does?"*

Dr. Forcier: *"It's a constellation."*

Matt Walsh: *"In reality, in truth."*

Dr. Forcier: *"Okay, whose truth are we talking about?"*

Matt Walsh: *"The same truth that we're sitting in this room right now, you and I."*

Dr. Forcier: *"No, you're not listening."*

Matt Walsh: *"If I see a chicken laying eggs and I say that's a female chicken laying eggs, did I assign female or am I just observing a physical reality that's happening in the world?"*

Dr. Forcier: *"Does a chicken have a gender identity? Does a chicken cry? Does a chicken commit suicide? Let's refrain because you're talking, you're trying ...*

Matt Walsh: *"Does a chicken have sex? Like any biological organisms?"*

Dr. Forcier: *"Chickens have an assigned gender, but a chicken doesn't have a gender identity."*

Matt Walsh: *So, we assign female to chickens when they lay eggs?"*

Dr. Forcier: *"We assume they are female, if they lay eggs."*

Back to Dr. Grossman's office.

Matt Walsh: *"Now I was told that really everyone agrees with the current approach to gender and transitioning kids and all of that. If you* *don't agree, then you are a dinosaur and a bigot. So, are you a bigoted dinosaur?"*

Dr. Grossman: *"I'm not bigoted and I'm not a dinosaur. I am rooted in reality and in science."*

Matt Walsh: *"Whose reality?"*

Dr. Grossman: *"There is one reality."*

School Track Competition

Selina Soule, Female runner: *"The first race that I competed against a transgender athlete was during my freshman year. Once the gun went off the two transgender athletes took off flying and left all of us girls in the dust. Throughout all four years of high school, I was forced to compete against biological males. I only competed against them in sprinting events, but I raced against these athletes over a dozen times throughout the years. Every single time I lost."*

Matt Walsh: *"Did they inch you out of medals that you would have won otherwise or trophies?"*

Selina Soule: *"They beat me out by 20 meters, out of medals, and qualifying spots. I missed out on qualifying for New England's. I had to go in the long jump and the 4X200 meter relay. So, I was forced on the sidelines in my own event. If they were not there, I would have been able to qualify. So, I missed out on so much throughout my high school career."*

Matt Walsh: *"Did they win all the events or almost all the events?"*

Selina Soule: *"Between the two of them, they won every single event they competed in."*

Matt Walsh: *"How does that feel?"*

Selina Soule: *"It is so frustrating and heartbreaking because we elite female athletes trained so hard to shave fractions of a second off of our time and going into races knowing that we will never be able to win."*

Matt Walsh: *"Feels like all that work has gone to waste?"*

Selina Soule: *"It does. After so many losses it just gets to the point of, why am I even doing this? Why do I keep training so hard and sacrificing so much, just to place third and beyond?"*

We are now in Washington, D.C.

Matt Walsh: *"A case in Connecticut, there were two male track runners."*

Rodridgo-Heng Lehtinen: "*Transitions girls."*

Matt Walsh: *"Right, who decided that they were going to race against the girls. You look at these individuals, you look at their times against the men, against the boys, they were kind of in the middle of the pack. They are racing the girls and they're, you know, first and second place. Is that indicative of some kind of, some kind of unfair advantage? That those individuals might have against the girls?"*

Lehtinen: *"No it's not indicative of an unfair advantage and I think part of the proof of this is that more transgender girls are coming out in high school and still playing sports and they're not winning. You know the Connecticut case is the exception and it got a lot of attention because those two trans girls performed well but there are many, many more trans girls competing in sports, and they don't excel. At the end of the day, whether or not you win a game is not about how hard you worked in your practice, because most of us aren't going to win. And that goes for transgender athletes too."*

Several other trans girls are competing in several different high school sports.

Lehtinen: *"The norm is that transgender youth don't win that much in sports games."*

Newscaster: *Alana McLaughlin was very appreciative for Provost to take this fight. I don't know how appreciative she is now, but she got a couple punches in."*

Lehtinen: *"It is very much the exception when a transgender young person does win. It's because there's not really an advantage to being trans. Only a few people are going to lead the pack. There are some slight differences, but does it translate to a competitive advantage?"*

Dr. Grossman: *"I think you'd be very hard-pressed to prove that."*

Lehtinen: *"If there was a big advantage to being transgender in sports then you would see transgender women totally dominate."*

College Coach: *"Over the last half of the pool, nobody will touch Leah Thomas."*

Newscaster: *"Transgender swimmer Leah Thomas breaking barriers and records but in a new article, Sports Illustrated calls the college senior the most controversial athlete in America."*

Teammate of Leah Thomas: *"Leah obviously helps us do better via swimming really fast. Leah's performance helps the University swim team. The feeling of winning doesn't feel good anymore. It feels tainted. There's a lot of things you couldn't talk about that were very concerning, like a locker room situation. If you even brought up concerns about it, you were transphobic. If you even bring up the fact that Leah swimming might not be fair we were immediately shut down. Being called a hateful person or transphobic."*

Matt Walsh: *"There's never any conversation? The coaches don't sit everyone down and acknowledge what everyone's really upset about?"*

Teammate: *"So Pat actually brought in people high up in the athletic department to talk to us. They brought in someone from like the LGBTQ center. They brought in someone from the psychological services."*

Matt Walsh: *"So, you're upset about what's happening and so you need psychological help."*

Teammate: *"Yeah, and they told us in this meeting, they said, 'Look we understand there's an array of emotions, but Leah's swimming is a non-negotiable, however we can help you make that okay. That's what we're here for."*

Matt Walsh: *"You're anonymous for this interview. Why did you decide that you can't have your face out there saying these things?"*

Teammate: *"They've made it pretty clear that if you speak up about it and you say anything negative, your life will be over in some way. Like you'll be blasted all over the internet as a transphobe. If you come out, and then you'll never be able to get a job. Like anyone who wants to hire you will look you up and down and see you're transphobic and your life will be over."*

New York City, New York speaking to people on the street.

Matt Walsh: *"Let's say that I identified as a woman tomorrow. I wanted to go into the same locker room where you are. Should I be allowed to do that? As long as I identify that way?"*

#1 passerby: *"I don't know. I just feel that other women would be uncomfortable by you walking in there."*

Matt Walsh: *"What do you think? Men that are transexual using the women's restroom? Do you think it's okay?"*

#2 passerby: *"No!"*

KCAL9 Newscaster #1: *"Controversy at a health club in Koreatown over the issue of gender."*

KCAL9 Newscaster #2: *"That's right. Video of spa goers complaining was posted on social media."*

Video of spa complaint.

"I just want to be clear with you that it's okay for a man to go into the women's section, show his penis around other women's young little girls' underage. Your spa, we don't condone that. Is that what you're saying? Like I asked. It's so he could stay there. He could stay there?"

KCAL9 Newscaster #2: *"Police identified the person involved as 52-year-old Darren McGregor of Riverside County. McGregor, who has been a registered sex offender since 2006 now faces five felony counts of indecent exposure."*

"Hello, I'm Congressman Mark Takano. Trans month of visibility is a time to recognize the strength diversity and resiliency of the transgender community. Together we can make our country and our world a more accepting place by speaking out against transphobia at the source and supporting the trans community by getting the equality act signed into law."

Matt Walsh: *"Congressman, thank you for being here. Thanks for joining us. You are the first member of congress who's a member of the LGBT community and also a person of Asian descent. You're also a big proponent of the equality act. What is the equality act if you were to just summarize it very briefly? I know it does a lot."*

Congressman Mark Takano: *"The simplest way to talk about the equality act is that it simply amends the 1964 Civil Rights Act to include sexual orientation and gender identity. So, public accommodations is one area."*

Matt Walsh: *"What's a way that someone that's LGBT could be discriminated in public accommodations?"*

Congressman Mark Takano: *"Currently public accommodations is the whole area of hotels and motels."*

Matt Walsh: *"And bathrooms and sports teams. Is that ..."*

Congressman Mark Takano: *"I say bathrooms, sports teams, athletic events."*

Matt Walsh: *"Let's get into more specific policy issues. There are some women who say, and I've talked to a few, who say this, 'Hey, I'd like some privacy in the bathroom. I'd prefer not to encounter naked penises.' Frankly, they say even that the penis is a telltale sign that someone is a male. There are people who kind of, really bought into the rumor that only men have penises. How do we account for that? How do you respond to that?"*

Congressman Mark Takano: *"Well, um. Well, um. Well, what I would say is that most transgender people, uh, that I know, um, and it's a very, I think minority of people. It's a, it is, it is a very, I think, uh, we're talking not about a lot of people. Um, I think a person that wants to use the woman's bathroom, who identifies as a transgender, who really does think of themselves as a female. So, how we go about trying to, uh, you know, respect their basic right to live. I think we'll be in, of course, an important part of this law and um ...*

Matt Walsh: *"Bathrooms?"*

Congressman Mark Takano: *"Bathrooms are, you know, where you want to take this conversation, instead of the basic right to just life, that I'm kind of mystified, that you're kind of not focusing on first. We're going straight to the controversy over bathrooms. Um, you know, I think this interview is over. Yeah, I think this is over."*

Matt Walsh: *"I just had one last question."*

Congressman Mark Takano: *"Uh, well I, this interview is over."*

Matt Walsh: *"I just want to know, what is a woman?"*

Congressman Mark Takano: *"Please turn off the cameras."*

Voice in the background: *"We're going to end the interview. If you guys could please pack up and return the office exactly ..."*

Matt Walsh: *"I just wanted to know, I came all this way to know what, I just wanted to know what is a woman?*

Voice in the background: *"And you're not going to find out!"*

San Francisco, California

Matt Walsh: *"My trip to California isn't providing many answers but at least I'm making new friends."*

Several naked men are walking down the street.

Matt Walsh: *"Are you worried about kids walking around out here?"*

Naked man #1: *"No, I raised two daughters. They are two of the most well-adjusted adults. They grew up around naked people, and there's been studies that have shown that children raised around non-sexual nudity, actually have fewer hang-ups when they're adults."*

Matt Walsh: *"People do have hang-ups. Can anyone be any gender they want to be? Can a man become a woman if they want?"*

Naked man #1: *"Somebody, I leave that, I mean what people do that's their personal choice. People can live the life they want to. I'm trying to* *live the life I want to, an authentic life. That's why I respect other people's rights and to choose what they want to do."*

Woman on the street: *"Why are you asking a gay man as to what it means to be a woman? You should be asking women what it means to be a woman. Especially trans women what it means."*

Matt Walsh: *"I'm asking all kinds of people. Can anyone have an opinion about it?"*

Woman on the street: *"Only people who are women. Men don't know nothing about what it means to be a woman."*

Matt Walsh: *"Have you told gay men here in San Francisco that they're not allowed to talk about this?"*

Woman on the street: *"No, it's not like I come around and say what a gay man is allowed to be."*

Matt Walsh: *"So, you're saying if you're not a woman you shouldn't have an opinion."*

Woman on the street: *"Where does a guy get a right to say what a woman is? Women only know what women are."*

Matt Walsh: *"Are you a cat?"*

Woman on the street: *"No."*

Matt Walsh: *"Can you tell me what a cat is?"*

Woman on the street: *"This is actually a genuine mistake. I'm sorry I even came up here."*

Matt Walsh: *"You want to tell me what a woman is?"*

He is now at the airport waiting for his luggage.

Matt Walsh: *"If my friend with the purple hat is correct and only women can tell me what a woman is, I guess I need to go where the women are.*

Now at a demonstration in favor of abortion, in front of the White House, he is asking the women,

Matt Walsh: *"What is a woman? Can you tell me that?" But they just look at each other and laugh.*

Matt Walsh: *"Well, you're at the women's march, you must have some idea. I see girls, I see vagina, does that mean they're the only people that can get pregnant?"*

Lady #1: *"If men can get pregnant too, I think they'd want the right to choose. "*

Matt Walsh: *"But they are saying men can get pregnant?"*

Lady #1: *"We're saying someone who was born as a woman but identifies as a man, that's a real man."*

Matt Walsh: *"It's a real man? So, men can get pregnant?"*

Lady #1: *"Yes, they have the parts to do so."*

Matt Walsh: *"Is it just women that give birth or is it ...?"*

Lady #2: *"I guess, yeah."*

Matt Walsh: *"So some men could give birth?"*

Lady #2: *"With a vagina."*

Matt Walsh: *"Well, that could be a man or a woman?"*

Lady #1: *"Well, I mean I think that's the whole point. Right? That it's fluid the way that we define these things, changes a lot."*

Lady #3: *"What are you doing?"*

Matt Walsh: *"I'm asking questions. I'm trying to figure out what a woman is, that's why I'm here. This is a women's march. I figured it's a good place to find out. I've come all this way to ask this question. Can anyone tell me what a woman is?"*

Lady #4: *"You are not here for women. We ask you to leave!"*

Matt Walsh: *"What is that?"*

Lady #4: *"He's going to harass you."*

Matt Walsh: *"How am I harassing? I am just asking a question. What is a woman? Can anyone here at the women's march tell me what a woman is?*

Someone in the crowd: *"Wear a mask!"*

Matt Walsh: *"Tell me what a woman is, and I'll put a mask on."*

Since he can't get anyone to answer this question, he is now walking around with a huge sign that asks, "What is a Woman?"

Matt Walsh: *"I've been all over America and I still can't find an answer. Maybe I'm looking too close to home.*

His next flight takes him to Nairobi. His trip to Africa is wonderful. He is seeing the animals in the wild while is heading for a certain tribe to find out if they can answer the question, "What is a Woman." When he arrives, the women are in their colorful dresses, and they are all lined up to welcome him to their village.

Matt Walsh: *"We came a long way to come and talk to you guys. Thousands of miles from America. Thank you for inviting us into your tribe first of all."*

Tribal man: *"I can say it is my pleasure to meet you and I feel most welcome but you're here to learn with me and I'm here to learn with you too."*

Matt Walsh: *"Great! What if a man decides to do the roles of a woman?"*

Tribal man: *"In Maasai community, it will not exist at all."*

Matt Walsh: *"It doesn't exist? What if a man decides that his gender identity is woman?"*

Tribal man: *"A woman has its own duty, and the man has its own duty, and a lady cannot do the duty of a man and a man cannot do the duty of a woman."*

Matt Walsh: *"Can a man become a woman?"*

Tribal man: *"NO!"*

Matt Walsh: *"What about a transgender?"*

Tribal man: *"NO! It looks like if you want to become a lady, but you are a man, you have something wrong."*

Matt Walsh: *"Something wrong?"*

Tribal man: *"Something wrong in your family, something wrong in you."*

Matt Walsh: *"Based on what I'm saying, would you ever want to move to America?"*

Tribal man: *"He says NO!" And they all laugh.*

Matt Walsh, to a lady in the tribe: *"What is a woman if you had to give a definition?"*

Tribal lady: *"A woman delivered, a man cannot."*

Matt Walsh: *"So, it sounds like you don't spend a lot of time thinking about gender, you just kind of live your lives and you don't think about it."*

Tribal man: *"No, because we believe that's a good plan, God's plan. I'm shocked with what you are telling me."*

"He's shocked. The Masai people don't think much about gender, but they have a firm sense of their identity. It's clear that gender ideology is a uniquely western phenomenon. So, where did all this come from? Who came up with it? And why?"

Notice how many times people will try to justify this insane, depraved, wicked, twisted relationship behavior with this mindset of do what is right in your own eyes. Truth is whatever you make it. It destroyed Israel and led to great misery. And if we are going to avoid it, we need to get back to God's truth. Doing what's right in His eyes. And that's what we'll be looking at next time. But again, I wanted to reiterate some hope.

During that time, (when everybody was doing what was right in their own eyes in Israel) the people of Israel would grow desperate and cry for help, (and hopefully we will too).

And then God would raise up some unlikely leader to conquer whatever enemy was oppressing them. These deliverers, known as "judges," weren't perfect by any means, but the Lord would empower and use them to deliver His people from servitude or national disaster.

And then when peace was restored, the nation would fall right back into another long stretch of sin and apostasy. It happened every time. The cycle is repeated over and over again.

Now, I don't know if we are in that last cycle of behavior heading towards captivity, or the 7-year Tribulation if you will, or maybe we have one last cycle of peace or revival before the hammer comes down. I don't know…

All I know is, if we're going to have one last genuine revival again before the hammer comes down, then we need to be those truth judges and stand for God's truth and His righteousness. The answer is not in condoning or compromising with the mindset of doing what is right in our own eyes. The answer is doing things God's way.

Chapter Ten

God's Judgment with a Woeful Destruction

If revival is ever going to happen, then we, the church, need to get rid of our own hypocrisy! In the last chapter we revisited the depraved mind issue and saw what causes that mindset to prevail. We had the transcription of the video "What is a Woman? Part 1." In that video we saw that this was the mindset that caused the same mistake that Israel made with "Everyone doing what was right in their own eyes." That's why people today can't even seem to define what a woman is, because they're making it up as they go, relativism, whatever is true to you. Unfortunately, that's not the only thing we're repeating of Israel's mistakes.

Now we're going to see the fruit of "doing whatever is right in your own eyes." It leads to woeful times and the destruction of your country!

Isaiah 5:3-15,18,20-25: "'Now you, dwellers in Jerusalem and men of Judah, judge between me and my vineyard. What more could have been done for my vineyard than I have done for it? When I looked for good grapes, why did it yield only bad? Now I will tell you what I am going to do to my vineyard: I will take away its hedge and it will be destroyed; I will break down its wall and it will be trampled. I will make it a wasteland neither pruned nor cultivated, and briers and thorns will grow there. I will command the clouds not to rain on it. The vineyard of the Lord Almighty is the house of Israel, and the men of Judah are the garden of his delight. And he looked for justice, but saw bloodshed; for righteousness, but heard cries of distress. Woe to you who add house to house and join field to field till no space is left and you live alone in the land. The Lord Almighty has declared in my hearing 'Surely the great houses will become desolate, the fine mansions left without occupants. A ten-acre vineyard will produce only a bath of wine, a homer of seed only an ephah of grain.' Woe to those who rise early in the morning to run after their drinks, who stay up late at night till they are inflamed with wine. They have harps and lyres at their banquets, tambourines and flutes and wine, but they have no regard for the deeds of the Lord, no respect for the work of his hands. Therefore, my people will go into exile for lack of understanding; their men of rank will die of hunger and their masses will be parched with thirst. Therefore, the grave enlarges its appetite and opens its mouth without limit; into it will descend their nobles and masses with all their brawlers and revelers. So, man will be brought low, and mankind humbled, the eyes of the arrogant humbled. Woe to those who draw sin along with cords of deceit, and wickedness as with cart ropes. Woe to those who call evil good and good evil, who put darkness for light and light for darkness, who put bitter for sweet and sweet for bitter. Woe to those who are wise in their own eyes and clever in their own sight. Woe to those who are heroes at drinking wine and champions at mixing drinks, who acquit the guilty for a bribe, but deny justice to the innocent. Therefore, as tongues of fire lick up straw and as dry grass sinks down in the flames so their roots will decay, and their flowers blow away like dust; for they have rejected the law of the Lord Almighty and spurned the word of the Holy One of Israel. Therefore, the Lord's anger burns against his people; his hand is raised, and he strikes them down. The mountains shake, and the dead bodies are like refuse in the streets. Yet for all this, his anger is not turned away, his hand is still upraised."

Now the word used there is "woe." How many realize that when God uses that, He does not mean slow down horsey. Woe in Hebrew is "hoi" as in "oy vey" and that's a common Jewish phrase, it's a Yiddish word which is common of Hebrew and German, and it comes from the Old Testament. It means, "a passionate cry of grief or despair." So, when you see this in the Scripture it is "Oh despair, grief is coming." Why? Because you rejected God, and you did whatever you said was right. How many of you would say, "doing whatever is right in your own eyes" and "rejecting God's Law" is not a good way to go? And yet, this is where we are, not only in the world but even in the so-called apostate church. Which means, we are headed for woeful times unless we start speaking up and speaking out. Which again, we'll get to in the next chapter.

Now, let's pick up where we left off. This is the fruit of a depraved mind but now we're going to figure out, where did it come from? How did this get instituted into our society where now it's at the point where people are afraid to even define what a woman is. So, now let's take a look at that.

What is a Woman?
Part 2

Matt Walsh: *"The Maasai people don't think much about gender, but they have a firm sense of their identity. It's clear that gender ideology is a uniquely Western phenomenon. So where did all this come from? Who came up with it? And why?"*

Dr. Grossman: *"Matt, I want to show you something. You're a parent, right?*

She holds up this book for him to look at.

Dr. Grossman: *"It's perfectly normal for 10 years and up. Here's just one page I want you to see here."*

Matt Walsh: *"For 10 and up, huh?"*

Dr. Grossman: *"It's unspeakable what these people have done to our children."*

Matt Walsh: *"When did that start? When was it decided that we need to start teaching kids about this stuff? At such a young age?"*

Dr. Grossman: *"So, I'll answer that with one word. Kinsey. Kinsey was a social reformer. He wanted to rid society of Judeo-Christian values when it came to sexuality, and he worked very hard to do that. And I would say he succeeded.*

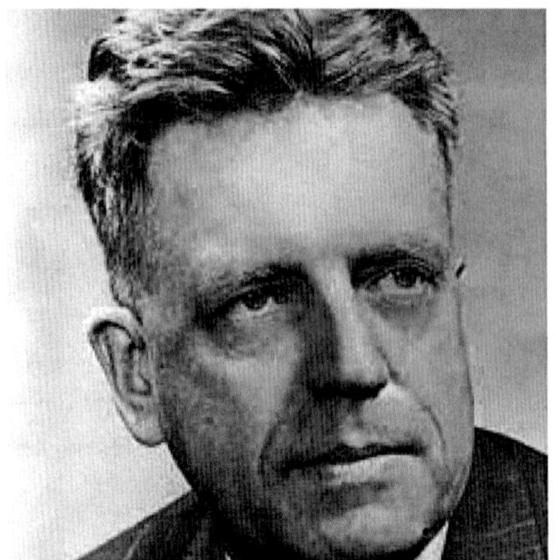

Matt Walsh: *"Kinsey would be very happy with our culture today. His idea was that children are sexual from birth. That we are all inherently sexual creatures from cradle to grave. He believed that true happiness is found in a life of perverse sexual experimentation. No matter the age."*

Dr. Grossman: *"What came out is that his research was fraudulent."*

Kinsey based his fraudulent conclusions on data he collected from convicted sex offenders and child molesters. His research was conducted in prisons, not everyday America. He also performed horrific sexual experiments on children, some under the age of one. His most influential book, 'Sexual Behavior in the Human Male,' contains an infamous chart called 'Table 34' which documents the orgasms of very young kids, including babies as young as 5 months old. But instead of suffering the consequences for his heinous actions he was and still is celebrated by academia and Hollywood. His ideas formed the foundation for sexual education in public schools today.

Matt Walsh: *"How do we get from this to, you can choose your own gender?"*

Dr. Grossman: *"Okay, now we have another very important character and his name was John Money.*

John Money was a psychologist and professor at Johns Hopkins University. Gender ideology was his brainchild. In fact, he coined the terms gender identity and gender roles. According to Money, babies are gender neutral at birth and ultimately environment determines whether a person is a man or a woman.

Dr. Grossman: *"Money was telling the world about his theory, that a boy could be raised as a girl and do just fine. And vice versa."*

So, Money tried out his theory on two young twin boys, the Reimer twins.

Dr. Grossman: *"When the twins were 8 months old, and they went to be circumcised, the first twin, whose name was Bruce, something went wrong with the machinery and his penis was burnt off. They stopped and didn't do a second circumcision on the other twin, as you might imagine. And the parents didn't know what to do. How are they going to raise this child?"*

John Money convinced Bruce's parents to transition him into a girl. Money also conducted sexually abusive experiments on the twins throughout their childhood. Including, forcing them to simulate sex acts on each other.

Dr. Grossman: *"He reported up to the age of 10 that it was a complete success. Well, it wasn't true."*

The results were a disaster. Bruce could never accept his female identity. Eventually his parents told him the truth and he chose to transition back to a boy. Taking the name David. As an adult David spoke out about the abuse and the damage done to him by John Money.

David Reimer: *"The girls would do their things with their barbies and things like that, and that wouldn't interest me. Things such as trucks and building forts and, you know, getting into the odd fist fights and climbing trees. That's the kind of stuff that I liked but it was unacceptable."*

Oprah Winfrey: *"As a girl?"*

David Reimer: *"As a girl, I had no place to fit in."*

Dr. Grossman: *"The trauma that he and his brother and his entire family went through left deep scars. His brother died of an overdose, when he was 38 and then David died by committing suicide."*

There was never a retraction or an apology from John Money. Instead, his ideas were adopted by mainstream psychology, and they formed the basis of gender ideology today.

Matt Walsh: *"Why don't more people know about John Money and Alfred Kinsey?"*

Dr. Grossman: *"Evidently, there are forces that don't want this information out."*

David Reimer: *"I never fit; I was an alpha female. A sales executive that kind of just didn't fit in any box. When psychologists or somebody that I was in love with or whatever, said I was in the wrong body, I started to think that, well maybe I am."*

Scott (Kellie) Newgent: *"I am a biological woman that medically transitioned to appear like a man through synthetic hormones and surgery. I will never be a man. Is it transphobic for me to tell the truth? Why is it that a couple hundred years from now, if you dug up my body, they're going to go, yep, that was a woman. Had babies."*

Matt Walsh: *"Can you tell me about the procedures that you had."*

Scott (Kellie) Newgent: *"I've had seven surgeries and I've had one stress heart attack. I had a helicopter life ride with a pulmonary embolism. I've had 17 rounds of antibiotics. I had six inches of hair on the inside of my urethra for 17 months. Nobody would help me, including the doctor who did this to me. Because I lost my insurance. I get infections every three to four months. I'm probably not going to live very long."*

Matt Walsh: *"Was there any real discussions of the risks and the side effects?*

Scott (Kellie) Newgent: *"No there's not. And I know that people want to think that there is, but there's not. The truth is that medical transition is experimental. We have studies that said medical transition helps mental health, helps mental health with kids. They've all been retracted, modified, changed. But the only long-term study tells us 7 to 10 years is when transgender people are the most suicidal. After surgery. But that's transphobic to say. For the first time in history a group has a huge dollar sign on the top of their head. We have five children's hospitals in the United States promoting that. (He raises his arm to show a long, huge scar on the inside of his arm)*

Matt Walsh: *"What is that?"*

Scott (Kellie) Newgent: *"That is a phalloplasty. That's a bottom surgery. We have five children's hospitals in the United States, telling girls that they can be boys at $70,000 a pop. In a surgery that has a 67 percent complication rate that will kill me from infection. That I can't sue on, that is butchering a generation of children because nobody's willing to talk about anything. I have three kids at the age that they are doing this to kids. I'm not transphobic! I love my kids and I love other people's kids and you should too. This is wrong on so many levels."*

Matt Walsh: *"Can kids consent? Do you think kids are capable of consenting to this?"*

Scott (Kellie) Newgent: *"No they're not! Being a parent, loving the h*** out of your kids, and helping them see around corners."*

Matt Walsh: *"What's the youngest patient that you've operated on?"*

Dr. Bowers: *"The youngest patient I've done a vaginoplasty on is age 16."*

Matt Walsh: *"Do you worry that minors just don't understand enough about themselves, they're not neurologically developed enough yet to make permanent life-altering decisions?"*

Dr. Bowers: *"Absolutely not!"*

Dr. Grossman: *"A young person's self-perception, one day they may be clear, the next day they may be totally confused and not sure and you're affirming it with hormones that have never been used in this way, in the field of medicine."*

Matt Walsh: *"You're talking about puberty blockers?"*

Dr. Grossman: *"Blockers and then opposite sex hormones."*

Matt Walsh: *"At what age does the medical transition begin with medication?"*

Dr. Forcier: *"So, medical affirmation begins when the patient says they're ready for it. So that could be a kiddo who is just starting puberty and panicking because they're getting breast buds, or their penis is getting bigger and busier, and they're worried about all kinds of masculine changes. That way, puberty blockers which are completely reversible and don't have permanent effects are wonderful because we can put that pause on puberty, just like you were listening to music. You put pause off and we stopped the blockers and puberty would go right back to where it was, the next note in the song. Just delayed that period of time."*

Matt Walsh: *"You can just pause puberty..."*

Scott (Kellie) Newgent: *"No you can't."*

Matt Walsh: *"And then pick it up in the future..."*

Scott (Kellie) Newgent: *"No, you can't. No, you can't! How many studies do they have? Long term studies on hormone blockers with children? None!"*

Dr. Grossman: *"I just spoke a month or two ago with a mother whose fourteen-year-old daughter was put on blockers. They discovered after two years, this 14-year-old girl has osteoporosis. That's something that old women get."*

Matt Walsh: *"How can doctors assure parents that a certain medicine is totally safe? Based on what you are saying, they can't possibly know that."*

Dr. Grossman: *"How can they be removing the healthy breasts of a 15-year-old girl? How can they be sterilizing kids? How can this whole thing be happening?"*

Scott Newgent: *"Every child that they convince is transgender and in need of medical transition, it generates 1.3 million dollars to pharma and we're believing a pharmaceutical company, that Lupron hormone blockers are reversible, so they say. Well, the truth is that in 2003, Lupron was sued and deemed a criminal enterprise by the US Government. They paid the highest fine of any pharmaceutical company at that time. $874 million dollars. Just wrote a check."*

Matt Walsh: *"Is Lupron chemical castration?"*

Scott (Kellie) Newgent: *"Yes. We're giving it to pedophiles aren't we? We're giving it to people who are dying and we're giving it to kids, telling them that they were born in the wrong body and it's completely safe."*

Matt Walsh: *"One of the drugs is Lupron, right? Which has actually been used to chemically castrate sex offenders."*

Dr. Forcier: *"You know what, I'm not sure we should continue with this interview because it seems like it's going in a particular direction."*

Matt Walsh: *"Well, you are a medical professional."*

Dr. Forcier: *"I am a medical professional."*

Matt Walsh: *"But you don't want to talk about the drugs that you give kids."*

Dr. Forcier: *"Again, I'm a physician and I use medication. You're choosing exploitative words, drugs I give."*

Matt Walsh: *"I'm choosing a chemical word that was in a dictionary."*

Dr. Forcier: *"That's not a correct term for puberty blocker."*

Matt Walsh: *"I could look it up on my phone. I'm pretty sure if I looked it up..."*

Dr. Forcier: *"You can look it up on your phone."*

Matt Walsh: *"Chemical castration: Medical definition; The administration of a drug to bring about a marked reduction in the body's production of androgens and especially testosterone."*

Dr. Forcier: *"And I said, as a pediatrician, who takes care of hundreds of these kids, when you use that terminology, you are being malignant and harmful."*

Matt Walsh: *"There are some who would say that giving chemical castration drugs to kids is malignant and harmful."*

Dr. Forcier: *"It's about the context of caring for a child and seeing the suffering that kids can have that have not been in an affirmative home situation."*

Matt Walsh: *"What do you say to the claim that we have to do this for these kids because if we don't, they'll kill themselves? They'll resort to drugs and self-harm?"*

Dr. Grossman: *"A lot of them were hurting themselves. A lot of them were suicidal before they even discovered gender. That is never part of the discussion. And they say, what would you rather have, a living daughter or a dead son? If this is what the professionals are saying, it's terrible emotional blackmail."*

His phone rings.

"Hello? Is this ....? This is, yes."

Matt Walsh: *"This is Matt Walsh, where are you right now?"*

Person on the phone: *"I'm in Vancouver, British Columbia, Canada right now."*

Matt Walsh: *"Are you able to leave?"*

Person on the phone: *"I'm not able to leave B.C. I can't even go to another province in Canada and it's because I'm technically out on bail."*

Matt Walsh: *"What happened exactly?"*

In 2018, a father in Canada was informed that a hospital would begin administering hormone-altering medication to his child. According to a recently passed Canadian law, doctors can administer these drugs to children without parental consent. When the father spoke out, he was arrested and fined $30,000 for misgendering his 13-year-old daughter.

Matt Walsh: *"How exactly did this get into the courts to begin with?"*

Person on the phone: *"Well, what happened is, we set up a meeting with BC children's hospital, and according to the BC Children's hospital's website there is going to be a thorough evaluation. And I'm thinking good. This is going to be the end of it all. You're going to clearly see that my child is not the opposite sex. So, my ex-wife brings my child into BC Children's Hospital. I get a call less than an hour into that appointment; they were going to pump her full cross-sex hormones within the hour. I put a halt to that. I said, NO! They agreed to stop for the moment. They figured, well, let's get the dad on board too. This is all going to be better. Let's just get everybody on the same page. I said it's not going to happen.*

So, I get a letter from BC Children's Hospital in December of 2018, and it says that under the BC Infant's Act they will start injecting my child with cross-sex hormones and I have two weeks to respond with legal action if I so choose. And so, that's how I ended up in court. Because I did respond with legal action."

Matt Walsh: *"So you called your daughter a she and you went to jail for that?"*

Person on the phone: *"It's considered criminal violence to not use the preferred pronouns. It's no different than, let's say if I were to take a broomstick and whack one of my kids over the head. So, they were treating it in a similar fashion that this misgendering, mis-pronouning my child was the equivalent of family violence."*

Matt Walsh: *"Is she on the hormone pills now?"*

Person on the phone: *"She is. The court order said that she could do whatever she wanted."*

Sara Stockton, Clinical Supervisor: *"From 2010 until I would say 2016, I would say 80 percent of my clients were trans youth. Now it is if you identify, you take hormones, you do surgery. There aren't any other pathways."*

Matt Walsh: *"So if you have two parents. One parent wants to affirm the trans identity, the other parent doesn't, who wins that battle?"*

Sara Stockton: *"The one who wants to affirm."*

Matt Walsh: *"Every time?"*

Sara Stockton: *"Every single time. The goal is to get the parents to affirm the kid."*

He has now flown to Toronto.

Dr. Jordan Peterson, Clinical Psychologist: *"There is no such thing as a gender affirming therapist. That's a contradiction in terms."*

Matt Walsh: *"Why?"*

Dr. Jordon Peterson: *"Because you don't affirm if you're a therapist, it's not your business to affirm. You come to see me because there is something wrong. Maybe you come to see me because a destructive* *element of you is wreaking havoc in your life. I'm on the side of the party that wants to aim up man. That's what I'm on the side of. Okay, now I don't know what that means in your case. We're going to talk about it. Am I going to affirm what you think? No, it's not up to me to affirm it. You don't get a casual pat on the back from the therapist for your pre-existing axiomatic conclusions. That's not therapy. That's a rubber stamp."*

Matt Walsh: *"Has anybody, at any point, explained to these kids the real long-term consequences of hormones and puberty blockers?"*

Sara Stockton: *"I don't think they are explaining it to the kids. So that has frightened me. That it's become, that we're even talking to the kids about it at ten. They're presenting it in schools."*

Matt Walsh: *"So, this generation, they're the lab rats?"*

Sara Stockton: *"Yes."*

Dr. Jordon Peterson: *"Biological sex, binary, it's been binary for like 100 million years, longer than that. Temperament is not binary, temperament or personality."*

Matt Walsh: *"So, that's gender? Temperament is gender?"*

Dr. Jordon Peterson: *"Well, gender is not a good word because it's vague and it isn't measurable."*

Matt Walsh: *"So, do we need it? Why can't we just say temperament? What do we even need the word gender for?"*

Dr. Jordon Peterson: *"Well, I don't need it. But what I would say is that people who talk about the diversity and gender are actually talking about diversity and personality and temperament, but they don't know it. You can have a masculine temperament if you're a woman. Maybe one in ten women have the average temperament of a man. And you can have feminine men temperamentally and it's not that uncommon. Because the* *differences between men and women temperamentally aren't that great. There are masculine girls, there are feminine boys. What are we going to do about that? Carve them up?"*

Matt Walsh: *"You, as someone who started your professional, you know, transgender care, now you're sitting here talking to me. I'm a dangerous man, I've been told. Are you worried about reprisals? Are you worried about how this is going to be, how this is going to play among your professional peers?"*

Sara Stockton: *"I am worried that I can't have conversations with any other peers. I don't know any other peer that will speak to me about these things that question it. I just don't think developmentally, this is helpful to our children."*

Dr. Jordon Peterson: *"You step wrong as a therapist; you say the wrong thing once and like your bloody career is over. Now it's the same with physicians. How's that going to work? You're going to go have an honest conversation with your physician when he's terrified out of his mind that he'll say something politically incorrect during the diagnostic processes? Hey man, you're sick with whatever you want to be. See ya later. You want a prescription for something?"*

Dr. Debra Soh, Author, The End of Gender: *"I left academia because the climate had become too stifling politically, especially when it comes to the topic of gender identity and the science of gender. It is absolutely impossible to do good research. You basically have to decide beforehand what you're going to find so that you don't upset activists and that is how you do science."*

Matt Walsh: *"Why has the shift occurred, where all of a sudden, gender and sex have become so politically and culturally charged?"*

Dr. Debra Soh: *"There is a really ugly history between sex researchers and transgender activists. In the past if any sex researcher spoke out about science and that went against activist orthodoxy or particular* *narratives that activists wanted to promote, they would basically have their personal and professional reputations ruined. So, what you see is that only experts who toe the party line and say the things activists like, those are the people who get attention, those are the people who get lifted up in the media. And also, I would say people are incentivized to go along with the activist narratives and gender ideology because that helps their career."*

Carl Trueman, Historian, Theologian and Author: *"Trans is very cool. Trans is a way of giving yourself value, given the way society at the moment is functioning. All of the things that used to give us anchors of identity have become very fluid or very volatile in recent years and into that context I think what you find then is new identities. Start to fill the void of the vacuum, whereas in the past I might have got my sense of self-worth from part of the village where I grew up. Now I might get my sense of self-worth through being part of the online community that I connect with or part of the sexual identity community."*

Sara Stockton: *"Now we are seeing kids that are identifying as animals going to school and they are purring instead of answering questions. They meow and the teachers are not allowed to question it because it's considered a queer identity."*

Matt Walsh: *"So, kids are going to school and they're saying, I'm a cat and the teachers have to affirm them as a cat. So, it's not just literal zoos now, basically they are."*

Wolf Woman: *"I am a 27-year-old transgender woman, I am a wolf therian and a member of the furry fandom."*

Matt Walsh: *"When and how did you discover this inner wolfness?"*

Wolf Woman: *"Probably around age 10 or 11. I was watching an anime about wolves and saw the wolf running across the screen and somehow just intrinsically like, oh, that's me."*

Matt Walsh: *"Have you spent any time around biological wolves?"*

Wolf Woman: *"Yes."*

Matt Walsh: *"That sounds dangerous, also what context?"*

Wolf Woman: *"I was a volunteer with the preserve, and I've also visited many wolf preserves."*

Matt Walsh: *"Are you able to communicate with the wolves?"*

Wolf Woman: *"Am I going to have a conversation with a wolf in the way I am communicating with you? Obviously not. Am I going to read their body language and respond appropriately to their behaviors and their nonverbal cues? Yes."*

Matt Walsh: *"Would you be able to give us an example of this wolf communication?"*

Wolf Woman: *"No. I'm not comfortable doing so."*

Matt Walsh: *"Okay."*

Matt Walsh: *"How exactly have these ideas become so pervasive?"*

Carl Trueman: *"First of all we need to remember that in the west at least, we have it drilled into our minds from childhood onwards that personal happiness is the key to individual flourishing. Secondly, we think of ourselves in psychological terms. I am my feelings and in order for me to be happy, I have to be able to express my feelings. I have to be outwardly, that which I feel myself to be inwardly. Thirdly, we're taught that interfering with somebody else's happiness is very bad. We need to acknowledge that there are powerful lobby groups, powerful cultural and political lobby groups driving this thing. Hollywood is pressing LGBTQ plus matters in so many movies. We are seeing it in the way Amazon sets up its algorithms. There are all kinds of factors in society that are pushing* *what would really be numerically a fairly minority interest into being one of the main political focal points of this generation."*

Clips of statements from Hollywood movies:

"After my operation I will be a woman."

"Why can't she just be a lesbian?"

"Because she's not a lesbian, mom. She's a boy."

"Because I was born in a girl's body."

"Can I ask you a question? Why don't you kiss me?"

Preston Sprinkle, Identity teens and gender: *"The whole idea of social contagion is that there could be something in one's social environment that could play some role in somebody coming out as trans. Would you say that is definitely part of your story?"*

Girl being interviewed by Preston: *"When I look back, I don't think I would have ever even considered seeing myself as a boy without these social aspects. Especially if I hadn't joined these online communities."*

Here are some statements from people that are changing their identities:

First girl: *"I identify as non-binary. I'll officially be changing my pronouns today."*

Second girl: *"Then my pronouns are 'him' and 'demon self."*

Third girl: *"I've been going by they and them pronouns for four years, now I'm pretty comfortable."*

Girl being interviewed by Preston: *"There are literally a period of a few weeks to a few months. I started out as an ally and eventually I was starting to identify as transgender."*

Fourth group of girls: *"We are trans models."*

Dr. Debra Soh: *"So they go on the internet, and they are told that all their problems will be solved if they become a man."*

Dr. Grossman: *"Kids are being taught that you might feel like you're a boy, even if you have a vagina and you're a girl, you are what you feel you are."*

Fifth girl: *"Some people are girls, some are boys, some are both, some are neither."*

Sixth girl: *"Gender is all about how we feel on the inside and how we express ourselves."*

Seventh person: *"As a queer and trans teacher my agenda is to show little boys that they don't have to be like as stereotypically masculine. That they can paint their nails and wear earrings and like still be a guy and like it could be cool."*

Matt Walsh: *"Do you worry that there could be a social contagion element of this?"*

Dr. Bowers: *"A teeny tiny bit, maybe."*

Girl being interviewed by Preston: *"Looking back on it, it was the same pattern, just kids that were really struggling, kids who were very alone and isolated."*

Dr. Grossman: *"They have anxiety. They don't fit in with their peers. They don't know where they belong."*

Girl being interviewed by Preston: *"Maybe they didn't have a welcoming family life. They just got caught up in these communities online."*

Dr. Grossman: *"Then they discover, hey, there's this group of people and they also don't fit in. They're different. They're not sure who they are. And 'Gee, that's where I fit in.'"*

Eighth girl: *"Today is the day before my top surgery. I am waking up tomorrow at 5:00 am to have a subcutaneous mastectomy."*

Scott (Kellie) Newgent*: "They're telling children, when they haven't fully developed, that all you have to do is medically transition and you fit in. I was one of those kids. It got me at 42. Your child doesn't have a chance."*

Nineth girl: *"Transgender. This is only going in one direction; you will respect us!"*

Rodridgo-Heng Lehtinen: *"As parents come to understand more about gender identity, kids are coming out at younger ages."*

Dr. Bowers: *"It's exciting. And you know who gets it right? This next generation."*

Dr. Forcier: *"The next generation who's already telling us that our antiquated ideas of things have to be a certain way, just don't apply to them."*

Dr. Bowers: *"They are rejecting a lot of our social mores; they're tweaking the system."*

Girl being interviewed by Preston: *"I just don't think it's realistic to put this decision on them. That is basically saying, 'Are you okay with the risk of permanent health effects that you can never ever reverse' How can you ask that of such a small child?"*

He finds himself in bed suddenly awakened by this horrible bad dream. It can't be real. He remembers all the statements that we made in the past interviews.

"I'm a physician and I use medication."
"Certainly, it's a bit of a Faustian bargain."
"Puberty blockers which are completely reversible."
"You keep invoking the word truth, which is condescending and rude."
"Some women have penises. Some men have vaginas."
"Does a chicken cry? Does a chicken commit suicide?"
"I'm a woman but I can't really answer that."

Matt Walsh: *"I guess because of that somehow this madness has infected our entire society. Am I the crazy one? I'm done asking questions."*

Developing Story: *"Tanner Cross is on administrative leave for what he said about gender identity. He said he would not call a student who's transgender by their preferred pronoun."*

Tanner Cross, Teacher, Loudoun County Public Schools: *"I can't lie to children, and I got to also represent a whole community that believes in biological facts and scientific facts. I just can't do that to kids."*

Kimberly Wright, Teacher, Loudoun County Public Schools: *"You get into teaching because you love kids. This policy started coming into play and I was like wait a minute. It's causing me to lie to my kids. The one's I've always wanted to protect."*

Fox News Reports:

Loudoun School Board: *"Do we have assaults in our bathrooms or locker rooms, regularly?"*

The response to the question: *"To my knowledge we don't have any records of assaults in our restrooms."*

In the courtroom a parent is disputing this claim.

Mother: *"My child was raped! And this is what happens."*

The police have tackled the father and have thrown him on the floor for standing up for his child.

Another response: *"The predator transgender student is or person simply, it does not exist."*

New Details from Fox 5: *"The Virginia Department of Education says it is now reviewing whether the Loudoun County School District has properly reported cases of assault. This comes after a 15-year-old was charged on two separate occasions for assaulting two different students at different schools."*

"Dozens rallying tonight in Loudoun County to protest the school's policies. That includes limiting who can talk during public comment portions of board meetings. One speaker leased property in the area just so he could speak tonight. Fox 5 Perris Jones is live with the details."

Perris Jones: *"That's right. Conservative commentator, Matt Walsh told me he's leasing out someone's basement in Loudoun County, so he'd be able to speak during tonight's meeting."*

Matt Walsh: *"I decided last week to fulfill my lifelong dream of being a Loudoun County resident. You know, I've always felt like, I've lived in Tennessee, I felt sort of like a Virginian trapped in a Tennessean's body. I identify as sort of state fluid, I guess."*

Fox 5 Reports: *"This is Matt Walsh,"* he tweeted, *"How do you do fellow Virginians?"*

Matt Walsh: *"Now I just have to explain to my wife and kids that we're going to be staying in someone's basement."*

Narrator: *"They tried to muzzle me by not allowing me to speak. And when that didn't work, they tried to muzzle me with a mask."*

Matt Walsh: *"I would thank you all for allowing me to speak to you tonight, but you tried not to allow it. But yet, here I am. You only give me 60 seconds so let me get to the point. You are all child abusers. You prey upon impressionable children and indoctrinate them into your insane ideological cult. A cult which holds many fanatical views, but none so deranged as the idea that boys are girls and girls are boys. By imposing this vile nonsense on students to the point of even forcing young girls to share locker rooms with boys, you deprive these kids of safety and privacy and something more fundamental too. Which is truth! If education is not grounded in truth, then it is worthless. Worse, it is poison! You are poison! You are predators! I can see why you try to stop us from speaking, you know that your ideas are indefensible. You silence the opposing side because you have no argument. You only hide under your beds like pathetic little gutless cowards hoping that we will shut up and go away. But we won't! I promise you that!"*

Dramatization, as he sits at a typewriter and starts to tell a story.
Johnny is a boy with a big imagination. One day he's a dog, the next day a crustacean. Johnny's mom loves her son's make-believe time. You're Johnny the Walrus, until you change your mind.

Tucker Carlson: *"Matt Walsh is out with a new children's book. The book is called Johnny the Walrus. What is this all about?*

Mike Huckabee: *"The book is called Johnny the Walrus. It sold out on Amazon in a few hours."*

Matt Walsh on the Tucker Carlson show: *"I have embraced my true calling as a children's author, hence the cardigan."*

Matt Walsh on the Mike Huckabee show: *"The book is about a little boy who's very imaginative and playful. I have four kids and they all have an imagination. He pretends to be different things and one day he pretends to be a walrus."*

Matt Walsh on the Tucker Carson show: *"Unfortunately, his mother is very progressive and thus confused. She is convinced by the internet and by society that if your child is identifying as something, then he really is that thing. And she tries to raise her child as a Walrus, as a sort of trans walrus, respecting his self-identity."*

Matt Walsh reading to a classroom of small children: *"One morning he came down the stairs, barking and clapping. Wood spoons for tusks and sock fins for flapping. With spoons in his mouth, he's pretending to be a walrus."*

All the kids laugh at that idea.

Matt Walsh reading to several small kids at the Maasai community: *"I'm Johnny the walrus, he said with a roar."*

As it is translated into their language the kids all laugh at such an idea.

Person escorting Matt to Dr. Phil's studio: *"This is a hot topic."*

Narrator: *"Yes, that's a good thing, right?"*

Escort: *"Yeah, absolutely."*

Addison, LGBTQ = advocate, consultant & community organizer on the Dr. Phil Show. *"It's good for us to have these conversations so people open their minds and relearn and unlearn to what we've been taught."*

Dr. Phil talking to Matt Walsh: *"So I want this to be a safe place to talk and learn."*

Addison: *"As you can see, there's an ongoing evolution of language and how people can identify."*

Dr. Phil: *"My next guest, author and conservative host of The Daily Wire's, The Matt Walsh Show, talking about his recently published children's book that has since been removed online by a popular large retail chain. Now Matt says gender is not a social construct but rooted firmly in biology. True?"*

Matt Walsh: *"True, as human beings we have a sex, male or female. That is a biological scientific fact. Now gender is a linguistic term. Words have gender, people don't. You can have whatever self-perception you want, but you cannot expect me to take part in that self-perception or to take part in this kind of charade, this theatrical production. You don't get your own pronouns, just like you don't get your own prepositions or your own adjectives. You know, it's like if I were to tell you my adjectives are handsome and brilliant. No matter, whenever you're talking about me, you have to describe me as handsome and brilliant because that's how I identify."*

Dr. Phil: *"So you think it's a delusion?"*

Matt Walsh: *"Well, this is one of the problems with this left-wing gender ideology is that no one who espouses it can even tell you what these words mean. Like, what is a woman? Can you tell me what a woman is?"*

Ethan, identifies as non-binary transmasculine: *"No, I can't."*

Addison: *"Womanhood is something that is an umbrella term."*

Matt Walsh: *"It includes people that describe what?"*

Addison: *"It describes people who identify as a woman."*

Matt Walsh: *"What is that?"*

Addison: *"To each their own. Each woman, each man, each person is going to have a different relation with their own gender identity and define it differently. So, you want to reduce women, you want to reduce men down to maybe their genetics, our genitals, our chromosomes, right?"*

Matt Walsh: *"What you want to do is appropriate women, you want to appropriate womanhood and turn it into basically a costume that could be worn."*

Dr. Phil: *"Joining us on stage is Dr. Suzy Denbo, associate professor at Kent State University. Dr. Denbo, how do you feel those who oppose using pronouns are taking the wrong approach in this conversation?"*

Dr. Denbo: *"There's the extreme approach that you are admittedly taking and then there's just ordinary people that might not be comfortable with the language change."*

Matt Walsh: *"She began with saying that my view is extreme. So, the view that every single person on earth has held up until 15 seconds ago is extreme? They are conflating gender and sex because on one hand they say well, you got your biological sex but then your gender is whatever social construct. Then they turn around and say that trans women are* *women. So, a man who identifies with the gender, the social construct of womanhood, actually is a woman."*

Dr. Denbo: *"Part of me wants to ask, why do you care so much? Because it's really not that big of a deal."*

Applause from the audience.

Matt Walsh: *"I care about the truth. So, basic truth matters. I want to live in a society where people care about the truth. I care about children and it's these insane ideas about gender that are being foisted on kids and that bothers me quite a bit. I care about the women who are having their opportunities stolen from them, I care quite a bit."*

Dr. Phil: *"I wanted us to have a safe place to be able to talk about this and it seems like we should just keep the dialogue going and hopefully find some middle ground."*

Days after this episode aired on the Dr. Phil Show, the other members on the panel complained they were emotionally damaged by the conversation. In response, CBS and HULU removed the episode from their platforms.

Scott Newgent founded TReVoices, an organization that helps young people who struggle with gender dysphoria. Despite death threats, Scott continues to warn the public about the dangers of transitioning children.

Matt Walsh: *"What do you say to parents; a parent comes to you and says my eight-year-old son is telling me he's a girl?"*

Scott Newgent: *"Great, you're gonna have him do an*

experimental procedure that creates the most suicidal ideation of any other population, seven to ten years after transition. And here's what I tell parents. You don't have the right to medically transition your child."

Sara Stockton: *"We have no research on long-term hormone use. We will be seeing the first generation of long-term hormone use and we already know at least 10 years of hormones you're giving yourself cancer."*

Matt Walsh: *"What's your message to parents who are trying to cope with this?"*

Man on the phone, stuck in Canada for trying to stop the cross-sex hormone shots: *"The first thing is, to tell parents that they are not alone. It is our responsibility as a parent to be the frontline defense for our children. And I know with my child, a lot of people will say, was it worth it? Because now, seemingly, you have lost your child. I'll say, yeah, but at least I've saved my conscience, my morals and my convictions. When my child turns 25 and says, 'Dad where were you?' I'll say, 'I was there, I was fighting as hard as I could. I was not prepared to let this happen.'"*

This Canadian father is currently free on bail. He is awaiting his trial in November of 2022.

Matt Walsh: *"So this really matters? Is another question."*

Dr. Peterson: *"This does matter for those who are getting double mastectomies when you're 16."*

Matt Walsh: *"So why should we care? If we live in a society where gender is ..."*

Dr. Peterson: *"Well I care because my government decided that I had to call people by the terms that they designated, or I'd be subject to legal penalties. It's like no, I'm not doing that, I don't care what your reason is. You don't get to control my tongue."*

Dr. Soh: *"We live in a climate now in which no one seems to care about the safety of women and girls who are going through a very developmentally challenging time in their lives. They may not want to share spaces with their male peers. I would not be surprised, in a few years, there will no longer be women's sports. It will literally be men's sports and transgender sports."*

Carl Trueman: *"The question being asked by the trans person is a legitimate one. 'How can I be happy?' The answer being given by having my body transformed to look like the other gender by having myself pumped full of hormones, clearly isn't working. We have to find a better and more humane way of dealing with individuals who are struggling with gender dysphoria."*

Dr. Grossman: *"I have the utmost compassion for people who suffer from gender dysphoria. It's a nightmare for them and their families. The vast majority, up to 90 percent of kids, as they go through a normal puberty, they're going to be okay. They will be at peace with their bodies. They will have avoided dangerous and experimental medical interventions and surgeries."*

Man on the phone in Canada: *"Maybe we're up against a battle up against a hill that perhaps we're not going to necessarily win today, but if we don't pave the way for a win, then we'll never get there."*

Matt Walsh: *"We are going on this journey, girls can boys, boys can be girls, men can be women, women can be men, it makes me wonder, 'What is a Woman?'"*

Dr. Forcier: *"What is a woman? A woman is someone who claims that as their identity. It could be many things to many people."*

Gert Comfrey: *"I think the question really brings up the fact that it is pretty relative, right? That if you ask women across race, across identities, across class, across culture, you will get a different answer."*

Dr. Bowers: *"Some of it is based on biology. Some is based on hormones. Some of it is based on what you wear and how you present yourself."*

Matt Walsh: *"A woman is not anything in particular. There's no one particular thing."*

Dr. Bowers: *"There is not one particular thing.*

Rodridgo-Heng Lehtinen: *"A woman is someone who says that she is a woman and transitions to be."*

Matt Walsh: *"Who says that she's what?"*

Back at the University

Matt Walsh: *"Can you define the word woman without using the word woman?"*

Dr. Patrick Grzanka: *"It's actually kind of like, it's a curious question. I um ..."*

Matt Walsh: *"We've been journaling across the country asking people this question and almost nobody can answer it. What is a woman?"*

Dr. Peterson: *"Marry one and find out."*

Matt Walsh: *"I should go home and ask my wife, I guess."*

Dr. Peterson: *"Yeah!"*

So, he flies back home to Nashville, Tennessee, to ask his wife.

Matt Walsh: *"Hey, I've been meaning to ask you something."*

His wife: *"Yes??"*

Matt Walsh: *"What is a woman?"*

His wife: *"An adult human female, who needs help opening this."* (a jar of pickles)

He shakes his head and turns around and walks away.

Took a while to get there but we finally figured it out. So, what does this sound like? Repeat after me. Homeschool. Get your kids out of the sewer pipe. That's what they're doing. Remember our study on Planned Parenthood and abortion a couple years ago? *Abortion, The Mass Murder of Children* and what we exposed of Planned Parenthood child murderers who have now gotten saved. They admitted that that's why they have put this Kinsey sex education in the school and why they're doing it as early on as even preschool now. They are doing it on purpose. It has nothing to do with sexual education, it's about getting the kids sexually active as early as possible so that they will commit fornication, get pregnant and then they have that, oh, Planned Parenthood and they'll go there to get an abortion. Because they will make thousands and thousands of dollars off the abortions. If it's in the first trimester, a few thousand, if they push it to the third it's upwards to ten to fifteen thousand and then even after that they sell the baby's body parts to the pharmaceutical companies and other medical and science industries. And they make a ton of money off of that. But they go into the schools to produce a future crop. And the same thing is happening with this.

What did he say? For every person that comes out as a transgender and begins that process of transitioning with chemicals, drugs and blockers and surgeries just for one person is a lot of money. So, we need to speak up and speak out about this. The Bible is clear we are headed for woeful destruction just like Israel. This is not just a moral issue it's a preservative issue. It's destroying us and the current administration is doing all they can to push it. Which means, we

CDC Directs Kids To Secretive Online Chat Space To Explore Sex Change Operations, 'Having Mulitiple Genders,' The Occult

The Centers for Disease Control and Prevention is hellbent on grooming, killing and castrating your better start speaking up about this or we will be destroyed, you can bank on it! Let me give you some of the reasons why they are pushing this destructive behavior.

The first is that they know this will destroy our country and that is the plan. And I think it is a planned destruction. Now one, God said when you go down this road you don't have to wonder where you're headed, **Romans 1**, the third state you're headed for the final stage of destruction. But I do believe that there is a deliberate attack on our nation to destroy us from within. And this fits in with that narrative. The current administration is cramming this everywhere they can. You see it with the CDC that they're secretly online encouraging kids to go down this route, to have multiple genders and all that stuff. So, the internet crowd, the CDC, the medical community, the same ones behind the lie with Covid. They are all pushing this agenda.

Biden's Woke Administration Invested $1.5 Million Into Programming Transgender Inmates

According to a recent report by The Washington Free Beacon, the Department of Justice invested almost $1.5 million into a "transgender programming curriculum" focused on transgender inmates' needs.

The curriculum is designed to help transgender inmates with their gender "identity," sexual health, and safety.

The Justice Department disbursed the funds for an outside firm to develop a tailored program aimed at helping transgender inmates "manage identity concerns during incarceration," according to a government summary of the contract. The contract also asks the firm to develop a program to help transgender inmates access hormone treatment after release.

Join The Gateway Pundit Newsletter

Sign up for our free email newsletter, and we'll make sure to keep you in the loop.

The current administration is spending 1.5 million dollars into programing transgender inmates. It's bad enough that you are in jail, now they are indoctrinating these people and spending our tax dollars on this agenda as well. Remember the people that the Biden

Transgender Biden administration health official to be sworn in as four-star admiral

Kaelan Deese

WATCH: Biden's SCOTUS Pick Says She 'Can't' Define What A Woman Is "I Can't, I'm Not a Biologist"

Judge Ketanji Brown Jackson, Biden's nominee for the Supreme Court, was eviscerated by Senator Marsha Blackburn in a series of questions that would have been so easy for anyone to answer just a few short years ago.

If you could travel back in time just fifteen years, it would be difficult to explain the line of questioning administration has been appointing to the Supreme Court? She cannot define what a woman is, she is a part of this narrative. She's a part of this mindset. And then, of course, remember this transgender person? The health person?

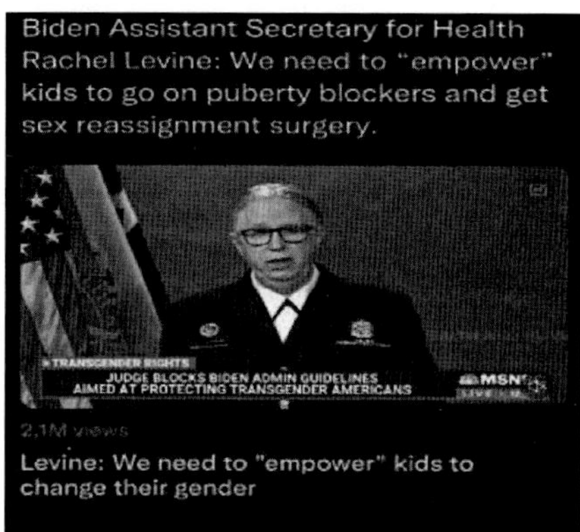

When sworn in, she said, "We need to empower kids to go on puberty blockers and get sex reassignment surgery." And that person is the Assistant Secretary of Health of the United States of America. Appointed by the current administration.

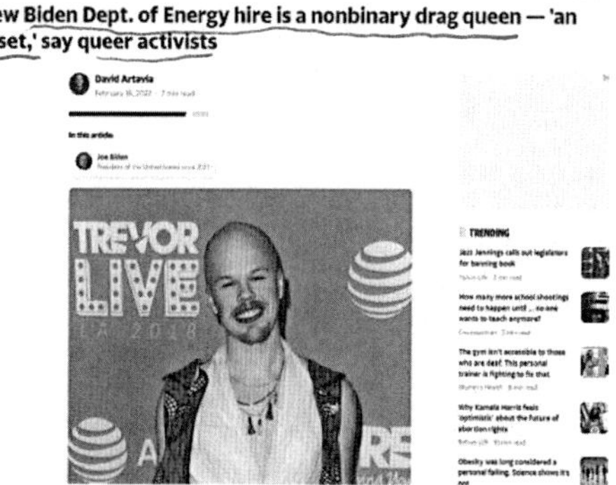

And this person is the new Department of Energy hire. This is a drag queen. They are in Europe representing the United States of America. We are a laughingstock to the other countries. But again, I think it is a deliberate attack on our country. Remember in the 50s what Nikita Khrushchev said? We will take America without firing a shot.

These two individuals are in Europe representing the United States.

Part of that is the re-education of America into communist ideals, we don't call it communism, we call it socialism. It's basically the same thing. And the other thing is to destroy the country internally, morally, and this is a moral issue that God warns about that once you go down this route you're going to a depraved mind! Things that ought not to be done. You're going to approve of those things, and you are done. So, I think it is a deliberate attack.

Now specifically, even from a military point of view, if you think that people have given up the desire to take over the United States from a military perspective you are fooling yourself. That has never gone away.

About Privacy ProTrumpNews AmericanGulag How To Help Store Login

Biden's America: Trans Soldiers Given Special Privileges in US Military While Christian Soldiers are Persecuted

Share Tweet Share to Gab Telegram Email

The left continues its assault on our country, our culture, our history, and our way of life.

In America today trans soldiers are given special privileges by the regime while Christian soldiers are persecuted and denied their religious rights.

At the same time the current administration is giving special privileges to trans soldiers, they are, at the exact same time, persecuting Christian soldiers. So, we are seeing transgenderization, a feminization, homosexual, and lesbianism, basically a neutering of our military. You don't want to do that to your military. From a security aspect, do you remember the recruiting commercial of the Russian army, full of testosterone and then the recruiting commercial of the Chinese army, full of testosterone, and then the current recruiting commercial for America was a girl wanting to go into the military who had two moms? There is where we are at. One guy said this. Isn't it comforting to know that China has amassed the largest Navy in the world while we focus on race, gender and which cartoon character could offend. Sleep well.

I really believe that this is as God says, "You're going to be destroyed if you don't turn around from this." But I also believe it's a deliberate attack on the military, on the people, we are being destroyed from within and they are going after the military. Call it what you want, but here comes Russia and China making an invasion on the United States and you have a bunch of transgender soldiers. Do you think that is going to strike fear in them? This is one of the dumbest things you could do. So that's one of the reasons, it's a destruction, the other one is money.

This industry has been turned into a money-making machine. Who isn't profiting would be faster to answer. Remember one transgender generates $1.3 million dollars. That's a lot of money. They have glamorized a mental illness, created a trend, pushed a narrative that "gender" is something you choose, and socially engineered it into every institution and across every TV screen. They have been training doctors across the globe in vaginoplasty, phalloplasty, facial feminization surgery, and urethral procedures. Clinics are popping up everywhere, every university is on board, and hospitals and medical institutions are frothing at the mouth to get in on the action.

So, who's profiting?

- Scientists and researchers
- Drug manufacturers
- Biogenetics
- Pharmaceutical companies
- Pharmacies
- Psychiatrists and psychologists
- Endocrinologists
- Surgeons
- Hospitals and clinics
- Planned Parenthood
- Universities
- NGOs
- Shareholders and investors

- Billionaires invested in all of the above
- All of the corrupt receiving kickbacks

Aside from surgery, one of the big cash cows is hormone therapy, because once they begin, they will spend a lifetime visiting doctors, having blood drawn, and pumping themselves with hormones. Repeat business is the name of their game. There has been a big shift over the past decade to target children with confusing them and causing them to question their own gender, by suggesting they can "choose" their gender. And if they want to "transition" they can begin with chemically sterilizing hormones.

This is how Planned Parenthood draws them in, under the guise of "reproductive rights," with no therapy required.

In 2016, Lupron alone generated revenue of $821 million.

Planned Parenthood is The Second Largest Provider of Gender Affirming Hormone Care in The Nation – A Big Profiteer

Just three years ago, Planned Parenthood was only offering hormone therapy in 27 of its clinics, and now they are the 2nd largest provider in the nation.

What does that say? Well, a few things. For one, this industry is growing fast, and they are in phase 3, which is the sales marketing push as they manufacture a reality. Second, Planned Parenthood is running this under the guise of "reproductive rights" while sterilizing thousands of people, which is their MO. Third, if Planned Parenthood has taken this on nationwide, that only means one thing – they will eventually expand to include surgical transitions in their clinics because it will expand their bottom line $$.

Who Are the Rich, White Men Institutionalizing Transgender Ideology?

As an environmental activist who was deplatformed from a speaking venue by transactivists, in 2013 I developed curiosity about the power of this group to force this development. A year later, when *Time* magazine announced a transgender tipping point on its cover, I had already begun to examine the money behind the transgender project.

I have watched as all-women's safe spaces, universities, and sports opened their doors to any man who chose to identify as a woman. Whereas men who identify as transwomen are at the forefront of this project, women who identify as transmen seem silent and invisible. I was astonished that such a huge cultural change as the opening of sex-protected spaces was happening at

Popular

1. Exclusive: In Private, Cassidy Hutchinson Joked About Riot, Called J6 Committee 'Phony,' Praised Trump Before Changing Story
2. FBI's False Labeling Of Biden Laptop As Disinformation Is Even Worse Than It Seems. Here's Why
3. Wokeism Is Collapsing On Itself
4. Why The Oncoming Recession Is Going To Be Worse Than You Think

Hospitals are not only profiting, but they are also driving This industry. I had already begun to examine the money behind the transgender project. I witnessed an overhaul in the English language with new pronouns and a near-tyrannical assault on those who did not use them.

Laws mandating new speech were passed. Laws overriding biological sex with the amorphous concept of gender identity are being instituted now. People who speak openly about these changes can find themselves, their families, and their livelihoods threatened. These elements, along with media saturation of the issue, had me wondering: Is there a bigger agenda with moneyed interests that we are not seeing?

Who Is Funding the Transgender Movement?

I found exceedingly rich, white men with enormous cultural influence are funding the transgender lobby and various transgender organizations. These includes but are not limited to Jennifer Pritzker (a male transgender billionaire who inherited stakes in the family's Hyatt Hotels chain); George Soros; Martine Rothblatt (a male who identifies as transgender and transhumanist); Tim Gill (a gay man retired computer programmer and multimillionaire); Drummond Pike; Warren and Peter Buffett; Jon Stryker (a gay man); Mark Bonham (a gay man) just to name a few.

These men and others, including pharmaceutical companies and the U.S. government, are sending millions of dollars to LGBT causes.

It is enough to change laws, uproot language, and force new speech on the public, to censor, to create an atmosphere of threat for those who do not comply with gender identity ideology. Along with support by pharmaceutical giants such as Janssen Therapeutics, Johnson and Johnson, Pfizer, Bristol-Meyers Squibb, and major technology corporations including Google, Microsoft, Amazon, Intel, Dell, and IBM are also funding the transgender project.

Now let me give you the third reason, there's another reason why and this is more of a long-term thing. It is preparing people for the transhumanist movement.

The LGBT Agenda Will Bring About Transhumanism and Artificial Wombs – 1971 Homosexual Manifesto

The ever-increasing reality that the LGBT movement is the tool of an agenda to destroy the family model and create an environment where transhumanists and technologists thrive is not a new idea, rather it was declared in a homosexual manifesto from 1971.

The radical document, which is a declaration of war against the morality of mankind, proclaims the end goal of a genderless dystopia, all made possible by the ever-increasing technological advances of society. Thus, the document brought about in 1971, aligns the ideology and timing of both the sexual devolution we are currently witnessing and the transhumanist movement that is brewing in the shadows of the LGBT movement.

The Fourth Industrial Revolution Is The Transhumanist Movement

Side by side the agenda of the LGBT has operated in collusion with the technological revolutions. While the mainstream organizers of the LGBT agenda may yet be clueless to the intentions of their leaders, this document lays bare the absolute intentions of the demoralizing agenda, to bring to an end the human and bring about the transhuman. Over and over again, the World Economic Forum has depicted that what comes in the next industrial revolution, will be, instead of mankind creating better tools, man himself will become the tool.

In addition to the aforementioned, out of the several things mentioned in the above manifesto, one stark point is outlined, the destruction of the patriarchal family. Ever since mankind was created, a profound structure has driven the population growth of this planet,

The Latest

[VIDEO] Drag Queen Drag Shows Are Now Infesting Churches

[VIDEO] Starbucks Worker Dumps Milkshake On Open Air Preachers Head

[VIDEO] Man Arrested For Threatening To Kill Female Abolitionist With Crowbar

St. Pete's Drag Queen Story Hour And Host REBUKED Out Of Existence. Answered Prayers!

SICKENING VIDEO! A Call To Action: Stop The Sexualization Of Children In Huntington West Virginia

By definition, a transhumanist is one who wants to use science and technology to transcend the so-called human limitations. They believe in the lie of evolution, and they believe that it is their job as the elite, because the trans humans, basically the billionaire elites around the world, believe it's their duty to speed up the process of human evolution and create, manipulate us, into their image. A better humanity. As we saw in our COVID study, that's what they did with the mRNA technology. Messenger RNA. You get injected with something that changes your identity, your genome, your structure. They believe they are going to create a new utopia on the planet. Part of their utopia goes like this: At least 90 percent of the world needs to be annihilated because we are overpopulated. Now the remaining 10 percent, someone put it lower to 5 percent, we have the privilege, as survivors of that, of serving these elites. But our current bodies aren't in the optimum as their worker bees. They are preparing us to be better worker bees for them.

A bigger brain with software and memory updates made possible.

Implanted ear wear to eliminate Bluetooth headsets and smartphones.

Larger stomach and backside.

Smaller sex organs as human interaction reduces.

Increased language skills to keep up with emerging economies and global working.

Smart fingers with chips that aid work or implement security protocols.

"It shouldn't come as a surprise to anyone that the LGBT movement and transhumanism have a lot in common. Nearly all transhumanists support the LGBT cause. Why?

Because after all, they too desire to be free to alter, express, and control one's sexual preference and identity which is a transhumanist concept."

"In the next few years, the human being will undergo a larger transformation. Men will be able to give birth with implanted uteri. Parents may choose to have designer babies without certain sexual organs."

And "Some religions (Roman Catholicism) *could encourage males to be born with genetically lowered sex drives so they can have a better chance at becoming celibate priests, which is a shrinking vocation in the U.S."*

"Or what about fembots and sexbots, which are already a growing 100-million-dollar market? Do we give them rights? Can we marry them? What if they're gay? What if we program them to not know if they're gay or not?"

"And cybersex will become a reality where Facebook's Oculus Rift and haptic suits will allow people from all corners of the world to have group sex if they want."

"Such actions may lead to a society where male and female traits disappear altogether as pleasure becomes 'on-demand,' and gene therapy is able to combine the most functional parts of both genders into one entity."

"Some institutions, like marriage, will go the way of the dinosaurs."

What's their end game?

Simple. To destabilize this country, divide and conquer, sterilize in every fashion possible, create a gender identity crisis, breed socialism, all while simultaneously relishing in their fantastical financial gain while aiming toward their one world governance they hope to achieve by 2030.

It is the same end game with all their agendas.

The 2030 agenda is not a joke. They openly speak about this. They want a one world governance with the UN in control.

People must open their eyes, especially if you are a parent, because they are coming for your children.

Chapter Eleven

The Twisting of Christian Pietism

We have already seen in our study, a kind of hodgepodge of videos and teachings and things, that there's an invasion going on in the church. We are dealing with why the world is so messed up. But not just the world, but the church. How are we in such high apostasy? Because there is an invasion going on by these people who are self-proclaimed atheists in a lot of cases. They're not Christians and they have taken over the seminaries, bible colleges, denominations, and churches. It spills downhill and that answers the question as to why things are so messed up. There are not just fakers in the pews, they've taken control of the church by and large. But then they moved on to the perversion.

They're not only invading the church, but they are here for a purpose and that purpose, is to change Christianity into "not Christianity." They are doing this by twisting the Scripture. That's what non-Christians do, and they started that with a twisted version of love. Their version of love is not the Biblical definition of love. Their definition is that you have to accept anyone, anything, no matter what you do, no matter what kind of sin or so-called lifestyle. That is being a loving Christian. No, it's not! They are using that to justify their twisted relationships. The Biblical love is God. God is love and He defines what true Biblical love is by demonstrating that love by giving us mercy, compassion, kindness, graciousness, patience, faithfulness, and goodness.

They use this to justify their twisted relationships. It started with twisting marriage. The Biblical definition of marriage was, and still is to this day, between a man and a woman. It's never going to change. That's it! You come together and you have a family and that's it! But they have twisted it, starting with homosexuality, lesbianism, and they didn't stop. In fact, the Bible tells us in **Romans 1**, they wouldn't stop, and then once you get to that level, you're going to get handed over to the final stage of what's called a depraved mind, and then you are going to start doing things that ought not be done. Because you have opened up Pandora's Box.

Now we've got polygamy that's being pushed, we've got pedophilia being pushed, this whole gender fluidity aspect. They don't even know what a woman is. Bestiality, and all of this kind of stuff is now being pushed. But that is exactly what the Bible said would happen. And then we took a deeper look at what this depraved mind looks like. We saw all kinds of depraved interviews, dolls, and cartoons. We even dealt with all the skeptical questions like, "Homosexuality isn't even mentioned in the Bible," or "You're interpreting that wrong," or "Love is love, what's the big deal," "If two people love each other, who cares?" etc.

Well, how did we get into this? Because we're making the same mistake as Israel, we've given into relativism. The Old Testament tells us that the reasons why they were all over the place and society was being destroyed, was because "everyone was doing what was right in their own eyes." What does that sound like? That is exactly what we are dealing with today. What does Isaiah say is coming? "Great times. It's incredible, the best time ever." No, woeful times. Woe does not mean, "Slow down horsey." It's where we get "hoi" as in "oy vey." It means, "doom and gloom, despair, bad things are coming, a passionate cry of grief or despair." It's not a good thing when you hit that route. It's woeful times and we're in a society where they're calling evil good and good evil, light

- dark, dark - light, etc. We are following the same rotten pattern. "Doing whatever is right in your own eyes," and "rejecting God's Law" is not a good way to go. Yet, this is where we are, not only in the world but even in the so-called Church.

As we saw, there are three things as to why they are doing this, promoting this perversion. Well, number one is a deliberate attack on our country to destroy America from within. Remember Khrushchev's warning in the 50s? "We're going to take you down without firing a shot." They've decayed us morally on purpose, so I think that's part of it as well as infecting our military.

Number two is that they are making a ton of money. Millions of dollars off this twisted, sick agenda; 1.3 million dollars is generated from one person who goes down the transgender route. It's a lifetime of medication, testing, and surgeries, and they are even starting to invest in it like it's a stock option.

And then, number three is to prepare people for transhumanism, for the transhumanist movement. That is where these global elites not only want to take control of the world, but they also want to genetically modify us into better worker bees for them, as crazy and as scientific-ish as that sounds. If that's a word, that's really what's going on. And this whole idea of gender fluidity, "I can be whoever I want to be" and "I can be this or that," and they'll say, "Yeah. We will genetically modify you into that." They want that mindset to permeate the planet because that helps them to cushion the blow when they say, "Oh, by the way, you had a choice, now we're going to tell you how to be and what we're going to genetically modify you with."

And if that wasn't bad enough. Now we have this lie in the Church saying that Christians should just keep your mouth shut and stay within your four walls and let the world do whatever it wants. Basically, this is called pietism. You have no rights, keep your mouth shut. Have you heard that mentality? Because that's actually there. It's called pietism. Now the problem with that is, that is one of the fastest ways to destroy your country, your home, your business, by a Christian who knows better. It's God's truth that sets people free, but if you never speak it, how cán they ever have the benefits of that? You'd think it would be common sense.

It will destroy your country in a heartbeat when you get conditioned and think, "Oh, that's right. I have no right to speak up. They can just do whatever they want to do." No, God calls us to engage our culture. In fact, this is cool. God actually calls us to be rebels. That is exactly what He says we are supposed to be. Not pietist. You may be thinking, "Are you serious, I'm called to be a rebel? I thought as Christians you are supposed to be lovey-dovey; you can't speak up; you just have to stay there in your corner and be quiet." No, we're supposed to rebel. God tells us specifically what we're supposed to rebel against.

Romans 12:1-2: "Therefore, I urge you, brothers, in view of God's mercy, to offer your bodies as living sacrifices, (in the Old Testament it was dead sacrifices) holy and pleasing to God."

If you are living an unholy life, then you're sending the wrong message to the lost. That is the first step in getting saved, you need to acknowledge that there is sin. Sin is harmful, sin hurts. I'm a sinner, I'm in need of a savior. But if we are loose with sin and living in sin, then what's the message to the lost? It must not be that big of a deal. No, you live a holy living sacrifice, that's pleasing to God. Again, the **Book of James** said the Modus Operandi, when you get out of bed, it's not pleasing myself, not pleasing my flesh, it's pleasing God. God, what do you want me to do? So that's the logical response. In fact, he uses that word logical.

Romans 12:1-2 cont.: "This is your spiritual act of worship."

Spiritual act is where we get the logical, and it makes total sense in the context. Therefore, in light of all that God has done, you're doomed straight to hell, there's nothing you can do, myself included, we all deserve to die and go straight to hell, but out of pure mercy, God gave you a gift called the gift of eternal life, Jesus Christ, who died on the cross to forgive you of all your sins. Rescued you from that place and then gives you the complete polar opposite on top. What's the logical response to that? That's what He says. Live your lives as a living sacrifice every day. You're a holy advertisement for Jesus and you're living like, "God how can I please you? I want to please you today for what you've done for me." Not because I have to, as Paul says elsewhere, it's Christ's love that compels us, not legalism. I want to please him.

Romans 12:1-2 cont.: "Do not conform any longer to the pattern of this world but be transformed by the renewing of your mind. Then you will be able to test and approve what God's will is - his good, pleasing, and perfect will."

The context here is basically that all have sinned and fallen short of the glory of God, the wages of sin is death, there is no one good, no one righteous, no not one. So, we are all basically doomed, going straight to hell, **Romans 3.** The good news is that God sent his son Jesus Christ to save us and rescue us. Purely as an act of His goodness and grace and mercy, and we are set free from that. We're no longer slaves to sin. We're not going to hell anymore and we didn't earn it, it's a gift from God. It's fantastic. Then R**omans 8** kicks in and He says it's guaranteed, nothing, height nor depth, angels, demons, suffering, nothing can separate us from the love of God in Christ Jesus. And then here comes **Romans 12.**

So, here we see the Bible says if we really appreciate God's mercy, and saving us from our sins through His sacrifice of His Son Jesus Christ, what are we going to do? We're going to sit on that pew until we die and go to Heaven. No, what did he say? Some people treat it like God's called us to do something. You don't just get your blessed insurance and your fire insurance and sit around on the premises. What do you do? He says you sacrifice your lives right back to Him. That's the logical response, right? According to our text, the Bible is clear. If we really appreciate God's mercy in saving us from our sins by sacrificing His Son, what are we going to do? We're going to sacrifice our lives right back at Him, right? And the question is, "How do we know when we're doing that?" Well, what did the text say? We know we're sacrificing our lives back unto God when we're no longer conforming our lives to this world, right?

And what do we usually call somebody who refuses to conform to something? We call them a what? A rebel, right? Therefore, God is giving us divine permission to be what? "Rebels for Jesus," right? Exactly!

And here's my point. Surely, we all know this, right? I mean, surely every Christian who's ever lived knows that the Church is to be a Body of Rebels, where people look at us and say, "Wow! Look at those people! They've got to be followers of Christ! They absolutely refuse to have anything to do with this world's wickedness. In fact, they'll face any threat and take any persecution just to stand up for God's truth." Surely, we know that, right? Well, you'd think so, but we've got some problems. Why? Because if you look at most churches, it doesn't look like we're Christian rebels with a cause. Are you kidding? We look like worldly conformists without a cause!

So why in the world do we do this? Why do we Christians no longer rebel against this world, and instead conform to this world, the exact opposite? Hey, great question. I'm glad you asked. It's pretty simple. This is basic Christianity, Romans 12, God's mercy, it's common sense. Christ's love compels us. You're thankful for being saved from eternal damnation in hell. You're going, "Hey, can I please you Jesus? What do you want me to do? I'm sick and tired of the filth and junk of this wicked world system." How many years was it before you got saved? For me, it was 25. Are you sick of it? Why would you want to go back to it? Like a dog to its vomit. How did we get into this?

Well, now the bulk of the Church is exactly mirroring the world. They act like the world. They speak like the world. They look like the world. It's like, where's Jesus? They don't even mention Jesus. How did we get into this? There's a lie spread through the Church called pietism which we're now going to expose. While all of this is going on, this invasion and this perversion, you would think Christians are finally going to speak up. We're at the final hour, it can't get any worse than this. Then they're conditioned with a lie to keep their mouth shut. And the world continues to go downhill. Let's take a look at this video transcript.

Pastor: *"My grandfather was taught that clergymen should not meddle in politics. My father was taught that clergymen should not meddle in politics. I was taught that clergymen should not meddle in politics. My father and grandfather were mostly obedient to the ideas of Christian pietism. But to their credit as good men, not always."*

Meaning of Pietism: Stresses personal devotion, internal holiness, and inward spiritual experience at the expense of an outward legal expression of Christianity in society.

Pastor: *"Pietism is a common doctrine of the western church. It has taught multiple generations that clergymen should never address the cultural controversies, much less the legal and political worlds, which naturally flow downstream from that culture."*

Matt Trewhella: *"Pietism essentially is, we take Christianity, and we boil it down to the personal. It's all about me, myself and I. We should have absolutely nothing to do with civil government matters and it stands in utter contrast to historic Biblical Christianity again, which said, 'Christ impacts every area of life.' August Francke, Founder of Pietism, Lutheran Theologian and Bible Scholar, was very strong on mission but on this matter of our relationship to civil government, they were deadly wrong. Somehow this teaching came to King Frederick, King of Prussia, and he immediately began to put the pietas, as they were called, into important positions of teaching in the universities."*

Dr. Kevin Baird: *"They began to have a theological construct which basically taught passivity. It taught compartmentalism. You deal with what you deal with, and we'll deal with what we deal with. Hitler's famous statement to the Church of Germany at that time was, 'You just be concerned with the souls of men, I'll take care of Germany.' And that was the fruit of pietism. It was the ability to sing louder as the trains rumbled by, carrying Jews to execution."*

Pastor: *"While Hitler was busy constructing his tyranny and his evil, Christian ministers of Germany were giving a wrong interpretation of* ***Romans 13****."*

Matt Trewhella: *"They were saying that* **Romans 13** *teaches that we are always to obey the civil authorities. You see that the agenda of the status, becomes the agenda of the Christian. They are easily influenced because they're not anchored to the law of God anymore."*

Bishop E.W. Jackson: *"Authority. The idea of authority is established by God. It doesn't mean every person in authority and everything they're doing is established by God and that you are somehow duty bound to obey them simply because they happen to hold a position of authority. In fact, I think we have a duty to rebel against authority, as our founding fathers did when that authority is unjust. When that authority is trying to turn us into slaves of man, rather than being children of God, there's a responsibility to stand up against it. Sometimes, even violently oppose it. And if that weren't true, then it was morally wrong for us to fight World War II. But it wasn't. It was the right thing to do."*

Matt Trewhella: *"If the state commands that which God forbids or forbids that which God commands, we are to obey God rather than man."*

Dr. Kevin Baird: *"None of us would dismiss the reality of a personal relationship with Jesus Christ. But when it is sealed, to only affect my personal ethic or life, that's when we begin to get into trouble."*

Trevor Loudon: *"It's no accident that the first communist revolution was in Germany in 1848. Karl Marx grew his movement in Germany, which had been neutralized, the politics were ripe because of pietism, and when that revolution failed, many thousands of German communists moved to the Midwest of the United States; to Milwaukee, Chicago, etc. And what eventually founded the communist party U.S.A. Communism followed pietism not just in Germany but into America."*

Michael O'Fallon: *"What you are being told by many that are in leadership, if your politics is involving itself in your Christian life, maybe your Christianity is too political. Maybe it's too American-centered. Now that is only applicable if what they're referring to is you really supporting conservative concepts. Constitutional concepts."*

Pastor: *"So, it's an aggression against conservative principles which are actually Biblical."*

Michael O'Fallon: *"Right."*

Matt Trewhella: *"The history of Christianity has been one where churchmen engaged the magistrates and instructed them from the law and word of God regarding their duty for their office as a magistrate. But now that we've abandoned them, they don't know what their purpose, their function, or their limits are."*

Pastor: *"The only way that pietism could do this, is by jettisoning the law. Antinomianism creates a vacuum if you don't have the law of God to lean on, as a basis for how you make decisions. Something else has to fill the void."*

Dr. Kevin Baird: *"This is the foundation of situational ethics and situationism. And that is, we no longer consider what is right and wrong. We now begin to determine most of the time, in and of ourselves, what we perceive to be the best possible outcome. I no longer look at a circumstance in my life and ask the question what is right and what is wrong. I immediately leap to the consequences of both of those decisions, and then I determine my decision on what I perceive to be the greatest possible benefit."*

Pastor: *"We did an outreach to inner city kids whose parents were unwilling to attend church. Hundreds and eventually thousands of kids in our town were successfully reached. Out of this sea of children emerged this little band of Hispanic kids and they were drawn to me. They stood out to me in every gathering. Smiling and well-dressed and always* *respectful to authority. They didn't have a dad and at the time, I had no kids of my own, so I, of course, fell in-love with them.*

Well, as the story goes, their mom came home one night to the house that they lived in, on the rough side of town, and their streetlight had burned out. Without a husband to keep her safe, she felt particularly vulnerable traversing the darkness with five little children. She called a male co-worker that she had grown fond of the next day. She asked him if he wouldn't mind staying at the house with her and the kids at least until the light bulb on the streetlamp outside was finally repaired.

He said yes, and he showed up with a hammer and killed all of the children in their sleep by crushing their precious skulls in just before he took a knife and slit the mother's throat and then used the hammer on her. He was eventually caught, and he committed suicide in prison. During that funeral with six white caskets, was the most difficult thing that I have ever done in 28 years of ministry.

Today I live two blocks from the park where I played with them for the last time before their murders. Now I take my own children there to play. As I stand there smiling at them on the outside, I have an everlasting pain hidden behind the smile. I'm glad that it still hurts. I don't ever want to forget it. It changed my life and changed my ministry because it forced me to question the teaching of pietism. Leticia probably had the purest of motives in asking for that man to come over to their home. But you see there was a time in American culture when a gentleman would never have even considered entering the home of an unmarried lady.

A hundred years earlier in a more Christian society, a gentleman would have probably climbed a ladder and replaced the bulb on the light pole in her alley. Why? Because the now vanishing western church, once upon a time, had a profound impact on western civilization. The mores and expectations of the Ten Commandments were a reliable fence erected around the cliffs of sin as a legal, political, and cultural protection. So, in the most horrific and traumatic way possible, I was forced, as a pastor, to look and see that the fence was gone.

What happened to the living, powerful, transformative, nation-shaking Christianity? You know what I'm talking about. The kind that Jesus brought the world. Something dressed up to look like Christianity is doing just fine here in the west. But is it a counterfeit? It certainly resembles Christianity, but most of the people I know sense that something is wrong."

And it is wrong because it's not the real Church. The Church has been invaded. But as you can see, what was his wake-up call to realize that it isn't just about preaching, teaching, which is what pastors and shepherds should do and teaching the word of God? But the whole point of that is we get equipped as saints to what? Keep our mouths shut? You go out into the world, and you affect the culture. You infect them, if you will, with God's truth. Why? Because they need the truth too in order to be set free. But that's not what's going on anymore with this lie of pietism.

What was one of the verses that are still being used today? And we saw this during the Covid thing. **Romans 13**. Really, so the government, we're supposed to obey everything they say. We're never supposed to be that rebel for Jesus. No! Just right after **Romans 12**, that we just read, he mentions this about the submission to the authorities.

Romans 13:1-4: "Everyone must submit himself to the governing authorities, for there is no authority except that which God has established. The authorities that exist have been established by God. Consequently, he who rebels against the authority is rebelling against what God has instituted, and those who do so will bring judgment on themselves. For rulers hold no terror for those who do right, but for those who do wrong. Do you want to be free from fear of the one in authority? Then do what is right and he will commend you. For he is God's servant to do you good. But if you do wrong, be afraid, for he does not bear the sword for nothing. He is God's servant, an agent of wrath to bring punishment on the wrongdoer."

You look, certainly in scripture, and you see early on, God is the one who instituted the government. Why? Because sin entered the world, and this was one of His protective measures. You get out of line, I don't know about you, but personally, I'm glad we have the police force, I'm glad we have the infrastructure and things that keep the city going normally. Those have been instituted by God as safeguards for sin. I'm glad we have the military. But the government and authorities, even though they were instituted by God, created by God for protective measures, if they ask you to do something, just do it. If they ask you to drive the speed limit, you drive the speed limit. If they ask you to pay your taxes, then pay your taxes.

But here's the point. Does that mean everything? What's the caveat? If the government, that God instituted begins to go against God, well then, we have to obey the government. No, that's the lie of pietism. That is the lie that was infiltrated during the Covid baloney. It's not true. I rebel against the government every single time, 100 percent of the time, when they disagree with God. In our ungodly society, it's happening more and more frequently. Which means we should be speaking up, engaging our culture, more and more frequently, just as much as they rebel against God, we rebel against them.

Now we go to the next verse to see the caveat. You don't obey the government in everything. You go the speed limit, you pay your taxes, right, you don't do donuts in the parking lot, but when they ask you to do something contrary to God, you would think it's common sense. You obey God. That is what we see with the apostles in this verse.

Acts 5:25-29: "Then someone came and said, 'Look! The men you put in jail are standing in the temple courts teaching the people.' At that, the captain went with his officers and brought the apostles. They did not use force, because they feared that the people would stone them. Having brought the apostles, they made them appear before the Sanhedrin to be questioned by the high priest. We gave you strict orders not to teach in this name,' he said. 'Yet you have filled Jerusalem with your teaching and are determined to make us guilty of this man's blood.' Peter and the other apostles replied, 'We must obey God rather than men!"

What did he say? "We must obey God," it's imperative, you have to, you're a Christian. You're a living sacrifice. You rebel against this wicked system. We must obey God rather than man. They went out, even though the government, the authority, threatened them, even with death, what did they say? "I'm a living sacrifice for Jesus Christ. I'll do what you say because authority is established by God, but the moment you disagree with God, I'm a rebel for Jesus." I am going to rebel against this wicked world system. I do not conform to it.

Now notice what was going on. Notice what we were being asked to do, and dare I say, even a massive number of churches unfortunately did. Scripture says we are not to conform to this world and certainly when it says to go against what God says. But we went from "not conform," to the word, "comply." The exact polar opposite. This was the crux of what was going on during the Covid baloney. This is God's divine salad. Do you like salad? This is the best salad you could ever have. This one is truly nutritious, healthy, and spiritual, all at the same time.

Hebrews 10:22-25: "Let us draw near to God with a sincere heart in full assurance of faith, having our hearts sprinkled to cleanse us from a guilty conscience and having our bodies washed with pure water. Let us hold unswervingly to the hope we profess, for He who promised is faithful. And let us consider how we may spur one another on toward love and good deeds. Let us not give up meeting together, as some are in the habit of doing, but let us encourage one another – and all the more as you see the day approaching."

So, as we see the return of Jesus Christ approaching, what does God tell us to do? Let us keep getting together. In fact, he even says the flip side of that. Let us not stop getting together as some are in the habit of doing. Remember when we busted out in the Greek, some are in the habit of doing? The Greek word for that literally means "as prescribed by law." That's a game-changer, isn't it? I looked it up in the Greek and every occurrence in the New Testament either applied to Jewish religious law or Roman civil law.

So, let's translate that. It says this, "let us not give up meeting together as prescribed by law but let us as Christians encourage one another and all the more as the day is approaching." So, if they are ever, and they could, unfortunately, our wicked government, say you need to close your doors again. Can I tell you straight up what we're not going to do? We're not going to close our doors. Do you know why? Because we obey God, rather than man. The way they got away with it last time, is not only because of lies, this lie of pietism, the abuse of **Romans 13**, without the **Acts 5** caveat. I obey them on certain things, but I never obey them when they ask me to disobey God.

Hebrew 10 says that we should not give up meeting together. Nobody, including the government, has the right to do that. Do you know what that is? It's called the First Amendment. The reason why you and I could support the Constitution, the Bill of Rights, is because if you know anything about the framers of the Constitution, the Bill of Rights, our founding fathers, it was based on what? Biblical principles. That's why we can support them. The very first one says we have not just the freedom of religion and press, but we have the right to assemble. What's that? **Hebrews 10**, we're assembling. You can't tell me not to assemble. And it didn't say until a "bug" shows up. Which was a whole bunch of baloney in the first place with that agenda. That's not what it says.

Historically, after the first amendment, I have the right as an American, I have exercised my religious expression, I can speak up, even against the government. I have that right. I have the right to assemble. And if you violate those three things, here comes the second one. I also have the right to keep and bear arms. We have the right to take our government back when they go back to tyranny. With force. You're not going to hear that in most pulpits, and you know why? Because they have fallen for the lie of pietism. Which is not Biblical.

So, how did we get into this mess? Well, these guys have come in, they have invaded the Church. Most of the Church, I'm convinced, is not even saved. Especially when you're going to see another stat. They have all the trappings. They have the stained-glass windows. They may wear a cool jacket. They may even wear robes and get really spiritual. They sound like it, they look like it, but they're not. They are in the church, and they are twisting the definition of love, bringing in sin, twisting relationships. We're going to eventually see how they are twisting Jesus. With them coming in with their twisting and perversion, they are infiltrating the Church and they're saying to the rest of you, "Keep your mouth shut! Keep in your four walls." And basically, just let the world go burn in hell. I don't see that in the Bible.

But that's what a lot of churches are all about. They are conforming to the world instead of conforming to God and they comply, comply, comply, instead of rebel, rebel, rebel. Now they come in and basically change the idea of twisted relationships. They've changed the definition of marriage, they've changed relationships, they've changed gender, they've changed male/female. Well, at the same time and this is where we are at now, they've changed the identity of the Church. The Scripture gives us three things that we're called to do. The identity that God calls us. Not just the Bride of Christ, that's not the only identity. There are three things that God calls us to do as our identity as Christians. Every single one is about impacting our culture. Not sitting there and keeping your mouth shut. This is what they have brainwashed people into not becoming.

The 1st reason why we're no longer rebels for Christ is that "We've lost Our Saltiness." So, let's look at the first label that's put on us.

Matthew 5:13: "You are the salt of the earth. But what good is salt if it has lost its flavor? Can you make it salty again? It will be thrown out and trampled underfoot as worthless."

So, here we see the reason that God doesn't take us to Heaven the moment we get saved, and he gives us an identity. Yes, we're the Bride of Christ, but here's another one. He's got a purpose for our lives before we get there, right? And what was that purpose? You guys get out there and you be that paprika of the earth. No, no, you be the pepper of the earth. Or even the pork-rub of the earth. No! What was it? We're called to be the preservative or the salt of the earth, right? Especially back in the day, they didn't have refrigerators and things if you wanted to preserve something. Used to, before refrigerators came along, you packed that baby in salt. Salt was a preservative.

And so, in context, surely the American Church knows this, right? I mean, surely, we know if our society is ever going to be preserved from absolute moral decay and wickedness, then the Church has got to stand for God's absolute righteousness, right? Get out there and start throwing salt on it. That's common sense, right? That's not just what we're supposed to do, it's what we are. We are the Bride of Christ. We're the Church. We're also the salt, which by definition means, get out there and start salting, preserving the culture. How do you do that if you sit there and keep your mouth shut? You don't. So, what's the payoff of that? If you weren't out there being the salt and preserving, guess what? We're headed for where we're at today. Moral decay. It's not the world's fault, it's the Church. The Church is not being the salt.

Let's be honest! We don't look like we're saltshakers preserving this earth. We look like sin shakers partying with the earth! Why? Because we're no longer rebels for Christ. We're no longer standing up for God's moral hierarchy of laws. We've conformed to the moral relativism of man. You might ask, "Do you think it's really that bad?" Yeah, it's that bad. And again, not just from the world, this is from the so-called Church. We have totally lost our saltiness. These are from people professing to be Christians.

HAVE WE LOST OUR SALTINESS?

- 55% say the Bible has errors in it.
- 50% of Christians say there is no absolute truth.
- 47% don't have a commitment to the Christian faith as a top priority.
- 58% don't have being active in a local church as one of their top goals in life.
- 35% of Christians say that to get by in life these days, sometimes you have to bend the rules for your own benefit.

- 65% say that satan does not exist.
- 29% say that when Jesus lived on earth, He committed sins like everybody else.
- Just under 70% agreed that it doesn't matter what faith you follow because all paths lead to Heaven.
- 49% of Pastors no longer have a Biblical worldview.
- 93% of Christians no longer have a Biblical worldview.

Out of 100 people, at an average church, only 7 people would be thinking Biblically who go to church services. That's what we're dealing with. I'm kind of thinking we lost our salt and yet we're supposed to be out there engaging the culture to preserve it from moral decay. Do you see the problem? How did this happen? The pietism keeps your mouth shut because of all this infection. The abuse of Romans 13, and now we're supposed to not conform to this world, but they are, with comply, comply, comply. They bought into a lie. If you act like the world, speak like the world, look like the world, the world will like you and that's the goal of the Christian and the Christian church today.

"Whatever's true for you is true for you, and whatever's true for me is true for me." And relativism is not just sinful, it's dumb! For instance, if there's no right and wrong then what's the difference between Adolf Hitler and Pastor Bobby? Who are we to judge? Or what's the difference between a psychopath murderer and a soccer Mom? Well actually, those ladies can get pretty violent at the games, especially if their kids are losing, but that's not my point! My point is this. If there is no right or wrong people, stop and think about it! Then all forms of behavior must be okay, be it murder, adultery, abortion, rape, etc. etc., right? But that would be dumb to think like that, right? Slightly!

That's why Isaiah said woeful times! That's what it leads to! So, what do we do? Is it too late? Is there any hope? Is it all over for us? No! Praise God, He's faithful. He's given us an antidote that has the ability to preserve our country just in the nick of time! And can anybody guess what that antidote is? Hey, that's right! It's you and I, the Church! We're the salt, the preservative of the earth, standing up for God's absolute righteousness in order to protect us from absolute wickedness, right? And so, here's the point. Surely, that's what we're doing, right? I mean, surely, we're standing up for God's absolute truth no matter what, right? I mean, after all, we're Christians!

But that's the state we're in. Charles Spurgeon said this, "We've come to a turning point."

Now folks, I don't know about you, but I'd say we're losing our saltiness, how about you? In fact, I'd say if something doesn't turn around quick, we're in a heap of trouble! And that's exactly what Charles Spurgeon said.

"We have come to a turning-point in the road. If we turn to the right, maybe our children and our children's children will go that way; but if we turn to the left, generations yet unborn will curse our names for having been unfaithful to God and to His Word."

Whoa! Wait a second! Could our behavior today really affect the next generation? Uh, slightly! But hey, if you don't want to listen to Charles Spurgeon, maybe you should listen to modern historians. Right now, we the Church are in what historians are calling the "terminal generation." In other words, unless this generation of Christians repent, turns around, and gets serious about proclaiming God's truth and impacting our culture, our once Christian nation is going down! We are over the precipice; we're not coming back this time. That's how serious it is. Why? Because what did Jesus say? If we lose our saltiness, we've not only lost our usefulness, but what? We'll eventually end up where? In the garbage, right?

Therefore, could this be the reason why our country is filled with garbage? Could it be that the problem isn't so much with the American people, as it is with the American Church? It kind of makes you wonder, doesn't it? Oh, but that's not all.

The 2nd reason why we're no longer rebels for Christ is that "We've lost our brightness." We are the Bride of Christ, with the Church, we're the salt, we're also the light of the world. This is another label given to us. We are to shine God's truth in this dark and dying world.

Matthew 5:14-16: "You are the light of the world—like a city on a hilltop that cannot be hidden. No one lights a lamp and then puts it under a basket. Instead, a lamp is placed on a stand, where it gives light to everyone in the house. In the same way, let your good deeds shine out for all to see, so that everyone will praise your Heavenly Father."

So, again before we get to Heaven, we are not only called the Church, the Bride of Christ, we're called to be the salt and moral preservatives, now we have another one. We're called the light of the world. So here we see the second reason why we don't go to Heaven the moment we get saved is why? It's because God's got another purpose for our lives, right? We're not just the salt of the earth. We're what? We're the light of the earth! And when we live bright and holy lives for God, what does it do? It exposes and repels the darkness of the world, right? And it's instantaneous.

Did you ever do that when you got home late? You grew up in Kansas like me and you had bugs everywhere. You come home late and you're starving to death, late at night, and you go to the kitchen, and you flip that light on. You just want to make a sandwich but then you found your first conundrum. Man, I'm starving but as soon as I flip that light on, all of a sudden, I saw we had a lot of guests all over the counter. Little guests with feet and legs. They are called cockroaches for those who've never been to Kansas. I hate those things, still to this day. So, when you flip on the light, what do they do? Not right away. Trust me, I know the procedure. I've seen it many times. You flip on that light and then they freeze in their tracks. It's just a momentary pause and then they're out of there. Did I yell at them? Did I say, "Don't make me get the Raid again?" No, it was natural critters of the dark, when you flip on the light, they can't take it and they flew.

Now I'm not calling people of the world cockroaches, but I am saying according to Romans 12, not only not conform, or to live Holy lives pleasing to God. When you're just out there as a Christian, living, speaking up, being the salt, speaking God's truth and living it, have you noticed that sometimes you don't even have to say a word and the light of your presence and how you live in Christ, makes the darkness flee? It makes people uncomfortable. So, we're not just the Church, a group of called out ones. By the way, ecclesia means called out of this wicked world system, gathered together, we're not just the Bride of Christ, but we are the salt and also the light to dispel the darkness in the world. How can you do that if you just stay here? How can you do that and keep your mouth shut? And how can you do that if you conform to this wicked world system? You can't!

And the point is this. Surely the American Church knows this, right? I mean, surely, we know if we're ever going to beat back society's wicked behavior it's not just believing the truth, it's by obeying the truth, right? Let's be honest! We don't look like we're shining for Jesus for all the world to see. We look like we're sinning with this world in hopes that God doesn't see! Why? Because whether you realize it or not, relativism not only affects your beliefs, causing you to lose your saltiness, it affects your behavior, causing you to lose your brightness! And for those of you who may not believe me, let's take a look at current Christian behavior, and you tell me if relativism hasn't affected it just a little bit. Let's check our lights.

HAVE WE LOST OUR BRIGHTNESS?

- 42% believe that it is more important to achieve success or win acceptance from other people than to please God.
- 49% of Christians don't have a problem with the distribution of pornography.
- Darryl, 17 – "Kids at school are pressuring me and my girlfriend to have sex. I want to wait until marriage, but I worry about how this makes me look."

FROM THE DESK OF

Greg King, Publisher

Dear Friend,

What if you had a crystal ball . . . and you could look ten years down the road at the future of cardiac care?

You'd be able to choose from the new heart drugs and discoveries available THEN — for your own heart health NOW.

In a way, you can.

How? The big breakthroughs in medicine are usually made at the top, at hospitals and research facilities like Cleveland Clinic. No surprise there.

But here's something that may shock you. These breakthroughs take, on average, ten years to filter into common medical practice.

So an entire decade could go by between a game-changing discovery for your health . . . and the day your doctor actually discusses it with you. And that's no reflection on your doctor. It's just how medicine works.

As a reader of *Heart Advisor*, you have a chance to jump the line. You'll be among the first to hear about the new drugs and amazing discoveries doctors are making at Cleveland Clinic Sydell and Arnold Miller Family Heart & Vascular Institute. Bring them up with your doctor. Connect the dots with your own heart health before a whole decade goes by.

I can't give you a crystal ball. But I can offer you the next best thing — a free issue of *Heart Advisor.* So you can look it over firsthand and assess its value for yourself.

There's no pressure, no obligation to subscribe. Just mail the reply card and I'll see to it that you get the next issue of *Heart Advisor* with my compliments.

Sincerely,

Greg King
Publisher

P.S. The one small step you take for your heart today can yield huge benefits right away — and for years to come. Send for your free issue of *Heart Advisor* and 3 free reports now and get a look at the future of cardiac care.

- Kendra, 14 – "I know the Bible says you can't have sex before marriage. But why can't you, if you're in love with the person? It doesn't feel wrong."
- 39% of Christians say it's okay for couples to live together before marriage.
- Christians are now more likely than non-Christians to get divorce (27% vs. 24%).
- 54% of Christians say homosexuality is okay.
- A United Methodist minister has written a book on Jesus that claims that Jesus not only condoned homosexual relationships, but that Jesus Himself was involved in one. The minister has not been reprimanded by his denomination.
- 4% of Christians and 3% of non-Christians said they had consulted a medium or spiritual advisory within the past month.
- Nearly 64% thought that was perfectly fine to be a wiccan. (That's a witch!)

Now folks, I don't know about you, but I'd say we're losing our brightness, how about you? In fact, I'd say if something doesn't turn around quick, we're in a heap of trouble! And that's exactly what this man said.

"It grieves me to say that, for the most part, the modern Christian, the modern pastor, and the modern Church have lost their savor. Taken as a whole, we have lost our inner character: the ability to resist decay and preserve the land.

Our churches are no longer places of respite from the world, they are mirrors of it. The same dress; the same attitudes, the same carnality, the same spirit, the same stubbornness, the same pride.

Churches are no longer bastions of truth, they are glorified social clubs, or mere corporations, where Christianity is never allowed to interfere with business. Instead of being watchmen on the wall, our pastors are CEOs or, even worse, politicians. Popularity and personal ambition far outweigh the commitment to truth.

We have a pandemic all right, but it's not Covid-19 or Monkeypox, it is a pandemic of spineless Christianity. Parents who cannot stand up to their own children, pastors who cannot stand up to their own congregations, religious leaders who cannot stand up to politicians, and churches that cannot stand up to unconstitutional government.

If one is looking for someone to blame America's demise on, don't look to the prostitutes, drug dealers, or crooked politicians, look no further than the doorsteps of America's churches. While the ominous clouds of oppression and tyranny boil overhead, our churches are content to play kid games and wallow in their own materialism and laziness.

Sadder still is the lack of anything on the horizon that points to any kind of spiritual awakening. Look at the churches that are growing: for the most part, they are of the Joel Osteen and Rick Warren variety, where conviction has been replaced with compromise, and principle with popularity.

And genuine Bible prophets now occupy the pulpits where hardly anyone attends. Truth has been replaced with entertainment and calls for repentance are drowned out by the clamor of prosperity.

I can tell you from personal experience that in more than 34 years of Gospel ministry, it has never been harder to continue to carry the torch of truth than it is today. It takes a toll on one's physical health and emotional being, and even on one's family.

Any pastor desiring to carry the torch of truth today need not expect to have many friends. And any evangelist desiring to carry the torch of truth today need not expect to get many meetings. Why? Because truth today is about as popular as a bad case of the measles, and yes, I mean among today's professing "Christians."

So, we are supposed to be the salt, we're supposed to be the light, but we look like, act like, speak like, we've been infiltrated by fakers. We're told to keep our mouths shut, and the goal of the church is to look like the world, act like the world, so the world will like you. And you wonder why we continue to go down. So, you know what the antidote is to the ills of our society? It's not a political change, it's Jesus. It's the truth. It's always been the truth. And when we are out there being the salt and the light, we're sharing God's truth and people get set free. You want to stop crying, get people saved. You want to stop these horrible statistics about family, then get people saved. Saved people, I'm not saying we're perfect. I'm not saying we don't ever sin, but by and large with saved people, you don't have to say, "I'm going to send you to jail." They're not going to rob a bank. God changes the heart. Instantly you start aligning and conforming to the Word of God. That's the answer.

Could our behavior today really affect the outcome of our country? Uh, slightly! And that's why I've said it before, and I'll say it again! We don't need revival in America. We need revival in the American Church! Why? Because what did Jesus say? If we lose our brightness, we're not only losing our purpose, but what? We'll eventually end up in a godless world. Therefore, could this be the reason why our country is looking so ungodly? Could it be that the problem isn't so much with the American people as it is the American Church? Kind of makes you wonder, doesn't it?

The 3rd reason why we're no longer rebels for Christ is because "we've lost our resistance." This is specifically our identity in the Scripture as we await the Rapture. We are called to be resistors.

2 Thessalonians 2:6-7: "And now you know what is holding him back, so that he may be revealed at the proper time. For the secret power of lawlessness is already at work; but the one who now holds it back will continue to do so till he is taken out of the way."

As we saw in our Rapture study, this is none other than the Church. The Holy Spirit's presence within the Church. When we leave at the Rapture there is nothing to stop the Antichrist from going hog-wild. So, now we see the third reason why we don't go to Heaven the moment we get saved is why? It's because God's got another purpose for our lives, right? What did it say? We're not just the salt of the earth, we're not just the light of the earth, we're the resistance to the earth…specifically as we see the rise of the Antichrist Kingdom!

"HOLDS BACK" is "katecho" in the Greek and it means to "hold back, or restrain, or hinder the course or progress thereof." So, now we are not only called the salt, we're not only called the light, the preservative, and the light to beat back the darkness, but God specifically says any time that we see any hint of this rise of antichrist, evil, satanic system, government, anywhere in our country or wherever, we're supposed to resist.

God says we are a hinderance to evil. We're to "hold back" evil. We're to restrain against evil. Specifically, as we await the Rapture! How can you do that if you keep your mouth shut? You have no right to speak up. Don't get involved. You just do your thing, and we'll do ours. Just keep your mouth shut. It's not Biblical. We are called to engage our culture. We're just to be the restraining influence specifically about evil. When we see it, we speak up. I didn't put this label on it. I'm not being a fanatic. This is what God says. This is our title. This is our identity. They've twisted Biblical identity. They can't even define what a woman is. The Church can't even define what the Church is. Yes, we are the salt, we're the light, and we are the resistors against wickedness, evil, tyranny during the rise of the antichrist kingdom.

Unfortunately, most so-called Christians, are worthless resistors as this man shares…

"Truth is not an opinion. Truth is a person. His Name is Jesus. But most Americans, can't handle the Truth. 'I'm OK, You're Ok,' was a best-selling book published in the 60's. It was the first genre of 'self-help' books that sold millions of copies and paved the way for Humanism's stealth-emergence into the Church.

Like most counterfeits, it looked authentic, but it was a lie. I'm not OK…and neither are you. And until we deal with that Truth, America, and

Americans, will continue to spiral down to a modern-day version of The Planet of the Apes.

This feel-good theology was popularized by Norman Vincent Peale (The Power of Positive Thinking), and handed off to Pseudo-Christians Zig Ziglar (See You at the Top) and Robert Schuller (Move Ahead With Possibility Thinking).

This deadly witch's brew of Humanistic messed with Christianity, created the wave for Author/Mega-Pastors like Rick Warren (The Purpose Driven Life), and Joel Osteen (Your Best Life Now) to present a sugar-coated, watered-down, sin-free version of the Gospel.

Ask yourself this. Why is it that CNN loves to give Osteen and Warren so much face time? Could it be that the media is doing their best to present to Biblically challenged Americans a "false gospel" instead of the true version of Christianity?

Could it be that CNN wants to sissify and pacify "Christians" by presenting Pastor Glitter Teeth as the establishment approved who-am-I-to-judge spokesman for the religiously weak?

Have you ever seen a "combative" Christian appear on any national TV show? Where are the Christian truth-bomb throwers willing to fight for our side?

Please understand the deception. Jesus is not a tolerant, go-along to get-along, I'm Ok you're Ok, if it feels good do it, come-sit-on-my-lap, passive Savior. A rude awakening is awaiting many.

Rather, He overcame death, hell, and the grave. He is a conquering King who will return and as the Bible says, 'in righteousness he does judge and makes war.'

He will not share His power, authority, or glory with another. You can take it to the bank.

That, my friends, is the Truth. And so why are so many Christians too intimidated to declare it? Why do we allow these lies to go unchallenged? Because most pastors are hirelings. Not one pastor in a thousand will speak out against public schools. They won't rock the boat. Best life Now, anyone?

But fighting is not evil. It's not fighting evil, is evil. We are to resist the evil rules that evil men make, otherwise evil will rule."

Now the good news is…for those who will resist…we're seeing some good results… There are still faithful shepherds, and this is the illusion. We think we're going to have to have a million trillion people to speak up to make a difference. No. You make a difference where you're at. It was a grassroots overtaking movement, communist, socialism, these atheists infecting the Church. It took decades. If we're still here and still alive, we could be gone tomorrow, I don't know. But we're supposed to be who we're called to be in the meantime. The salt, the light and the resistors. Rebels for Jesus. But if it's going to happen, we have to speak up. There are results. Some unthinkable things have happened recently. We should be encouraged. If anything, we have no excuse. Don't be apathetic. Apathy doesn't help anything. Don't go AWOL, that's not in the Scripture, don't get cynical. Get active, share the truth, we're the antidote. We're the antidote, do you get that too the ills of society? It's God's truth. We've got God's truth, and we give out the antidote, but there are some good results that we should be encouraged. First of all, Roe v. Wade. Now that didn't stop abortion, the murder of children, but at least it made a huge step back to the states and many states are outlawing it. But that's just the first thing. It's such a big deal that these

WHYY

Donate

With Roe dead, some fear rollback of LGBTQ and other rights

A person walks past Planned Parenthood Friday, June 24, 2022, in St. Louis. (AP Photo/Jeff Roberson)

people who have come in and twisted love and relationships and marriage and identities, they're freaking out. Because they could see the writing on the wall. But wait a second, if you're going to overturn Roe v. Wade back to the states on the issue of abortion, maybe they'll do it with LBGT issues. Aah, that couldn't happen. Did you think they would do this with Roe v. Wade? Apathy, keeping your mouth shut, pietism, is never an option for Christians. We should really be in third gear now. I'm really going to kick it into gear, speaking out, because guess what? It's making a difference. And we are called to make a difference until he comes and gets us, which could be in 5 minutes, it could be in 5 years, I don't know. But we're supposed to make a difference.

About Privacy ProTrumpNews AmericanGulag How To Help Store Login

Judge Blocks Biden's LGBTQ Guidance that Allows Transgender in Girls' Sports and Bathroom Access

Share Tweet Share to Gab Telegram Email

PROBLEM SOLVED.

A Trump-appointed judge in Tennessee temporarily blocked Biden's woke LGBTQ policy on Friday, including transgender workers and students to use gender-appropriate bathrooms, and participate i sports teams, **Reuters** reported.

U.S. District Judge Charles Atchley Jr. ruled in favor of the 20 state attorneys general who sued the Biden administration saying the directives infringe on states' freedom to establish laws governing

DeSantis Threatens CPS Investigations Into Parents Bringing Children To Drag Shows

by PAUL AUBERT

Anyway, they are freaking out and they're trying their best to pass laws to somehow prevent the Supreme Court from overturning that one. Another one, DeSantis is threatening CPS investigations into parents when they bring their kids to drag shows.

Just when you thought they're never going to get any kickbacks, people are speaking up, they're resisting, joining the resistance. We are called to resist when they disagree with God. He's also got another thing now with girls' sports that you have to have a biological affidavit. That's another good news thing to prevent what is going on. Also, a judge blocks

Biden's LGBTQ guidance that allows transgenders in girls' sports and public bathroom access. And that judge was appointed by Trump.

So, some of the investments made back then is paying off today. So, there is kickback, even in our government, there's kickback. So, what do you do? "I give up, I just get an apathetic attitude." No. First of all, that's not your identity as a Christian. But that's what they want. They want you to keep your mouth shut, if they can't get you to live like the world.

Now this is even happening across the pond. UK ministers to make single-sex toilets compulsory in new public buildings. So, they're resisting against that.

UK ministers to make single-sex toilets compulsory in new public buildings

Government sources confirm move to curb the sole installation of gender-neutral facilities

The new rules will act to prevent non-residential buildings from being built solely with 'universal' lavatories. Photograph: Loop Images Ltd/Alamy

New offices, schools, hospitals and entertainment venues will be expected to have separate male and female lavatories, government sources have confirmed, in a move to curb the sole installation of gender-neutral facilities.

Ministers will formally announce this week that they will prevent non-residential buildings from being built solely with "universal" lavatories. The move will involve changes to building regulations and planning guidance.

The plans, headed by the equalities minister, Kemi Badenoch, were quietly approved last month, the Sunday Telegraph reported. The government has said some children are avoiding using lavatories at school because they only have access to gender-neutral facilities.

Now you're not going to get this in the "lame stream media," the sewer pipes of ABC, American Broadcasting Communism, whatever they call that or Nothing But Communism, NBC, or Communist News Now, CNN, whatever you want to call it. But you're not going to get that there. It's out there, but that's the illusion. If we're going to make a difference and be who we're called to be… we're not just the Church, we're not just the Body of Christ, we're the salt, we're the light, and we're the resistors. And we need to get busy being who God has called us to be in the meantime.

So, to encourage us to not go back to the lie of pietism and speak up, even against threats, even the threat of our lives, let's remind ourselves what that first part of that video said. Hitler told the churches, "You take care of the souls. I'll take care of Germany." Basically, keep your mouth shut, it's none of your business what I do, while people are being hauled off in trains. I will say this. How could the German people do that? Even the one's professing to be Christians? They knew about the camps, but they kept their mouths shut. How could they do that? Just do your thing and hopefully you'll arrive at death safely.

There's been another holocaust that's been going on for two years. It's called the Covid-19 jabs. Killing millions of people and we haven't seen the half of it yet. Injuries, tons and tons more like the holocaust. If we see somebody being murdered unjustly, murdered period, kids, adults, you name it, by anybody or even physically harmed for life, maimed forever, what do you think the Scripture says we should do? Speak up. The Bible says you shall not murder. Where is everybody on this issue? We've been told to comply and keep your mouth shut. Don't speak up with this current holocaust that's going on.

But let's remind ourselves of the fruit of pietism. If you don't think another holocaust is coming, oh, it will. Certainly, as long as we fall for this lie. But let's remind ourselves of what pietism got for Germany.

Proverbs 24:12: "If you say, 'But we knew nothing about this,' does not he who weighs the heart perceive it?"

An old man is suddenly awakened by a bad dream. He sits up in bed in a state of alarm, but when he remembers it's only a dream, he realizes that it's not a dream. It's a past memory of when he was a boy.

The old man: *"This dream has haunted me for decades. There are some things that time does not erase. Sometimes the only way forward is by facing the past. This is my story.*

I lived in Germany during the Nazi holocaust. A railroad track ran behind our small church. Each Sunday morning at the exact same time, we heard the whistle from the distance. And then the clacking of the wheels, moving over the track. It was at the same time every Sunday. We felt the rattling of the trail of cattle cars accompanied by the screeching of metal that would echo through our church walls. It was a Sunday in the spring that would change my life forever."

Minister: *"Jesus said, 'Do not resist an evildoer. If anyone strikes you on the right cheek, turn the other also.' Loving your enemy, this is a far better way. This is how we were called to live. To understand this unnatural virtue, we must look to Jesus Christ as our model and our guide. His meekness was his strength. His silence, his statement to the world.* (During this sermon, the train can be heard arriving at the church, so the minister preaches louder to try to drown out the noise of the train whistle) *We must pray for those who persecute us. Prayer is the mechanism that reaches Heaven and moves mankind. Prayer is easy to underestimate but that is quiet action.* (Suddenly, the train is screeching to a stop outside the door of the church.

Everyone looks up as the train rubs against the metal tracks. As they are looking up and no longer listening to the sermon, they can hear moaning and cries coming from the train. They all go to the window to see what is going on outside.) *Christ is the Prince of Peace. As we better come to know Jesus, we learn to choose, to choose as He chooses. We learn to love our enemies and allow God's peace to rule within our hearts.* (The minister realizes that his voice can't be heard above all the noise coming in from the outside, so he motions for the music leader to start leading the congregation in song.)

This is the old man's remembrance of that day. As a little boy, he was in the congregation and his curiosity got the best of him. As the congregation is standing to sing and without anyone noticing, he slips out of the church to see what is going on in that train. Standing outside looking at the train, he can hear that the congregation is singing louder and louder to try to cover what is happening outside. No matter how loud they sing, it doesn't seem to take away the noise coming from the train.

Suddenly his mother looks down and realizes that her son is missing and runs outside to find him looking up at the people on the train. Since this is a cattle car, it is made of wooden boards. Only one board is missing, and he can see a girl trying to get some fresh air from that opening. She looks directly at him, and they make eye contact. She says something to him, but he doesn't reply. German soldiers are getting off the train to run him off.

As his mother is walking up to him to get him away from the train, he is sobbing. How can humans do this to humans? His mother also makes eye contact with the girl on the train. The soldiers are yelling to get back into the church.

The old man: *"Years have passed, and no one talks about it much anymore. I still hear that train whistle in my sleep. I can still hear them crying out for help. God forgive all of us who called ourselves Christians yet did nothing to intervene."*

Proverbs 24:11: "Rescue those being led away to death."

"This video is in remembrance of Christian heroes like Corrie Ten Boom, St. Maximilian Kolbe, and Dietrich Bonhoeffer who helped save countless Jewish people."

Speaker #1: *"Do believe me when I tell you that the reality was indescribably worse than these pictures. You cannot photograph suffering, only its results."*

Speaker #2: *"In just the last 24 hours, more than a quarter people have fled Rwanda and its terror. Lines at some border crossings stretch for five miles."*

Speaker #3: *"Anyone who ventures outdoors is fair game. Red Cross and UN relief convoys, even men and women in breadlines are targeted."*

I John 3:18: "Let us not love with words or speech but with actions and in truth."

That's the fruit of pietism and you can see it's still going on today because you fell for another lie. Keep your mouth shut, you have no right to speak against the government. You do your thing, we'll do ours. And that's what you get. It's a lie. I like the meme that's out there referring to the last couple years of the Covid plandemic. Did you ever wonder what you would have done as a Christian in 1933? Now you know. Did you speak up or did you just keep your mouth shut? Are you speaking up? Or are you complying? Are you more worried about yourself, your self-preservation instead of being the salt, the preservation, to stop this wickedness from happening?

We need to get back to who we're called to be and stop falling for these lies that have purposely come in, and by the enemies in the Church that have infected the Church and get busy being the salt and the light and the resistance. Because if we don't, Hitler not only killed nearly six million Jews, and this doesn't usually get shared, but he killed about seven million professing Christians. And if you don't think that will ever happen to us, we are starting to see the underpinnings of that. And all they have done is this. We are soon going to be guilty of hate crimes. They will call the Bible hate speech and a hate book. The only thing you can speak from this book will be what the government tells you to speak about. That's going on today. We're starting to see signs of it.

I don't know how much longer before we're out of here at the Rapture, and I'm very excited about that. I look forward to that. It could be 5 minutes. it could be 5 days. It could be 5 years. I don't know. You don't know. But what I do know is what are we supposed to do in the meantime. Stop being a bunch of chicken livers, get out there and be who we're called to be, speak up, or this level of wickedness is going to come back and make what happened the first time look like chump change.

Chapter Twelve

God's Judgment with a Woeful Destruction

God said that once you start going down that road and you reject Him, **Romans 1**, and you get to that last stage of a depraved mind, it didn't stop at lesbianism and homosexuality, not even in the so-called Church today. Now it is leading to polygamy, gender fluidity, bestiality and pedophilia. We are going to see that again in this chapter. But we can see that this is the last stage of destruction of our society.

We have dealt with all the skeptical questions like, "Homosexuality isn't even mentioned in the Bible," or "You're interpreting that wrong," or "Love is love, what's the big deal?" etc. Well, we answered all those questions. But then we dealt with the big, hot question, "What is a Woman?" Apparently, people are having a hard time answering that one. Why is it that people in the Biden administration, these "Woke" churches, "Woke" people, people in the medical industry say, "I just don't know." We saw that was the mindset that caused the same mistake that Israel made back in the day, with "everyone was doing what was right in their own eyes."

That's why people today can't even seem to define what a woman is, because they're making it up as they go. Relativism: whatever is true to you. The Bible says it's leading to woeful times, just like Israel. "Doing whatever is right in your own eyes," and "rejecting God's Law" is not a good way to go. Yet, this is where we're at. Not only in the world, but even in the so-called Church. And why is this being done? Promoting this perversion?

Number one, they are trying to destroy our country morally, because this will destroy us. This is depravity. You're not going to last long if you keep this up. Number two, they are making a ton of money off this. Remember, 1.3 million dollars is being made off of every person that goes down the transgender route - for just one person - because they are on a lifetime of surgeries and drugs. And then number three, they are preparing people for transhumanism. Preparing the world for what the transhumanists wants to do. (For those that are allowed to live). They are genetically going to modify humanity into a post-human species, "Human 2.0" they call it, to be better worker bees for them.

You might think, "Maybe I will be a cat, or maybe I'll be this or that." That is the mindset they need to justify what they want to do. When at first, they let you choose. Then the choice is taken away, and they say, "No, we want to modify you the way we want you, genetically." As sick as that sounds that's the mindset.

And if that wasn't bad enough, we saw they're also promoting this lie in the Church, saying that Christians should just keep their mouths shut and stay within your four walls. You shouldn't get involved in politics. Let the world do whatever it wants, burn, and go straight to hell. The lie is called pietism! That you shouldn't get involved. The problem is that's not what the Bible says! We are to be the salt – the preservative against moral decay. We are to be the light – to dispel the darkness. And we are to be the resistance – to restrain against the Antichrist Kingdom. That's by not keeping your mouth shut! And being a pietist! That helps nothing! All it does is give these guys free reign, and it gets worse and worse. You're not going to stop the 7-year Tribulation, but if there is going to be any kind of reprieve, we have to speak up. Apathy, going AWOL, fearful, that is not an option, and that is not from God. That is not what He has called us to do.

So, now we're going to take a look at what these enemies within the Church are going to do to these resisters. I mean, are they just forever going to let us get away with resisting? Are they going to let us go on forever being a thorn in their side? Remember, the restraining influence in **II Thess. 2**, the identity of the Church, and what that word means in the Greek? It means to hinder the course of progress thereof. Do you think they are just going to let us keep hindering things, throwing a wrench into the works? They say, "Every time we get so close, and then those Christians speak up and expose what we are doing, and it gets put back on the drawing board." Do you think they are going to let that happen forever? No!

Now, what we do know Scripturally, is eventually, this whole movement that has affected the Church, is going to lead towards a One World Religion, a twisted version of Christianity that is Christian in name only. Because did you know that there are going to be Christians left behind in the 7-year Tribulation? They're not real Christians, because the real Christians go in the Rapture. There will be a lot of people still going to Church services, who are left behind. All this fake Jesus, fake gospel, false God, twisted love is not how you get saved, and they are going to be left behind. Christianity in name only will continue on. And that's the main theme you see in the Scripture. If we are going to have a One World Religion, then how are we going to get all religions, that are diametrically opposed to each other, to get along?

Well, we are going to see in the coming chapters, some of the things that are going to corral that, and one of them is this twisted love. Like the Beatles song, "All we Need is Love." Just love each other. The Christians can love each other, the Muslims can love each other, and the "Woke" Church can love each other. And we'll love everybody, that's something we can corral around. And then we can have the Pope run the whole thing. That's the plan. But my point is, there are going to be real

Christians today who are going to resist against that. What are you going to do with those people?

The Scripture says it's going to ultimately lead to persecution. It's going to lead to death. That is what is going to happen in the 7-year Tribulation. Anybody who rejects this coming system, and the One World Religion is just a part of it. There is going to be a One World Government, One World Economy, cashless, Mark of the Beast system. All of these things are being put into play right now. But this whole "Woke," twisted thing is preparing the fake Church to go along with the One World Religion in the 7-year Tribulation. That's really the deeper issue of what is going on. It isn't only, "Gee, wow! It's really getting wicked. They are making some really poor choices." No, this is where it is headed. I want to give you the bigger picture of what is going on.

We are going to see eventually there is going to be a filter as in who's with them and who's not. I call it, "The Big Switcheroo." What they are doing is - and it's been going on in the Muslim community for quite some time - basically, what they have been doing in the Church to prepare people for this One World Religion, it's all love, love, love, twisted love. But this has been going on in the Muslim community. You have the true Muslims, and they are the ones who are out there killing people, because that is what the Koran says to do. The infidels, not just the Jewish people, but us, the Church too, by the way. Now I don't condone that. It's horrible, it's wicked, it's wrong. But they're being true to their religion because that is what they are told to do.

Then you have what is called the moderate, or basically, the fake or false Muslim, and those are the ones that the media keep saying, "Oh, this religion is a religion of peace. These are wonderful people." No, it's not! Those are the fakers. But here's my point. What they are doing, and we know this is going to happen, at one point the true Muslims are going to be taken out, because they'll never go along. They are monotheistic. They will never go along with worshiping of all different religions. I think a lot of them will be taken out according to **Ezekiel 38,** when they come down and try to work with Russia against Israel. They are going to become the bad guys. And then the fake ones will continue. The seemingly impossible will take place. Islam, a monotheistic religion, that will never go along with a One World Religion, they will continue in name only in the 7-year Tribulation. They have been doing this for a long time.

And that is the exact same thing that is happening to the Church. They are taking the true Christians, now known as the new terrorists, radical extremists, radical fundamentalists - the same term they used on the Muslims, and they are now applying it to us. Why? Because we have to get out of the way. Because we'll never go along with their One World Religion. They are subverting the Church. They are taking the fake Christians, and the new word for the fakers is "Woke." They are taking the "Woke" churches and the "Woke" churches will go along with the One World Religion. They are saying that the "Woke" Christians are the real Christians, because they love, and they tolerate.

But what I want to focus on is what I call the "filters." How are you going to "filter" whether you have a true or a fake to prepare for the One World Religion? Well, there are a couple of ways. They use climate change. Climate change is not only this fake definition of love, but it's "what we can all corral around." Save the planet! Another one is the Ecumenical Movement, "all paths lead to Heaven." That one statistic, it's almost up to 70 percent of people professing to be Christians, believe all paths lead to Heaven. I'm sorry, you're not saved if you believe that. And then also, is the homosexual, lesbianism, transgender, pedophilia, bestiality, twisted, perverted love that is being used as a filter. If you don't go along with that, then you are going to be targeted, you are going to be persecuted, and if they have their way, they are going to kill you. Because you will never go along with the One World Religion. That is really the arching umbrella that is going on.

If you think they are going to back down on this homosexual and lesbianism thing, as God says, once you go down that route, you will go over to that final stage, the depraved mind, and it's going to get worse and worse, and you will begin to do things that ought not to be done. I am telling you; we have got to wake up. We don't need to go "Woke." It is getting way worse. If you think it's wicked now, you ain't seen nothing yet! Remember the Supreme Court decision? We said that they would eventually legalize pedophilia and bestiality.

Well, have you seen the news? Pedophilia is what they are pushing now. We thought it was only homosexuality and lesbianism. Now in the last two years, it's that transgender issue. Is it going to stop? No. Take a look at this transcript of a video clip. Oh, and by the way, this is from Great Britain. They will report on it, but you're not going to see it reported here. But this is happening here in the United States, in Pennsylvania. This is nuts.

GBNEWS.UK Reports: *"Before I report this, the first topic of the day, I just want to give parents a warning because the next few minutes of conversation is of an adult nature. You might want to remove your children from the room, if you feel that is appropriate for you. Now I want to bring your attention to a clip that I ran across online this week that has been watched nearly 2 ½ million times. And although it could be dismissed as just a one off of just one woman, I just can't help but suspect that it's a signpost of a potentially horrific social change of which we just need to be aware.*

It features a sex therapist who works for the Keystone state of Pennsylvania, in America, which described herself as proudly founded in 1681 as a place of tolerance and freedom. Now don't get me wrong. Tolerance, co-existing with people, will cause no harm, but not like her, is good. Freedom, if we mean as being the architect of our own destiny as far as possible, is of course all good. But I fear that the clip I am about to show you might be the start of an insidious creep towards the normalizing of sexual contact with children."

Miranda: *"I am a licensed professional counselor, sex therapist in Erie, Pennsylvania. And today I want to talk about minor attracted persons. I want to talk about minor attracted persons because they are probably the most vilified population of folks in our culture."*

GBNEWS.UK Reports: *"There is a reason for that. Now when this lady is talking about minor attractive persons, what she means is pedophiles. The Latin derivation of that word is 'philia' love and 'pais' child. Of course, we know that there is no love involved in damaging behaviors that we quite perceive as criminal. She goes on:"*

Miranda: *"Most folks are making incorrect assumptions about them without actually knowing much about them. And those assumptions create harm for an already marginalized population."*

GBNEWS.UK Reports: *"You see, it's one thing to argue that abusers require help. They do. You will never hear me advocating castration or public flogging. But remember, abusers are commonly victims of abuses themselves, but there is a difference between arguing for understanding, and the victim that manages or contains these people, and blaming others for judging them. Or trying to make us feel guilty for rejecting in the harshest term for such a horrific act."*

Miranda: *"We are all people first. We have many different facets or parts of ourselves, and this includes folks who are attracted to minors."*

GBNEWS.UK Reports: *"Do you see where this is going? You may think a "minor attracted person" is wrong, because they are not the same as you, but everyone has rights. There's no such thing as good or bad anymore. Just a murky, moral relativity in which you don't have a right to judge someone who is different than you. Furthermore, I think we need a very clear, firm line in the sand when it comes to the sexual interference of children. Successful civilizations are built upon the protections of the next generation. A society which does not pride itself on keeping kids happy and safe is one that is heading for annihilation. Sexual assault - unwanted, coerced, or forceful contact of any form - is the most effective way of psychologically damaging a young person in both the long and the short term. Some survivors will cope better than others, but a full recovery from such a violation is rare."*

Miranda: *"Let's talk about what a minor attracted person is. Or who they are. This term means that this person has an endearing or sexual or romantic attraction to minors. They have not chosen this attraction, just as the rest of us have not chosen whatever our attraction is. You don't get to choose to be heterosexual, or to be gay or whatever you are."*

GBNEWS.UK Reports: *"She's just trying to humanize pedophiles. In some ways, that's okay, if you are truly trying to understand what drives people to act so abnormally. It's critical if we want to stop future crimes. But aligning a criminal act with normal sexual preferences is potentially very dangerous. She makes no effort to eliminate the abnormality of these people. She makes no mention that this is most commonly the result of learned behavior - a pathological, psychological disorder, which people like this therapist are apparently seeking to normalize.*

And this is from TikTok, a social media platform owned by the Chinese government, aimed at children. Imagine your daughter or granddaughter experiencing unwanted molestation from an adult and is just wondering if she should bring it to someone's attention. Over 90 percent of child victims know their offender, with almost half of them being a family member.

Most certainly, this poor child wonders whether she should complain. Maybe this is okay. Maybe this is just like being gay or straight. Maybe she doesn't want to be judged for making a fuss. I don't know. Maybe there are people hoping that by the time that the guest list of the Epstein-Maxwell parties is released, we will have all bought into the idea that pedophiles are minor attracted people who deserve our understanding. So, all I'm saying is let's just be awake to this phenomenon, shall we?"

The problem is, we are not, and the Church - who should know better and who should be on the front lines speaking out against it - they are not awake, they have gone "Woke." Which basically is the code word, "they're going along with this." "Well, my church isn't going along with this." Are you complying? Are you compromising? And here's a form of going "Woke." You keep your mouth shut. Right? What's that? Pietism, which is what we saw in the last chapter and is unbiblical. We should be on the front lines. This is what is really going on. And basically, on the other hand, this is something that we shouldn't be surprised at. This is wickedness unrestrained.

There was an old-fashioned term we used to use in the Church back in the day. We became "Hedonistic." You heathen! Now hedonistic, actually, believe it or not, is a Biblical term. In the next few verses, Paul gives a whole list of rotten behaviors in the last days. Wickedness unrestrained. But what I like about it is that he also tells us why. How did you get into this shape? It's everything that we are dealing with right now in the so-called "woke" Church.

II Timothy 3:1-5: "But mark this: There will be terrible times in the last days. People will be lovers of themselves, lovers of money, boastful, proud, abusive, disobedient to their parents, ungrateful, unholy, without love, unforgiving, slanderous, without self-control, brutal, not lovers of the good, treacherous, rash, conceited, lovers of pleasure rather than lovers of God – having a form of godliness but denying its power. Have nothing to do with them."

The Greek word for terrible means "savage." Terrible, brutal, times in the last days. These verses were written 2,000 years ago. It's a good thing we don't see anyone walking around the planet saying, "I need to love myself. I need to love myself more than anyone." What is the number one virtue of our society today? It's all about self, as we saw in our other study, that's satanism. "Do what you want shall be the whole of the law." Self-love came from satan. And then, from then on, does it help your society? No. You fall for that lie, which we have for a couple of decades now, and I'm talking about the Church. Does this sound familiar? That's our society.

Tell me that's our marching orders every day when we get out of bed! We are so enamored with self-love that there is a word for it. "Selfie." Self is doing this, and self is doing that. We've been there for quite some time. But what does the scripture say? Once you go down that route, it's downhill from there.

Paul said, on the one hand, he wasn't condoning it. But God loves us enough to tell us the future so we aren't caught off guard. It's not to freak us out but to show us that, "Hey, you're in the last days, you better get ready. The Rapture is coming." So, finish strong, don't procrastinate. Certainly, don't partake in this. Come out from among them. Be separate and do what God has called you to do. But He's telling us, guess what? It's getting close when you see all this. And every single one of those is commonplace today.

But notice, what was the last behavior that was mentioned there? What did it say? It said people would be lovers of pleasure rather than lovers of God! The phrase, "lovers of pleasure," comes from the Greek word, "philedonos," made up of two words: "phile," meaning "love," and "donos," which comes from the root word, "hedone." Which is where we get our word "hedonism," which means "pleasure." And "Hedone" was the Greek goddess of pleasure, enjoyment, delight, or entertainment! And "Hedon-ism" was the movement that argued one's life consists of seeking pleasure at all costs to avoid all suffering!

That's the fruit of what's going to happen when you go down the route of "self," and you will get greedy, lovers of money, which is what we all take for granted, and it's ungodly. It will destroy you and everything it touches. But it will get to the point where? Love pleasure more than even God himself. If it's all about me, then what's the logical conclusion? I need to please, deal with pleasure, whatever self wants at all times, at all costs. That becomes my way of life. That is "hedone" worship, which is where we get hedonism. Now, I said all that to get to this. That is where we're at. We're in not just a messed-up society, a wicked society in America, we haven't just gone south. We don't just have people who love pleasure more than God, even in the Church. But we live in a hedonistic society.

If you read the Scripture, you will see that God judged two societies once they reached this level. Not just depravity in **Romans 1**, but once you reach this level where it is "self" at all costs, pleasure at all costs, wickedness, totally unrestrained. Literally old-fashioned "hedone" worship, it's judgment time. That's why we know where we are headed. If we don't speak up, and we keep giving in to the lie of "wokism," pietism, keeping your mouth shut, we are headed 100 percent to judgment. And I'm talking even here in America. Now let me prove it to you. Look at this and remember the video clip on pedophilia. The first society that got hedonistic and God judged, was in the days of Lot.

Genesis 19:4-7,24-25: "Before they had gone to bed, all the men from every part of the city of Sodom – both young (Hebrew – Nah-ar "boy, lad, youth, child") and old – surrounded the house.

Now, the sin of Sodom and Gomorrah was not just homosexuality. What was it? Young and old alike, surrounded the house. It was pedophilia. We just saw the it in the video transcript. We are there. And what did Jesus say? This isn't just the days of Noah, before He comes back, it will be like the days of Lot. So, on the one hand, we certainly don't condone this, but on the other hand, we know that our society is going to accept pedophilia because it's going to be like the days of Lot.

Genesis 19:4-7,24-25 cont.: "They called to Lot, 'Where are the men who came to you tonight? Bring them out to us so that we can have sex with them.' Lot went outside to meet them and shut the door behind him and said, 'No, my friends. Don't do this wicked thing.' Then the LORD rained down burning sulfur on Sodom and Gomorrah – from the LORD out of the heavens. Thus, He overthrew those cities and the entire plain, including all those living in the cities – and also the vegetation in the land."

Yet, when you talk about Sodom and Gomorrah, people, and even the Church, want to downplay it and say that's just an allegory. "That didn't really happen. There wasn't really sulfur coming down and fire burned everybody to a crisp. God is a God of love. They are just teaching us the moral truth." No, that really did happen. They really were judged by

God for homosexuality and pedophilia, exactly like He said. In fact, here is a recent archaeological thing, that you once again, you won't see in the American media.

Joel P Kramer, Archaeologist: *"So, I am up here at the site called Cali Numeira. This is the site that the archaeologist associated with Gomorrah. Here you can see the ashy layer that is just underneath the surface. This is full of burnt pottery. It's full of the fragments of human bones. The question is, what evidence is there of this burning sulfur that rained down? Well, it seems that the culprits are these sulfur balls that are also found in this area. These would not be preserved on land. They would only be preserved in water. So, he encouraged me to go look for them in areas that were once under the Dead Sea. So, I went down near the shore of the Dead Sea and looked in these areas where the waters have receded. This is when I started finding sulfur balls.*

To give you an idea of how many sulfur balls there are. All these are sulfur balls.
They are everywhere. This is one

of the reasons why sulfur balls would only be preserved in water. If they strike the land, you can see they burn up, it's burning down to goo and then dripping off.

So, anywhere that they would have landed on land, they would have burned up like this and

burned anything flammable around them. This is how the cities were burned. However, if they were to hit the waters of the Dead Sea, that would have extinguished them, and therefore they wouldn't have burned up. They would have sunk down to the bottom of the floor of the Dead Sea and been preserved in the geological layer.

I've lived in the Biblical world now for over 15 years. Things just always end up being so much more obvious than mysterious. So, when you have something described in the Bible, you go to that place and you look at the excavation work that's been done, there's always not just a fit, but an obvious fit. The more that I explore this land, the more that I excavate in it, the more that I understand the different places and what the Bible describes in them, the more the Biblical account comes to life, and it's substantiated. This is a perfect example of this. We're not talking about a burned destruction over a layer of one city. We are talking about multiple cities. We are talking about burn layers over graves and cemeteries where they are talking about historical stories in the Bible that gives us a description of what happened. Describing the burning sulfur that is coming down like rain out of the sky."

So much for NOT BEING REAL… God in His divine sovereignty made sure that some of them went into the Dead Sea, and then in our lifetime when we are seeing the push of pedophilia, He let the waters recede so we could find them. Was that by chance? No.

Now, the other passage of God judging a society that was full of Hedonism was in Noah's day. Let's take a look at what God did there and why did God judge that time.

Genesis 6:5-7 "The LORD saw how great man's wickedness on the earth had become, and that every inclination of the thoughts of his heart was only evil all the time. The LORD was grieved that He had made man on the earth, and His heart was filled with pain. So, the LORD said, "I will wipe mankind, whom I have created, from the face of the earth – men and animals, and creatures that move along the ground, and birds of the air – for I am grieved that I have made them."

Why? Because of their wickedness unrestrained. Again, that's your term, hedonistic. It's whatever you want to do, it's all about self. Whatever wicked thing you can come up with, it's all about pleasing self. So, here's the point. What do you think is going to happen to us? Do we not think that God is not grieved over our wicked behavior, even here in America? We are approaching the same days as Lot, and He did judge them. Do we not think He's not going to judge us too? Yes, He is. But with Lot and with Noah, the thoughts were continually wicked all the time.

But you might be thinking, "Well hey, it's not as bad as it was in Sodom and Gomorrah or in Noah's day. I mean, yeah, it's kind of bad, but it's really not that bad, is it?" Uh…yes, it is! Folks, you tell me if our hearts haven't already gotten just as wicked as Sodom and Gomorrah, and just as evil all the time like in Noah's day that God wiped out. We're headed for judgment and here's the proof. I'm just going to give you some headlines. Are we at that point, not just with Lot and homosexuality and lesbianism, but isn't it just wicked everywhere you go?

MODERN DAY WICKEDNESS

- Schools are teaching kids that religion is a "disease" and entertainers are saying that, "the Bible is a work of fiction."
- New York City principal nixes the song 'God Bless the USA' at kindergarten graduation, but when the kids went ahead to sing it anyway, adults chanted back "Burn in Hell."
- Divorce cakes are now the new trend.
- Epidemic growth of Internet porn cited.
- Sexually transmitted disease rates have hit record highs in U.S.
- Girl Scouts are now supporting abortion and sexual promiscuity.
- MTV wants you to lose your virginity in a new reality show.
- The U.N. is calling for the legalization of prostitution worldwide.
- A PC game has been released called Rapelay that allows players to gang rape virtual women and then force them to have an abortion.

- A chastity ring has become the source of a new problem in school. A Christian teenage girl was banned for wearing a celibacy ring on school grounds.
- Live baby treated as "medical waste." Crematorium workers found an infant crying in a "medical waste" receptacle on its way to being cremated.
- Planned Parenthood kills 329,445 babies in one year using $487.4 million in taxpayer's funds. In fact, since 1973, we have now murdered over 64,000,000 babies in America alone. This is over 10 times the amount of people killed in Hitler's Holocaust of the Jews. We've also murdered almost 1.7 billion babies worldwide just since 1980.
- The government wants pro-life Americans to be forced to pay for other people's abortions. And British teens are having as many as seven abortions.
- And these murderous people are rabid as seen here. You tell me, this isn't evil. Take a look at this transcript of a video clip.

A security guard is standing outside an abortion clinic. A doctor comes out on break, drinking a cup of coffee. The person holding the camera begins to speak to this doctor.

Man with the camera: *"You need to repent for murdering babies."*

Doctor: *"Why?"* (He comes over to the cameraman and again repeats) "*Why?!"*

Man with the camera: *"Because it's a sin against God."*

Doctor: *"Why?"*

Man with the camera: *"It's pretty evil of you. Sir."*

Doctor: *"Yeah, I am."*

Man with the camera: *"You're in an abortion clinic and that's what you're doing to babies."*

Doctor: *"Yeah, and I love it."*

Man with the camera: *"You love it, huh?"*

Doctor: *"Yeah, I do!"*

Man with the camera: *"I hope you come to Christ, sir."*

Doctor: *"No, I'll never come to Christ."*

Man with the camera: *"I hope you come to Christ."*

Doctor: *"No, I don't listen to Christ."*

Man with the camera: *"You have a darkened heart."*

Doctor: *"I do have a dark heart, I do, I do, very much so."*

Man with a camera: *"You will stand before God in judgment."*

Doctor: *"Yes, I will. Every day."*

Man with the camera: *"You will stand before God."*

Doctor: *"I will, I will, I love it."*

Man with a camera: *"You are tearing babies apart."*

Doctor: *"Yes, I love it, I love it."*

The security guard comes to tell the doctor to go back inside.

Man with the camera: *"The babies, their blood screams from the ground."*

Since 2002, Planned Parenthood and other abortion providers have received over $1 billion in taxpayer's funding.

The next scene is a demonstration where people are holding up signs that read "Fund Planned Parenthood."

Lady holding a sign: *"You want to talk about morality? Look at what we represent right now. Abortions on demand, without apology."*

Another sign being held up reads: "How can you trust me with a child?"

Female doctor in demonstration: *"I am so proud to be a doctor here. I will perform abortions and be proud of it."*

Lady on the street: *"There is no shame in abortions. I had an abortion a few weeks ago. My insurance actually covered it.* (Everyone cheers)

According to Planned Parenthood's 2009 Annual Report, abortion accounted for 98 percent of its services to pregnant women.

Bus Driver: *"I agree!"*

Lady #2 on the street: *"Abortion is health care."*

What is Planned Parenthood's vision for our future?

Lady #3 on the street: *"Unless you are going to start adopting all these kids that are going to be born, I don't know what we are going to do. The maintenance."*

Cameraman: *"Kids, you're killing kids."*

Planned Parenthood says that they are not anti-Christian.

Lady #4 on the street: *"I really want them to stop making decisions about my body. It's my body. Keep your rosaries off my ovaries."*

Lady #5 on the street: *"It is not a baby. A baby is a fetus that has been born."*

Lady #6 on the street: *"A baby gets in the way of a job that I want to get to pay off my loans."*

Another sign reads: "Pro-choice is Pro-life. I stand with Planned Parenthood."

Why should we fund Planned Parenthood?

Lady #7 on the street: *"Because we can't wait until tomorrow. If I get pregnant tomorrow, I'd want an abortion. If I got pregnant today, I would abort the baby. And I wouldn't feel bad about that."*

Man on the street: *"I want Planned Parenthood to be like Starbucks. I want Planned Parenthood on every corner."*

And their hearts were continually wicked all the time. But it's a good thing that the Church is speaking up on this. No, the Church has gone "Woke." In fact, churches are actually promoting abortion. I was sent a video, taken in New York. He was in the pulpit. He said men should get vasectomies, but he supported choice for abortions. From the pulpit, it's sick. But it's worse than that. There are churches that are taking people to have kids murdered, and having so-called religious services, asking God to bless that.

Catherine Szeltner, EWTN Pro-Life Weekly Reports: "*This next story is an example of so-called religious leaders, leading their flock astray and twisting God's Word to feed an agenda of death and destruction. Based on a Facebook post by Whole Woman's Health and an article in the Texas Observer earlier this month, a group of so-called clergies gathered at an abortion clinic in Fort Worth, Texas to 'bless' abortion providers, clinic* *staff, and patients. The group reportedly sang 'Hallelujah' and prayed. When we sing 'Hallelujah,' we should be praising God, not praising abortion, which goes directly against God, the Author of Life. If it's going to debate abortion on Biblical grounds, it's clear where the Good Book stands. 'Thou shall not kill,' 'Before you were formed in the womb, I knew you,' and many more verses. It's not up for debate.*

The Ohio Religious Coalition for Reproductive Choice will host a 'Clinic Blessing' at an Ohio Planned Parenthood Abortion facility next Friday. Organizers want 'to show that anti-abortion advocates do not have the monopoly on Faith or God. Many Faith leaders, and people of faith, will hold that accessing and providing abortions is a good and Godly decision.'

What these so-called religious leaders are doing is dishonest and deceitful but using ministers and twisting truth to persuade the faithful to support abortion is nothing new for the industry. In a 1939 letter, Planned Parenthood founder Margaret Sanger wrote, 'We do not want the word to go out that we want to exterminate the negro population, and the minister is the man who can straighten out that idea, if it ever occurs to any of their more rebellious members.'

Just because you put a collar on it doesn't mean it's true. Be warned, my friends that this event is a perversion of faith, and these clergy members are false shepherds."

Clip from The View:

Host: *"We've seen the progressive church that has drawn huge millennial crowds, but it's still evangelical. So, where do you stand on social issues that young people are particularly passionate about, like gay marriage, abortion? How do you address those things? It's not against your church to have an abortion?"*

Pastor Carl Lentz: *"That is the kind of conversation we would have to have, finding out your story, where you're from. God's the judge. But you have to live by your own convictions."*

How many ways can you mess that up? It's called dancing around the issue. Yes, it's called sin. It's called the sin of murder. You're murdering a child and the Bible says it here and here and here and here. Next question. It's not hard. It's like throwing somebody a softball, or a wiffle ball. But not in the "Woke" church. These are the kinds of people that will be left behind. These are the kinds of people that will submit under the Vatican and join this One World Religion. In Christian name only. This is nuts. But wickedness all the time, look at this:

- A female senior student believes that abortion is a medium for art, and will be displaying her senior art project, a documentation of a nine-month process, during which she artificially inseminated herself "as often as possible," while periodically taking abortion drugs to induce miscarriages. Her exhibition will feature video recordings of these forced miscarriages as well as preserved collections of the blood from the process.

And that's art?

- Undertakers are now washing dead bodies down the drain by dissolving them in a caustic solution and flushing them into the sewer.

- A publicly funded exhibition encouraged people to deface the Bible in the name of art. Visitors responded with abuse and obscenity such as "This is all sexist [blank] so disregard it all," and another wrote on the first page of Genesis, "I am Bi, Female & Proud. I want no god who is disappointed in this."

- The U.S. is using foreign aid to promote gay rights.

Dare I say this has been done around the world and Trump did the same thing. One of the things that I really disagree with him on, is he and his administration promoted homosexuality and were penalizing nations that didn't go along with it. I have a problem with that. Just being consistent.

- Pentagon held its first gay pride event.

- Politicians say they're okay with second grade teacher reading gay prince fairytale called, "King and King."

- Thousands of schools across the nation are now observing the homosexual sponsored 'Day of Silence' in a nationwide push to promote the homosexual lifestyle in public schools. Students are taught that homosexuality is a worthy lifestyle, and that it has few or no risks, and that individuals are born homosexual and cannot change. Those who oppose such teaching are characterized as ignorant hateful bigots.

- California laws require all public-school instruction to positively portray homosexuals, transsexuals, and bisexuals to children as young as kindergarten. Another California law barring people from 'curing' gay children was signed into law."

- Proposed law would force churches to host gay weddings.

- There is another law on the books that's coming. They are wanting to make it permanent in our country. They are freaking out over the Roe v. Wade thing. And that was good news. At least it got back to the states. It didn't stop abortions, but at least it got back to the states. And states are starting to ban the majority of them and that's good. But they see the writing on the wall, this community, and now they want to make it permanent.

- A play depicting Jesus as gay packs church.

- A lesbian nativity is being promoted by another church. And when the Holy Family arrived, it was two women with their baby.

- A new version of 'The Last Supper' has come out in San Francisco. Amidst black leather, tattoos, and feather boas, homosexuals pose as the apostles, who in the original painting, are depicted gathered at a table with Jesus to partake of the last meal together.

- In the 'new version,' the table no longer has the traditional bread and wine symbolizing Christ's body and blood being given for us, but rather sex toys symbolizing the god of sex and unlicensed physical pleasure. And Nancy Pelosi stated, "Christianity has not been harmed by this."

  Do that in a Muslim Mosque and see what Nancy says.

- A publication is now promoting incestuous pedophilia as healthy sex-ed. Booklets for Family Affairs encourage parents to sexually massage their children as young as 1 to 3 years of age, and psychologists are pushing to decriminalize pedophilia.

On the one hand, we shouldn't be surprised. We certainly don't support it and we better speak up, as long as we have breath. We shouldn't be surprised because if we read the Genesis account, how many times have we read it, but we haven't read into it what is all there. In the days of Lot, it isn't just homosexuality, it was young and old alike, pedophilia. And Jesus said there's going to be a repeat of that. And we don't think we're going to be judged? I like what this man said:

"It seems that America has become the land of the special interest and the home of the double standard. If we lie to Congress, it's a felony, but if Congress lies to us, it's just politics.

The government spends millions to rehabilitate criminals, but they do almost nothing for the victims. In public schools, you can teach that homosexuality is OK, but you better not use the Word of God.

You can kill an unborn child, but it's wrong to execute a mass murderer. We don't burn books; we simply rewrite them. We got rid of the communist socialist threat by renaming them progressives.

If you protest the president, you're a terrorist, but if you burn an American flag, it's your 1st Amendment right. You can have pornography on TV or the internet, but you better not put a nativity scene in a public park during Christmas time! We can use aborted, murdered babies for medical research, but it's wrong to use an animal. We take money from those who work hard for it and give it to those who don't want to work.

We still have freedom of speech, but only if we are being politically correct. And parenting has been replaced with Ritalin and video games. What has happened to the land of the free and the home of the brave?"

I'll tell you what has happened. Not only has God given us over to a depraved mind, but we have allowed this to go on for so long: satanism, self-first. And God says once you go down that route, it's not just depraved, and it will destroy your society, but it's going to get to the point where you are going to love pleasure. Pleasing yourself in as many different ways as you can think of. You become hedonistic. Ouch! I'll tell you! We've turned into Sodom and Gomorrah! We have gone into a full-blown hedonistic society, and the Bible says we are headed for judgment! This is why one guy said this, he said, *"If God doesn't judge us, He needs to apologize to Sodom & Gomorrah."*

But can I tell you something? God's not in the apology-making business. And unless we, here in America, turn around and repent now as a nation and it starts with the Church, He will judge us! Why? Because we have become just as wicked as Sodom and Gomorrah, and our hearts are just as evil, all the time, like in Noah's Day. We've turned hedonistic! And if you don't want to listen to me, about the coming judgment, then listen to Jesus. He clearly told us that once this level of wickedness happens again, to the planet, it's a sign He's getting ready to come back and judge us!

Luke 17:26-30: "Just as it was in the days of Noah, so also will it be in the days of the Son of Man. People were eating, drinking, marrying and being given in marriage up to the day Noah entered the ark. Then the flood came and destroyed them all. It was the same in the days of Lot. People were eating and drinking, buying and selling, planting and building. But the day Lot left Sodom, fire and sulfur rained down from heaven and destroyed them all. It will be just like this on the day the Son of Man is revealed."

We are there. So, we don't have to be a prophet. If we read the Scripture, we know where it's headed. You're not going to stop the 7-year Tribulation. And being apathetic and fearful is not an option. God told us what to do. Noah was a preacher of righteousness. That is the opposite of wickedness. For 120 years. That's what we need to do. We need to be that salt, be that light, stop this lie of pietism, keeping your mouth shut, staying in your four walls. We need to be those resistors. We need to be preachers of righteousness. Because one day, God is going to say, "Get into the ark, you're going home." But until then we need to preach righteousness. No matter how bad it gets. There's no other option and we need to wake-up to that. Unfortunately, again, the Church is not waking up. The Church is going "Woke." Which is a code word for complying, compromising, keeping your mouth shut.

Narrator: *"When God said come into the ark, you and all your household. Noah saw God close the ark. The people on the outside wondered, 7 days before the rains came. I know if it were me, I would wonder, there are sleepless nights that I have. I am pondering the things of God and what He has shown me what is coming to this country. Can you sleep? I can't see how you could sleep at night. The Bingo Halls are full, the churches are empty.*

You may say, 'My church is full.' Full of what? Dead men's bones? The casinos are full, but no one will give to God. Concerts are packed, but no one will praise the Almighty. You will scream and shout for a rock star, but sit quietly bored when hearing about God Almighty. You will sit through a movie for two hours, but will you sit and pray for two hours?

We will drive out of state for a game or a race, but we can't even get up Sunday morning or Sunday night or Wednesday night, to hear the Word of God. And these are so-called Christians that do this. Not only is the world asleep while there is a fire coming upon this earth, but the Christians are asleep. These are Christians that do this.

They give God crumbs while they dine on the fruits of the world. They demand unconditional love, and they give God lip service. They demand blessings though they curse His name. They demand the flesh, yet they crucify the spirit. They say they can't go to church every time the doors are open, but they can take their kids to football, basketball, baseball, dance or to the fair, or just sit in front of the TV all night long. But to go to the presence of the Heavenly Father is just too much to ask. We will work 8 to 10 hours a day to pay the bills and to buy the bass boat. But for the one that breathes life into us, one hour is for you, God.

We sit in church like we are godly, we have a form of godliness, but we deny the power thereof. I don't see how the Christians can sleep at night. Before the rains came, I believe Noah couldn't sleep but the world outside was sleeping just fine. They fell asleep, watching TV. They just got home from their favorite game or movie. They would be doing everything under the sun - eating, drinking and being merry - not knowing that tomorrow they shall die.

You cannot say you were not warned. In **Luke 21:11** *it says there will be earthquakes in diverse places, and famines and pestilence and fearful events and great signs from Heaven. In verse 25, nations will be in anguish and perplexity at the roaring and tossing of the sea. You cannot say that you were not warned. Did not Noah preach to you for 120 years and you ignored him? They asked, 'Who is that man?' 'Oh, that's just Noah. That's just Noah, he's always talking negative. That's just Noah. Let's go back to sleep.'*

At least when Jesus was praying in the garden, when the disciples slept, at least they woke up. When the servants slept, and the enemy came and stole the wares, at least the servants woke up. But when Jesus Christ comes back, the kingdom it will be like the virgins, 5 wise and 5 foolish. And they will be sleeping. All of them. Oh, that we may open our eyes and see what is coming. And yet, we sleep on. God have mercy."

Yes, may God have mercy on us. Why God, why? Why did we fall? How did this happen? How did our great and mighty Christian nation turn into such a society of wickedness and rebellion just like Sodom and Gomorrah?" And not just in the world, but in the professing Church. And the irony is they are asleep, but they have the audacity to call themselves "Woke." The exact opposite of what they really are. They're asleep. They invaded the church, perverted God's truth, created their own god. That's not the real Biblical God. And Christianity in name only is going to march us right in to the 7-year Tribulation.

Another thing they want to twist is, they want to twist who Jesus is. But on this aspect, what I want to move forward with, is what do they do with us that are faithful, who are not asleep? "Woke." Who are not going to comply, who are not going to compromise, who are going to be like Noah, and I'm going to preach righteousness until God shuts the door. We don't know how far it's going to go but what we do know, scripturally, they're going to persecute, and they are even going to take you out. And again, they are going to filter who's real and who's not. Remember, their version of real is really the fakers. The real ones that they are going to call fakers, they will ostracize them and propagandize them as being mean terrorists, as an excuse to haul them away and/or get rid of them. That's the old switcheroo that's going on.

The filters that we are going to take a look at, who's going to be a part and who's not? Who are we going to give a label to? Who's dangerous? And now we have to take them out. Climate change, the ecumenical movement, and the whole thing we are primarily seeing now, homosexuality, lesbianism, transgenderism, now pedophilia. And if you don't go along with that, you are going to become dangerous to society. And your beliefs and all that you believe in will eventually become a hate crime. The Bible will become a hate book. That will become the justification as to why you need to be rounded up and hauled away or killed.

If you don't think that will ever come, we're going to see this in Scripture where it says this will happen. And it's going to culminate in the 7-year Tribulation, which we're not going to be in, but we are starting to see signs of it. And frankly, persecuting and killing Christians has been going on for quite some time. Another thing you will not see in the media.

Narrator: *"On October 25, 2005, this girl was walking to a Christian school with three friends. They were attacked by two men with machetes. She was the only survivor. The girl was 10 when her house was bombed for being a Christian.*

This boy was thrown into the fire by soldiers for refusing to renounce Jesus Christ.

Another person was flogged for being Christian. Church buildings are being burned down. Christian homes are being destroyed. 'A mob of Hindus came at midnight. They burned our homes and destroyed our church. We had to hide in the jungle to survive.'

Believers of a home church that was attacked and the pastor beaten. 'I would have been dead long back if it were not for the grace of Jesus Christ. Pastor Simon prayed for me, and I am a witness today of the healing power of God.' This young man was asked, 'So, will you stand firmly for Jesus Christ in any situation?' His answer is, 'Even if they kill me, I am not going to leave Jesus.'

In the House of Prayer, Pastor Walter Masih is beaten with clubs by several men with masks. When they leave him bloodied, they destroy his church.

Pastor Masih says, 'As Jesus had told us we have to practice to show the other cheek. I have forgiven them, let them be blessed. They are ignorant.'

In August 2008, in Orissa, India, an uproar of anti-Christian violence swept through 300 villages. Over 50 Christians were beaten to death, cut to pieces, or burned. There are more than 26 million documented cases of martyrdom in the 20th Century alone. More than in the prior 1,900 years combined. Close to 185,000 Christians are martyred every year. One Christian is martyred every 3 minutes. More than 250 million Christians in over 80 nations are currently living under the threat of persecution, 60 percent are children. Stop tolerating sin!"

That's what "Woke" will get you. That's the fruit of pietism. That's what you get when you chicken out and keep your mouth shut. You won't be like that preacher and do what he did. Or you compromise and comply. And if you don't think that's coming, that's already happening. That's why I wanted to let you see that. It's already happening. It's just not here yet. But don't mark my word, mark God's Word. Do you think it's insensitive to be who we are called to be? To be the salt, the light, the resisters? If we don't, that will come here. People will be after us, because we are haters for preaching God's truth that homosexuality is wrong, that pedophilia is gross, and a wicked sin. We need to speak up.

Chapter Thirteen

The Persecution of Biblical Christianity

What is love? God is love. And God tells us what Biblical love is. The Biblical love that God has given us is mercy, compassion, kindness, graciousness, patience, faithfulness, and goodness. I'll take that any time of the week over their twisted, perverted love. Their twisted, perverted definition of love (and this is in the so-called church), is saying that Christian love is accepting and tolerating anything. Any kind of immoral behavior. You shouldn't say anything. Just accept one and all. But that's not what God says. In the previous chapters we saw not only are they twisting the definition of love, but they also are also twisting relationships - i.e., Biblical identities, male and female, Biblical marriage between a man and a woman.

Once you hit that route, the Bible says in **Romans 1**, if you don't turn away from that, God's going to give you over to that last stage of a depraved mind, and it will destroy your society. And that's where we are today in America. If we look at Israel, we see that we are following the same mistake they did with that mindset, called relativism. The Bible says, "Everyone was doing what was right in their own eyes." And that is why today, they can't seem to define what a woman is, as basic as that is.

Because they are just making it up as they go. Relativism, whatever is true to you. Whatever feels right to you. But that is not what the Bible says. The Bible says it's leading to woeful times just like Israel.

"Doing whatever is right in your own eyes," and "rejecting God's Law" is not a good way to go!! Those that call good evil, evil good, and that is exactly where we are at today. But why are they doing this? Number one, it's going to destroy our country from the inside out. Number two, they are making a ton of money off this. Pushing this agenda. It has gone beyond the twisted relationship of homosexuality and lesbianism, to bestiality and pedophilia, and this whole transgender movement, fluidity, etc. But the reason they are pushing it, is because it's going to not only destroy the country, but it will also bring them a lot of money; 1.3 million dollars is generated off each person that comes out as a transgender. Going through that procedure brings in big bucks.

It is also preparing people for the transhumanist movement goal, which is number three. They want to make us into a post-human species, human 2.0, non-humans. As crazy as that sounds that's what they want. So, if you have a whole group of people that say, "Hey, yeah. I'm not a male or female, a male that wants to be a female, a female that wants to be a male, but remember, that female that wanted to be a wolf? Remember that one? Well, believe it or not, that mentality is needed, because one day the elites, very soon, are going to come and say, "Yes, we're going to honor all your fluidity, and whatever you want to be. We will make you that genetically because you don't get to choose now. We're going to do it for you." It's a set up.

As bad as that is, you would think that people would start speaking up. Well, the Church is falling for another lie called pietism. Basically, it says to the Church, "Shut your mouth. You guys stay within your four walls and keep quiet." No, that's not what the Bible says. The Bible tells us we are to be the salt, we are to be the light, and, specifically, **2 Thessalonians 2**, as we see the underpinnings of the rise of the antichrist that'll culminate in the 7-year Tribulation, we are to be the restrainers, the restraining influence. Keeping your mouth shut, pietism, doesn't help and it goes against what God says to do. How can you engage the culture if you sit there and stay behind your four walls or go hide out in the hills? You can't! You can't be the salt, the light, you can't be the resistors if you are hiding out and keeping your mouth shut.

Now what are they going to do with all these resistors? The real born-again Christians - who are being obedient to God's word, being the salt and the light and being resistors - are they going to just let us keep getting away with it? No, they are going to, basically, figure out how to not only persecute us, but eventually execute us. Anyone who doesn't go along with their wicked agenda. And that is what God said would happen. What these people have created, not only in our society, but in the world, is a Hedonistic society. That Hedonistic society had two other societies that hit that route. It was called the days of Lot, which included pedophilia, and the days of Noah. Once your society hits the Hedonistic route (and that is where we're at, and what's being pushed in the Church by the fakers), it is judgment time! And that is where our society is today.

It isn't that these people just want their so-called freedom to do what they want to do by twisting the definition of God's love, but there is a bigger picture that we are going to expose. They are using this Hedonistic lifestyle, if you will, the LGBT, as an excuse to filter out any and all resistors of the coming One World Religion. Because that's where it's ultimately headed. It isn't just these fakers that come into the Church, it isn't just that they are pushing this Hedonistic LGBT message. I'm telling you; it's going to be used as a tool to force the real Christian to pop his head out because you can't go along with it. They are going to use that as an excuse to get rid of us.

These people are going to march into the 7-year Tribulation claiming to be Christians, but they're not, and their so-called lifestyle will expose anybody who won't go along with their agenda and the One World Government. You might be saying, "Wait a second. Do you mean to tell me that we're really headed for a One World Religion?" Yes, and homosexuality is the first filter to expose those who will never go along with it. I want to explain why by taking a look at that One World Religion aspect. Are we really headed for that time, and are these enemies within the Church - these fakers, these phonies - are they really going to march into the 7-year Tribulation and be a part of that? And will they be used to take out anybody who doesn't go along with their agenda?

Revelations 13:3-9: "One of the heads of the beast [the antichrist] seemed to have had a fatal wound, but the fatal wound had been healed. The whole world was astonished and followed the beast. Men worshiped the dragon [satan] because he had given authority to the beast, and they also worshiped the beast and asked, 'Who is like the beast? Who can make war against him?' The beast was given a mouth to utter proud words and blasphemies and to exercise his authority for forty-two months. He opened his mouth to blaspheme God, and to slander His name and His dwelling place and those who live in Heaven. He was given power to make war against the saints [the people who do get saved during the 7-year Tribulation] and to conquer them. And he was given authority over every tribe, people, language and nation. All inhabitants of the earth will worship the beast – all whose names have not been written in the book of life belonging to the Lamb that was slain from the creation of the word. He who has an ear, let him hear."

In other words, you better pay attention to this! But folks, according to our text, the Bible clearly says that there's really coming a day when all the inhabitants of the earth are going to be busy worshiping who? The actual antichrist himself, right? One day, the Bible says, the whole world will be unified into a One World Religion that is actually satanically inspired. This will be satan's religion, and it will be headed up by the antichrist. But that's the question. Could this really happen? Could the whole world really be deceived into creating a One World Religion that the antichrist is going to hijack and take over and say, "Now worship me?!" Uh, yeah! In fact, it's happening right now before our very eyes! We know that halfway into it he goes up into the rebuilt Jewish temple, and he does what is called the "abomination of desolation," **Matthew 24**, and **Daniel** mentions it as well, Paul mentions this in **Thessalonians,** when he goes up into the temple, he says, "Worship me. I am God." That's the “abomination of desolation.”

It says all the inhabitants of the earth, which is a code phrase in **Revelation** for those who do not belong to God. So, people who do not belong to God will worship the antichrist. They will be a part of this One World Religion. We are going to see that these enemies within the Church - if the Rapture were to happen here in our lifetime, which it sure seems like it is going to - Christianity in name only, these fakers, are going to march right in and they’re going to be a part of this One World Religion.

In fact, the Bible also says the antichrist is going to kill people who don’t go along with this One World Religion, that is, those who turn to God during this time! Jesus mentions it here:

Matthew 24:3-10: “As Jesus was sitting on the Mount of Olives, the disciples came to Him privately. ‘Tell us,’ They said, ‘when will this happen, and what will be the sign of Your coming and of the end of the age?’”

Number one, the Church is not born yet, and He’s talking to His Jewish disciples, and the coming that they are talking about is the Second Coming, which is at the end of the 7-year Tribulation. So, Jesus, is speaking about the very beginning of the 7-year Tribulation, which is a perfect parallel of Revelation 6, which goes through the beginning point of the 7-year Tribulation and moves forward. That’s why He says:

Matthew 24:3-10, cont.: “Jesus answered: ‘Watch out that no one deceives you. For many will come in My Name, claiming, ‘I am the Christ,’ and will deceive many.”

That is how **Revelation 6:1**, the white horse rider, the false peace, utopia, the antichrist, rides in on. That’s what starts the 7-year Tribulation and then the second seal is the war. Again, this is a parallel passage to **Revelation 6:1**. That’s why Jesus says wars after that.

Matthew 24:3-10, cont.: "You will hear of wars and rumors of wars but see to it that you are not alarmed. Such things must happen, but the end is still to come. Nation will rise against nation, and kingdom against kingdom. There will be famines and earthquakes in various places."

Again, parallel with that passage, He's talking about the events in the 7-year Tribulation in chronological order.

Matthew 24:3-10, cont.: "All these are the beginning of birth pains. Then you will be handed over to be persecuted and put to death, and you will be hated by all nations because of Me. At that time many will turn away from the faith and will betray and hate each other."

So, Jesus clearly says that not only one day, the whole planet is going to hate followers of Him - specifically in the 7-year Tribulation - but that many people who claim to be "in the faith" (i.e., posing as Christians) will actually betray and hate others who are "really in the faith" (i.e., true followers of God).

Does that sound familiar? That's the fakers who are invading the Church right now. I'm telling you, Christianity in name only is going to march into the 7-year Tribulation. If anybody during that time turns to God, these fakers are going to turn them in.

I've said this phrase for so many years and I'll say it again. You better be careful - the person sitting next to you in the pew, may one day be the death of you. They might turn you into the authorities! Why? Because all these churches that are enamored with numbers and who could care less if there's a bunch of fakers and only have five genuine Christians, they are not only going to continue to march the fakers into the 7-year Tribulation, but your reward is, one day these fakers will betray anybody who really does turn to God. Praise God, you got saved during the 7-year Tribulation, but now these fakers that you were so enamored with are going to turn you in.

If you think I'm joking, that's actually what's happening. There is a great book called "Tortured for Christ," written by Richard Wurmbrand, where he documents how the Communists, when they took over the Church, they did the same thing that's happening now. "Oh, no, we're going to let you do your own thing. We're going to honor that." But they didn't. They came in and took over everything in society, and then they began to send fakers into churches posing as Christians. They sat there and began to take names of anybody who said anything about the Communist state. If they couldn't get the pastor to preach state-approved sermons, then he disappeared, and they put a guy in there who would. This is all on record. Then you go to church services one day and say, "Hey, where's Bob Jones?" "He's gone. I don't know. He just hasn't been here in a month." It's because they hauled him off and killed him. Because Bob Jones was talking smack about the communists. This is what went on.

The Church continued on, but you see what's happening. The same thing is happening today. It's being supplanted. True Biblical Christianity is being eradicated before our eyes with fakers coming into the Church, and the way they're getting away with it, is because the Church is bonding to a lie. Numerical growth is more important than spiritual growth. One day your payday is coming. They're going to turn you in. Those who didn't get saved, found themselves now left behind in the 7-year Tribulation. You got saved but, guess what? They're going to turn you in. They're going to go along with a One World Religion. That's what's been going on, on a massive scale. So, my question is, do we see any signs of a hatred developing? Because it's going to culminate in the 7-year Tribulation. Do we see signs now of the hatred towards true followers of Christ? Even to the point where they would literally turn us into the government authorities and haul us away or even kill us? Yes, and that is what is being, and has been laid for a long time. And the reason why is because you have got to get rid of the true believers if you are going to pull off a One World Religion.

Logically, if you are going to have a One World Religion, that's called pantheism. The word pan means "all," and theism means "all gods, all religions get you to God." Is that lie here today? Yes, and we saw that one stat poll where nearly 70 percent of people who profess to be Christians are already believing that lie. That shows how many we have that are fakers in the Church, and they are going to march right into the 7-year Tribulation. But that is what you need. If you are going to have a One World Religion, you have to accept all religions. Well, wait a second. We have a problem. You have religions out there, that by definition, are called "monotheistic." What does that mean? There is only one God, and that's it.

Guess who happens to be the three monotheistic religions on the planet? Us, real Christians. Not the enemies, not the fakers. I didn't say it, Jesus did, **John 14:6**, "I am the way, the truth, the life, nobody comes to the Father except by Me." He's the only way to Heaven.

Islam is another one. Their way is the only way. It's a false way, but that's what they believe. They're monotheistic. And guess who else? Judaism. So, if you're going to have a One World Religion, then you've got to get rid of these three monotheistic religions. Why are you going to do that? Because, by definition, of all religions, you've got to have Islam, Christianity, and Judaism be a part of that. But they'll never go along with that. So how are you going to pull it off? Bingo! You're going to take the real ones and say they're the bad ones, and you're going to take the fake ones and say they're the real ones. It's called the old switcheroo.

This is what's been going on ever since 9-11. Starting with Islam, let's take a look at that. Just draw a line. This is what's been going on for the last several decades and the true Muslims, who actually follow the Koran, who actually kill people, who murder people because they

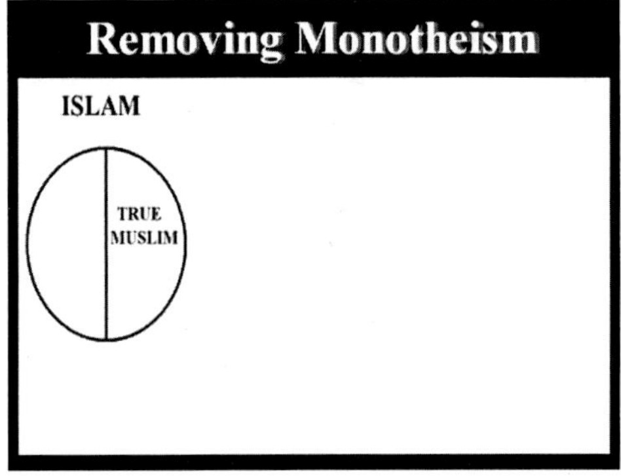

think they're doing good for Allah, and their reward is for the men to satisfy your lust forever in Heaven with virgins. That's really what it teaches. I don't condone that. I don't recommend that and it's wrong but that's what it believes. So, that's why they do what they do, because that's what they're told to do in their religion.

Well, the media is out there saying, "Oh, you guys are bad!" And what's the terms they're using? You're terrorists. You're fundamentalists extremists, Muslim extremists. Fundamental Muslim terrorists, right?

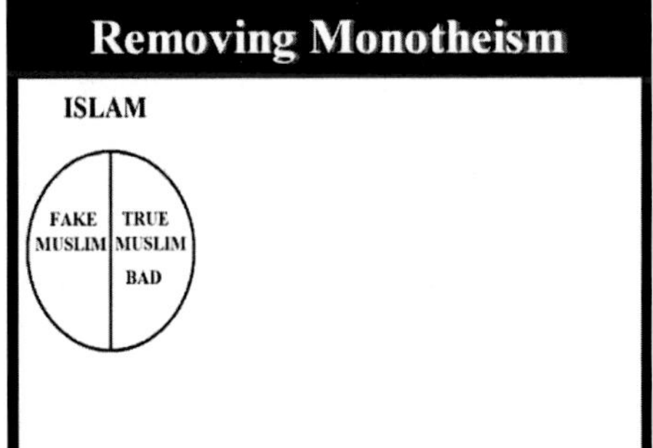

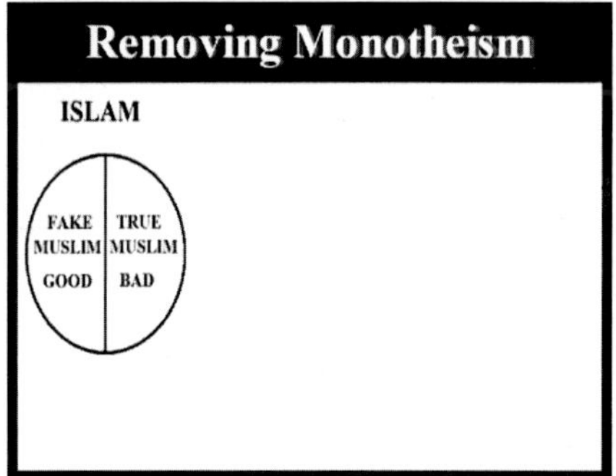

And then at the same time, you and I, who've been scratching our heads with the fake Muslims that the media is saying, "Oh no. These are the real ones." The moderate Muslims, the ones who say, "Oh no, Islam is a religion of peace." No, it's not. The reason that they say that is because they're fake Muslims, if you will. They're not following the Koran and they are not doing what it says you're supposed to do, which I'm not recommending. So, the media right now is touting and promoting, and has been for decades, that the fake Muslims are the real Muslims. The other guys are bad. They're not just bad, we need to exterminate them. That's actually one of my concerns. I remember after 9-11, I saw, coming out of the mouths of professing Christians, "We need to go over there and kill those people."

I'm all about defending our country, but the best things you can do for a person who is a true Muslim, believing in the Koran, is to share Jesus Christ with them. Because God can save them too. In fact, right now, one of the fastest places that people are getting saved, is in Iran. That's the power of the gospel. But when Christians jumped on the bandwagon saying, "Yeah, go kill them, they're extremists, they're bad, they're dangerous," again, they promoted these fakers. So, guess what? That fake version of Islam will continue on in the One World Religion. Can you see how they are doing it? That way, they get away with it. Because we accept everything, including Islam or the fake version.

Now if you've been paying attention, the same thing has been happening with you and me. And dare I say, at the same time. Draw a line down the middle and here's what's going on. We've got the true Christians, you and I, who follow the Scripture. They're saying that we are bad. In fact, they are using the exact same terminology that they used on the Muslims, on you and I.

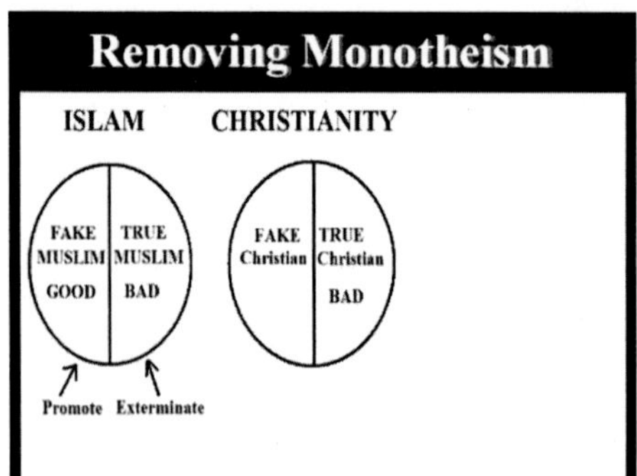

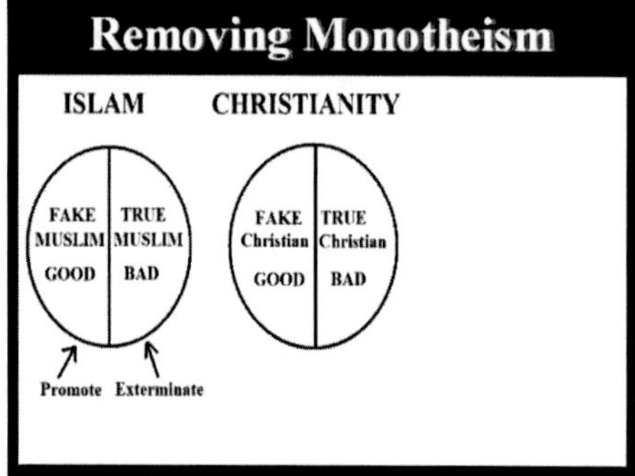

We're fundamental extremist, right-wing terrorists. This is propaganda. Hitler was a master of it, and that is what he used before he began to slaughter the Jews. Well, the same thing is happening with you and I. They're taking the fake Christians, all these enemies within the Church who will go along with this One World Religion - the whole LGBT, do whatever you want to do, all paths lead to Heaven. These fakers, who say there is no hell, we all go to Heaven and it's all that fakery. Those guys are fake, they're not Christians.

They're saying, "No, see, that's the real Christianity. That's the real Jesus. That's the real love." This perverted one. Now they are going to say we need to get rid of those dangerous, fundamental, extremist Christians, just like those Muslims. "We can't let this continue. They're a danger to society. They're guilty of hate crimes." And then they continue to promote these fakers as the real, loving, true Christians. So, Christianity in name only will continue in your pantheistic One World Religion. You can see the ruse that is going on.

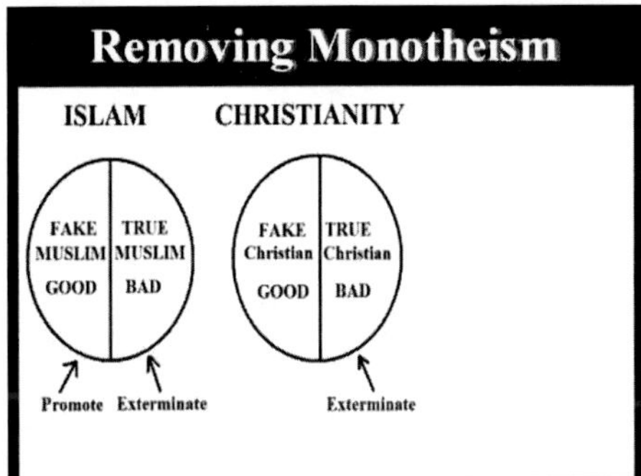

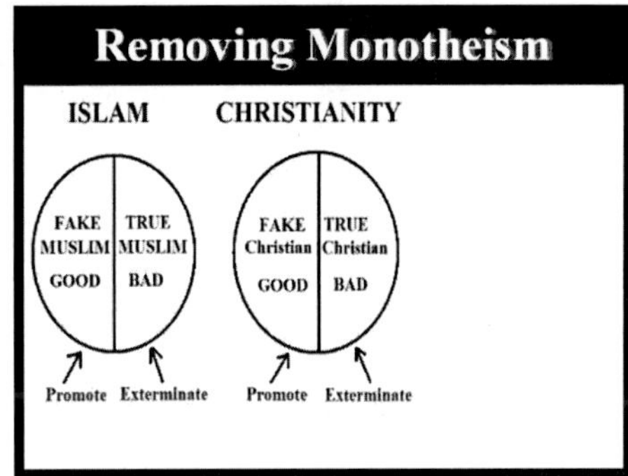

Now that leads us to the final one and that's Judaism. The Bible gives us a different little slice. Instead of down the middle. The Bible says that Israel is in such a state spiritually, which is not good, that they actually strike a deal with the antichrist himself. They think the antichrist is going to be their savior, and they cut a deal with him, (**Daniel 9:27**). And that's what starts the 7-year Tribulation. He eventually shows his true colors halfway into it. Again, he goes up into the temple and declares himself to be God. And, at that point, are the Jewish people going to do that?

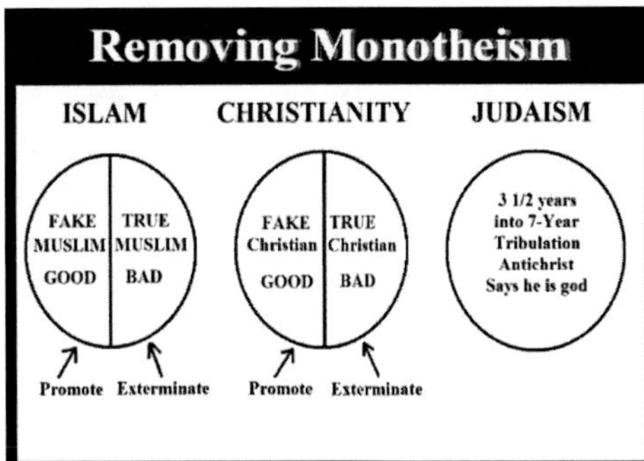

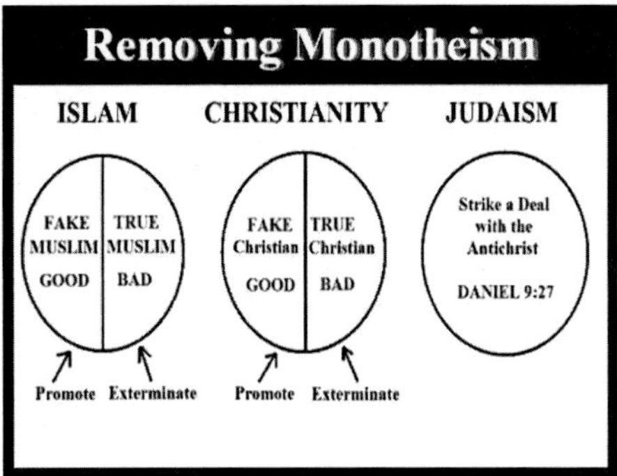

No, they're monotheistic. They're not going to worship a man as a god. There's only one God and they know that. Even though currently they deny Jesus Christ. But this is their big wake up, the Bible says. At this point they go, "Oy vey! Hey man, we've been duped!" So, the good news/bad news is that they finally turn to God at this point, the veil is removed, and they see that Jesus is the one and only Christ. But the bad news is the antichrist is going to slaughter them.

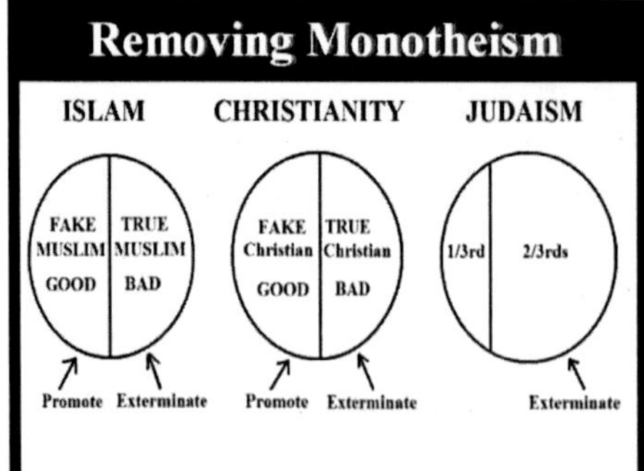

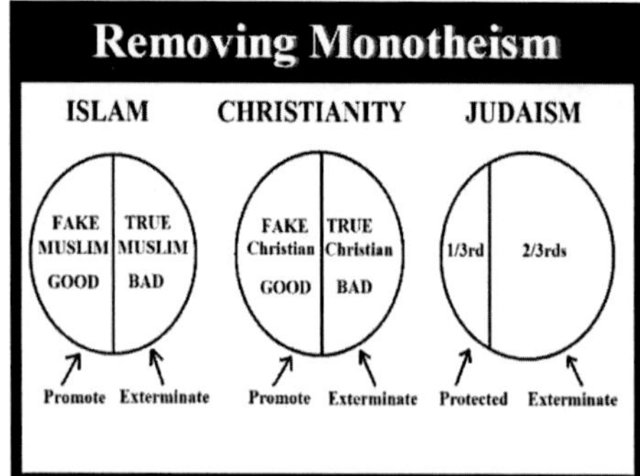

And that is what we see. Two-thirds are going to be slaughtered, and one-third will be sovereignly protected. **Zechariah 13** talks about two-thirds being taken out and one-third is sovereignly protected with (**Revelation 12**), with the archangel, Michael. God is not done with the Jewish people. This One World Religion will continue on, even with the monotheistic religions in the 7-year Tribulation, but you've got to get rid of the three monotheistic ones, and that is already under play. Now you know what they are doing.

These fakers are coming in, and they are going to be the fakers that are going to march straight into the 7-year Tribulation, in name only, as Islam, Christianity, and then Judaism will be dealt with as one of the major players in the 7-year Tribulation. Now, how are they going to force the real believers to rear their heads, to expose themselves? We are all mixed together, fakers and real. So, we are going to talk about two issues, and the first one is already in play. The first one is the hedonistic issue (a moral issue) - homosexuality, lesbianism, pedophilia, transgenderism, the whole LGBT thing. etc. And the other is the pluralism issue (a spiritual issue). The ecumenical movement that says all paths lead to Heaven. Both are being used to force the true Christian to pop their head out so they can be identified, targeted, vilified, persecuted, then hauled away for execution. And the so-called worshipers around you will turn you in.

So, how are they going to do this? Well, let's take a look at true believers in Jesus Christ. What does God say that we're supposed to do when it comes to this moral issue? Well, let's take a look at the Scripture.

1 Corinthians 5:9-13: "I have written you in my letter not to associate with sexually immoral people – not at all meaning the people of this world who are immoral, or the greedy and swindlers, or idolaters. In that case you would have to leave this world. But now I am writing you that you must not associate with anyone who calls himself a brother but is sexually immoral or greedy, an idolater or a slanderer, a drunkard, or a swindler. With such a man do not even eat. What business is it of mine to judge those outside the church? Are you not to judge those inside? God will judge those outside. Expel the wicked man from among you."

So, here we see the Bible's response to sexual immorality in the Church - like in the case of homosexuality or lesbianism among others - is to, what? Do not associate with them! Don't even eat with them! Why? So, they'd be ashamed of their behavior! How can you say you're a Christian and keep doing this, let alone expect us to condone this? However, for the non-Christian in the world, it doesn't say we can't hang out with them, because somebody's got to witness to them, right? Otherwise, you'd have to leave the world, as Paul says. But in the Church, different story.

Those who would say they're a Christian and they continue to engage in this behavior, and refuse to repent, what do we do? We don't associate with them! We don't even eat with them! Why? So, they would be ashamed of their behavior! God has a standard. And for those of you who don't believe me, that they should be ashamed of their behavior, listen to what Paul says. Paul uses the exact same word in **Thessalonians**.

2 Thessalonians 3:14: "If anyone does not obey our instruction in this letter, take special note of that person and do not associate with him, so that he will be put to shame."

People, the Bible says that shame is not bad, it's good. Why? Because it helps bring about conviction. You need to acknowledge that what you're doing is wrong, so you can repent of it and be healed! But if you don't, I'm not supposed to hang out with you, so you'll feel bad about it, so you'll get right with God. It's meant for your good! But this is exactly what the Church is not doing! You talk about apostasy! They're helping people keep locked into the bondage of sin! This is how far it's gone! This is how far we have fallen! We're not only still associating with those who say they're Christians in the Church - who are committing immorality, let alone homosexuality - but we're also removing any sense of shame for sinful behavior, and even saying that those who oppose are the real sinners! I'm not making this up! How are you going to know who these people are who never go along with the One World Religion? They are using this moral issue to force true Christians to pop their heads up. You can't go along with this, and the fakers will promote it. It's the old switcheroo. So, let's take a look at that.

"We all know that major denominations across America have been sliding on this issue of homosexuality Biblically for a long time now. And that they have actually moved to the point where they are now approving homosexual behavior and homosexual marriages, as well as homosexual pastors behind the pulpit. But it's getting so bad in the Church that the Washington National Cathedral not only hosted its first transgender priest celebrating 'LGBT month.' Gary Hall, the chief ecclesiastical leader, and executive officer of the National Cathedral said that 'homophobia and heterosexism is a sin.'"

It's on tape, here is the video clip:

Alyona Minkovski, Huffpost.Live: *"If the Washington National Cathedral's recent decision to celebrate same sex marriages didn't make their stance on the LGBT community clear, then Reverend Gary Hall's* *statements during his Sunday sermon definitely should. Hall told congregants on Sunday, that the church must have the courage to call homophobia and heterosexism what they are, a sin. The Reverend also called the church's role in oppressing the LGBT community shameful."*

Reverend Gary Hall: *"It's wisdom. The church came to its senses over time and labeled both racism and sexism as sinful. And now we find ourselves at this last barrier about human identity. You can call that barrier homophobia. You can call that barrier heterosexism. But we must now have the courage to take the final step and to call homophobia and heterosexism what they are. They are sin. Homophobia is a sin. Heterosexism is a sin. Shaming people for whom they love is a sin. Shaming people because their gender identity does not fit neatly into your sense of what it should be is a sin."*

A sin? God's standard has now become a sin in the Church? This is not the world; it is the fakers in the Church. If the Rapture were to happen tonight that gentleman right there, I'm convinced, will march straight into the 7-year Tribulation and probably be excited that we just disappeared. And here's what's sad. Those who turn to Jesus during that time, got saved. Maybe that guy, that's what it'll take for him to really get saved. But guess what? The fakers around you are going to betray you and turn you in. And then they will kill you. That's what Jesus said is coming.

But, who in the world would have thought that we'd see in our lifetime, the Church being flooded with fake apostate pastors, filling pulpits in droves? And now the Church is actually saying that homosexuality is not a sin, and those who oppose it are the real sinners. Can you believe that? The days of apostasy are here! In fact, apparently, so is the arrival of the antichrist! Little do these people know that they're not only not following God's Word, the Words of Christ, but they're actually preparing people to be part of the One World Religion and the worship of the antichrist. And the reason that he is helping is because of this moral issue. Many people believe that the antichrist himself will be a homosexual.

Daniel 11:36-37: "Then the king will do as he pleases, and he will exalt and magnify himself above every god and will speak monstrous things against the God of gods; and he will prosper until the indignation is finished, for that which is decreed will be done. He will show no regard for the gods of his fathers or for the desire of women."

Interesting…you mean to tell me the antichrist has no desire for women? What do you call that? Oh yeah, that's homosexuality. I've heard a lot of people say, "Oh no, that's not what it means." I think it's pretty plain. If you are a man and you don't desire women, then you're desiring something that's not a woman. You have to call it what it is, because everybody's so sheepish to call out this immorality. But these guys who are promoting this aren't just being a part of ushering people into the One World Religion, but they are preparing them to worship the antichrist. And that doesn't surprise me, because the antichrist means the opposer of Christ, and this is what satan does. Anything that God says, he does the exact opposite. As we saw in our Satanism study, it's called the Law of Reversal. They do it on purpose, just to get back at God, so to speak. Here's God's design, male and female, and so what's the reverse of that? Male/male and female/female, bestiality, pedophilia, all that. It's all perverted. Right? So, it fits that satanic agenda.

And now, the Church is helping to promote it…just in time for the antichrist's arrival. Can you believe it? 20 years ago, this would never have been possible! But today, right now, it's progressed so far that "66% of Americans, right now, said they would vote for a Gay President." You know, a political leader, like the antichrist!

But now because we disagree with this immoral behavior, it's become the excuse to label us and it's already started to play out all around the world. I think it's going to culminate in the 7-year Tribulation, but we are starting to see telltale signs of it. Just like we are starting to see rumors of wars, famines and pestilence, and earthquakes in various places. We're not in the 7-year Tribulation but we are seeing things ramp up.

Well, this hatred towards followers of Jesus is also starting to ramp up over this issue of LGBT. So, we are now being labeled as being mean, and judgmental, and intolerant, and dangerous to the point where they now say we are guilty of a hate crime and we need to go to jail! Don't believe me? The groundwork has been laid here in America for quite some time now. Even way back in the days of Obamanation. Check it out:

George Thomas, Christian World News Reports: *"A new hate crimes law raises disturbing questions about freedom of speech and religion in the United States. Hello, everyone, I'm George Thomas."*

Wendy Griffith: *"And I'm Wendy Griffith. This week U.S. President Barack Obama signed hate crimes legislation into law and later he hosted a reception at the White House for gay rights supporters."*

Barack Obama: *"We must stand against crimes that are meant not only to break bones, but to break spirits. Not only to inflict harm, but to instill fear."*

Wendy Griffith: *"The new law expands federal hate crimes legislation to include homosexuals. Gay activists have been pushing for this for nearly a decade and Democrats attached the measure to an unrelated defense spending bill. Opponents are afraid the new law threatens freedom of religion and speech. Here's Jennifer Wishon from Washington."*

Jennifer Wishon: *"Despite added language meant to strengthen free speech protections for Christians who preach Biblically held beliefs against homosexuality, many Republicans fear it is not enough."*

Rep. Mike Pence: *"Whatever language they add, it has an escape hatch, and we know from the experience at the state level and around the globe, that this represents a real infringement on the First Amendment, freedom of religion, freedom of expression of Americans."*

Jennifer Wishon: *"Many predict the new law could land Christians in jail."*

Rep. Mike Pence: *"If you aid or abet or induce in the commission of a federal crime, you're guilty of that crime and so, as the scenario goes, someone could preach a sermon out of* ***Romans 1****, for instance, about sexual practices; and if someone was inspired by malevolent intent in some way to go out and commit an act of violence, that pastor, that minister, or priest could be held liable under existing federal law."*

And by the way, don't think it's just going to stop with just the pastor…it's going to be any Christian who speaks out against it! This was back in the Obamanation days, and shocker! The current administration who was a part of Obamanation is doing the same thing. Which, by the way, I saw this on the internet. I didn't come up with it. But one person is out there saying that BIDEN, based on behavior, now stands for: Bumbling, Imbecile, Destroying the Entire Nation. Now, I don't know if that's true, but maybe that should be put on a T-shirt. You'd probably sell a billion.

The current administration is pushing the same thing. If you disagree with this, you're going to be guilty of a hate crime.

Isaiah 5:20: "Woe to those who call evil good and good evil, who put darkness for light and light for darkness, who put bitter for sweet and sweet for bitter!"

Laura Ingraham, The Angle: *"Americans recoil as dems sell perversion."*

Unidentified Speaker: *"Trans youth are vulnerable."*

Rachel Levine, Assistant Secretary for Health: *"You really want to base our treatment to affirm and to support and empower these youth, not to limit their participation in activities and sports and even limit their ability to get gender affirmation treatment in their state."*

Laura Ingraham: *"No, it's not Halloween. It's the Biden administration's version of normal. As inflation continues to tear through* *household budgets and weaken America, they trot out Rachel Levine from HHS to promote dangerous hormone blockers and life-altering trans surgery for minors. This is sick. Adults preying on our children under the guise of providing health care, claiming anyone who criticizes their tactics and their goals is bigoted or intolerant. And their twisted forces that are backing them? Yeah, they're well-funded, and they are fanning out across America. In New York, the homosexual deviants' drag story hour, DSH NYC, a taxpayer-funded nonprofit puts on shows for children as young as three. And one of its more prominent performers has social media accounts filled with nudity and other sexually explicit content. Oliver Herface, who also goes by Angel Izaguirre, is one of the talents listed on the DSH website. The organization's sanitized bio of Herface describes him as a drag king and a former daycare teacher who has a passion for working with children, especially what it means to be queer and trans, the education of that.*

But one video posted on his social media profile shows Herface pretending to stab his breasts while wearing a chest binder. But don't worry, he warns his followers to not bind longer than six to eight hours and urges them to be safe. Of course, lefty lawmakers, they defend this garbage, claiming that this drag queen group, DSH, is an opportunity for children as young as three to engage in play of gender fluidity in childhood. It also helps them learn about love in a safe space. And across the country in Washington State, we found the most maddening story of the week. An 80-year-old grandmother was banned there from her YMCA after demanding that a biological male leave the women's locker room where little girls were undressing. Addressing the Port Townsend City Council last Monday, here's how Julie Jaman, who's the banned senior citizen, described what happened."

Julie Jaman: *"In an effort by the city and the YMCA to apply the neocultural gender rules at Mountainview Pool dressing/shower room facilities, women and children are being put at risk. My experience while showering after my swim was hearing a man's voice in the women's dressing area and seeing a man in a women's swimsuit, watching little girls pull down their bathing suits in order to use the toilets in the* *dressing room. I reacted by telling him to leave. And the consequence is that I have been banned from the pool. The Y has not provided any dressing/shower room options for women who do not want to be exposed to men who identify as women. It is unconscionable that the YMCA would instigate these new policies without clearly informing pool patrons and parents."*

Laura Ingraham: *"Once again the left is encouraging this insanity. Biden's expansion of the categories of the people protected under Title IX requires now that men who identify as women be allowed full access to the women and girl's restrooms and locker rooms of K through 12 facilities and other higher ed facilities."*

And this is happening all over the world. Our current administration is taking it even further. At first, it was just you're guilty of a hate crime towards homosexuality, but now they are adding transgenderism and, as you are going to see, they're getting ready for pedophilia. And if you disagree with that, you're the person who's not only going to get shamed - complete opposite of the Scripture, (shocker!) but they are going to haul you away. You're the bad guy. You're the "faker." You're a danger to society. Now, to show you how far this went, this was pre-Covid days, a couple of years ago.

I was doing some conferences in Canada, and there's still a good Christian conservative element up there. Great brothers and sisters in Christ. But the last two conferences I did there, before they shut it down with the Covid plandemic, do you know what the border patrol agents asked us when crossing the border? It was not do have any guns? It was not, do you have a nuclear bomb in your trunk? Do you have any C4 that you're getting ready to blow up our embassy? Or something like that. Something that would be dangerous, whatever. The very first thing that came out of their mouths was, "Do you have any material in this vehicle that is against homosexuality?" Not a gun, not a bomb. Thought police at the border. If so, you're in trouble. That was two years or so ago. It's nuts, but this is where all this is heading.

Because fewer people, in general, see homosexuality as a sin; and then fewer churches are either taken over by fakers or they have given into pietism, keep your mouth shut or, dare I say, they are a bunch of chickens, and they won't preach God's truth, and that's why this is happening. It's paving the way. In fact, churches are not only not preaching on it, but they're also "accepting it" and "condoning it," and they're actually saying, "Homosexuality is a gift, not a sin." And it reminds me of what this man said.

A.W. Tozer: *"This version of the Christian religion is not transforming people; rather, it is being transformed by the people. It is not raising the moral level of society; it is descending to the society's level and congratulating itself as if it scored a victory when society is actually smiling, accepting their surrender."*

It's beyond just accepting the behavior; it's now moving into your need to be hauled away. This issue is identifying the true Christians, true believers, and we have got to get rid of you.

Right now, churches in the UK are fearful they are going to be forced to have to perform same sex marriages, and one man who has opposed it is facing losing his home. And another Christian couple is now being told they can't adopt because they oppose homosexuality. And another preacher in England has been arrested for saying homosexuality is a sin. It's already begun.

And here in America there are bills out there that are seeking to deny the tax-exempt status of any group that opposes gay marriage, and reports are out there that say, "Those who oppose gay marriage are now considered Domestic Hate Groups." And now they are expanding. It's not just homosexuality, it's any and all perversion that God said would happen once you get to this depraved mind issue and reject Him. You ain't seen nothing yet! It's going to be bestiality, transgenderism, pedophilia, you name it.

And folks, I'm telling you, this is the first filter, homosexuality, the whole LGBT movement - in getting rid of anyone who won't go along with a One World Religion. This has become their first excuse! They're weeding out the true ones, Christians, from the fake ones, the apostates, who will now go along with this.

And now they're saying the fake ones who go along with this are the "real Christians" and the true ones are dangerous ones and need to be gotten rid of. True Biblical, evangelical Christianity is being eradicated and replaced with a fake, phony, apostate church who will go along with a One World Religion; and the tool they're using to get the job done is homosexuality! Now, let me show you just how far this tactic to eradicate true Christians from society has infiltrated all sectors of society.

EDUCATION SECTOR

For those of you who think you're going to get a good education so you can equip others on the dangers of this moral issue and help them out, think again. You may not get that chance. Right now, Christians are being kicked out of graduate school counseling programs because they object to homosexuality. Also, Christian schools are under fire, like Gordon College, who's kept its Biblical code since 1889. But they were given an ultimatum by the New England Association of Schools (NEASC): "Be an accredited institution by accepting homosexual practices or you will lose your school accreditation." As one person stated, "If a secular agency can dictate the religious beliefs and worldviews of a Christian institution of higher learning, then religious freedom in this nation is over."

BUSINESS SECTOR

For those of you who think you're just going to start your own business and provide a great, godly environment for your employees, think again. You may not get that chance. For years we've seen business owners like this baker being fined $150,000 and told he needs 'rehabilitation' for his beliefs, because he refused to bake a wedding cake for a gay couple as seen here.

Channel 4 News Reports: *"Developments now involving a Lakewood bakery accused of discriminating against a gay couple by refusing to sell them a wedding cake. Well, the state civil rights commission says that bakery did violate discrimination laws. The wedding cakes at Masterpiece Cake Shop are detailed and attractive. The conflict between some customers and the owner has become ugly and complicated."*

Bakery Owner: *"We will close down the bakery before we compromise our beliefs."*

Channel 4 News Reports: *"He says he doesn't believe in gay marriage and refused to make this marrying gay couple a wedding cake."*

Purchaser: *"We've already been discriminated against there. We were already treated badly."*

Channel 4 News Reports: *"A judge ruled that a business owner cannot refuse service to a customer on the basis of sexual preference and that decision was upheld today by the Colorado Civil Rights Commission. This commission is also ordering the baker to submit quarterly reports on who he refuses to serve and how he retrains his employees to serve all customers."*

So, this moral issue is what? It's forcing the real Christians to take a stand, and it forces their head out, so to speak, to be identified, vilified, and taken down. So, they can do the old switcheroo. But it's not just him. That's been going on for many years if we've been paying attention.

"We also saw another business owner, a florist in Washington, also pursued by the State Attorney General for declining to make a floral arrangement for a same-sex wedding. A photographer in New Mexico was fined $6,700 for declining to do a photo shoot for a lesbian wedding.
A Christian T-shirt company was ordered to produce T-shirts to promote a gay pride event in Kentucky, and all employees were ordered to attend diversity training. And, if Chuck Schumer gets his way, true Christians

won't even be allowed to own a business anymore. He said this from New York:

Chuck Schumer: "Anyone whose religion teaches that the murder of an unborn child is wrong should simply not open a business in America." What about homosexuality? Is that next? What's around his neck?" (He's wearing a rainbow-colored ribbon around his neck in a photo.)

And it's because if you don't believe in this moral issue - which is immoral, ungodly, and unbiblical - you're already starting to see we're being ostracized.

GOVERNMENT SECTOR

For those of you who think you're going to just run for office and help overturn some of these laws that are harming people, think again. You may not get a chance. In Canada, Christians with Biblical values are being blocked from running for office. Canada's Liberal Party recently announced that they will not allow anyone to run in any national election who does not pledge to vote for "pro-choice," without exception. They also hinted they may also take a similar stance on other "social" issues, like homosexuality. In fact, one town in Canada, Nanaimo, at one point even moved to ban Christians who disagree with homosexuals from using public facilities."

Newscaster: *"Last month Nanaimo City Council passed a shockingly bigoted motion. A motion to ban Christians who they find 'divisive' from using publicly funded facilities, like the convention center in town. Just days before a Christian convention of sorts was being hosted at that convention center, this city council voted to cancel it. Seriously, they had a debate. Well, debate's the wrong word. It was really a series of shocking rants against Christians that culminated in making Nanaimo's public buildings Christian free zones."*

Christian-free zones? That's the kind of stuff that's going to culminate in the 7-year Tribulation. This is nuts!

LEGAL SECTOR

But that's not all. Canada also has started to ban Christians from the legal realm in case they want to overturn these homosexual laws."

Newscaster: *"Two Canadian law societies have decided to ban Christian school lawyers from practicing law in their provinces. The Law Society of Upper Canada voted 28 to 21 to ban them. And just last week, the Nova Scotia Barrister Society voted 10 to 9 to effectively blacklist Christians from that province too. The ban applies in advance to any and every lawyer who graduates from a law school of B.C.'s Trinity Western University."*

"Well, why would they do that? Because Trinity Western School is a Christian School that holds to the Biblical view of marriage between a man and a woman. And for years now, in the United States, it's gotten so bad against Christians in the government sector, that a former U.S. military general admitted this:

"Given the violation of religious liberties that have been going on in America, ironically, Christians are being forced into the closet. It's now become a policy of don't ask, don't tell, if you're a Christian. It used to be that you had to come out of the closet to admit you're homosexual, but now you have to come out of the closet to admit you're a Christian.'"

MEDIA SECTOR

"For those of you who think you're just going to get the word out on the airwaves and help others to see the dangers of this behavior, think again. You won't get that chance. Back in the Obama administration, they pushed for what's called 'The Hate Crime Reporting Act' which would task the Telecommunications and Information Administration to, 'begin scouring the Internet, TV, and radio for speech it finds threatening. Where, 'we will find ourselves in the same situation as our founding fathers were in under British rule.' You know, where we won't be allowed to speak out against the government, homosexuals, illegals, other religions, etc."

That's why we have the First Amendment - the right to free speech, the right to religion and the right to assemble - because that is not a part of what they were in England. You couldn't say what you want. If you disagreed, you were drowned, hung, burned at the stake, killed, murdered. You were even told what religion you had to be a part of. That's why we have what we have set up. And now they say they are going to scour electronically anything that disagrees to again identify, and websites will be shut down, Churches will be forced to compromise on the Word of God or close their doors or go into hiding and meet in underground locations.

You know, like when the Communists took over in Europe.

CHURCH SECTOR

"For those of you who think you're just going to go into ministry or just be a vocal Christian and equip God's people with God's truth and warn them, think again. You may not get that chance. Right now, thanks to Obamanation and the current Biden administration, they have, and are passing dozens of laws and executive orders in favor of homosexuality, which has created such an atmosphere of 'hatred' towards Biblical Christianity and the Bible, that we are now seeing the day where preachers in the United States of America, who preach the gospel will soon watch helplessly as their churches are taken from them, and they themselves are placed in jail. And, at one point, even the city of Houston subpoenaed Pastor's sermons, emails, and text messages to make sure no one is opposing the gay agenda." Remember this?

Sean Hannity: *"It is a shocking story out of Texas, where the city of Houston has issued subpoenas demanding that a group of pastors turn over their sermons as part of a battle to enforce an equal rights ordinance in the city. Now, ministers who failed to comply with the subpoena could be held in contempt of court. Pastor we'll start with you. Did you get one of the letters, subpoenas?"*

Grace Church Co-Founder: *"I did. Yes, I did."*

Sean Hannity: *"What did it say?"*

Grace Church Co-Founder: *"Well, it wanted my sermons and texts and anything that had been said about the equal rights ordinance or homosexuality or including Mayor Parker, if I'd ever said anything about her. Communication with the congregation, they wanted any of that."*

Pastor #2: *"And, contrary to the media reports, the city is not backing off. The mayor actually tweeted on her page that if the pastors were talking about this issue from the pulpit, their sermons are fair game."*

Grace Church Co-Founder: *"And I'll tell you this, with all due respect. There's no one that knows the mayor or the city attorney who would believe that they did not know about those subpoenas until yesterday."*

That already happened. Do you think they won't keep doing it? That they won't press it with this administration? That worked with the Obamanation that started all of this. You can see the writing on the wall.

And this is why one church leader stated, "The U.S. Creed on gay marriage is just like Sharia Law. Just as Jews and Christians are being fined in countries governed by Muslims for their religion, so all citizens in the United States of America are being required to approve of the gay marriage agenda, and sexual agenda, and sexual practices or be punished by the state."

And if you don't think churches will ever be forced into marrying homosexuals, think again. It's already happened in Denmark. They have recently won 'the right' to be married in any church they want. The government actually voted to make it 'mandatory' for all churches in that country to conduct gay marriages.

It's coming, and you know why it's coming? Because we have become enamored with numbers at all costs. They don't share God's truth anymore, and you got your reward. You got a lot of fakers now in the Church. You got your big congregations and your big buildings, big numbers. But now those people are not content to sit in the pews, and now they've taken over, and they're not even Christians. And then, they went from the churches and took over the seminaries, Bible colleges, denominations; and this is where we're at. Of course, those people are not speaking up because they are going along with this. And then the ones that are true, born-again Christians in churches, you're guilty of pietism or you're a bunch of chickens. That's why we are in this mess. Because we're not doing what God says. But this is the first excuse. They're weeding out the true believers in God to supplant them and replace them with the fake ones.

WHERE ARE WE HEADED?

Believe it or not, a court case has already been brought forth that claims that since same-sex marriage restrictions are being lifted, so should restrictions on multiple-partner marriages. They say the concept of marriage between a man and a woman is outdated. The new concept proposes the acceptance of multiple partners without the stigma of adultery, as seen here:

Newscaster: *"Details tonight about an historic court ruling having to do with two volatile subjects. Sex and religion. Correspondent, Shannon Bream explains."*

Jonathan Turley, Brown Family Attorney: *"What the opinion means for polygamist families is really something quite transformative."*

Shannon Bream: *"In response to a lawsuit brought by a polygamist, reality TV family, a federal judge in Utah has ruled that polygamy will no longer be criminalized in that state. A victory, the plaintiff's lead attorney says, is no surprise."*

Jonathan Turley: *"If you look at the trend of the law, it has been towards greater protection of individual choices to get the government out of homes and bedrooms to prevent the majority from dictating the moral code that everyone must live by."*

Shannon Bream: *"Those who oppose the Supreme Court's recent opinions on sodomy and gay marriage say they're not surprised either. That they predicted this very turn of events."*

Just like God said would happen. Now, why is that first starting in Utah? Mormonism, as we saw in our Mormonism study. Do they teach that in the Book of Mormon? Yes, they do. Again, you'll have people that say, "No, they don't." But they really do. We dealt with that in great detail. In fact, Brigham Young and the early, so-called apostles, along with Joseph Smith, they were all polygamists. In fact, that's the reason Joseph Smith was murdered. Because he was sleeping with so many other men's wives. He was not, as they would say, some martyr who was trying to defend the truth, and they, unfortunately, shot him as he was jumping out of a jail house window. They shot him in the back as he was trying to flee because they were invading the jail. They were holding him in the jail cell because he was sleeping with their wives. Making it spiritual. And it still goes on today. But that's why it's being promoted there first because that's a natural place to get that kick-started. And dare I say, Mormons - which are not Christians, although they profess to be, because it's a false gospel - they are going to march into the 7-year Tribulation as well.

But that's not all. Certain people in Congress want to 'federalize' a state law to prohibit counseling to change a person's sexual orientation, even if the person requests it. Now they have already done that in California. Now they want to federalize it. You can't counsel somebody and say you shouldn't be a homosexual or LGBT or trans. They want to make this nationwide.

"The bill says this would be 'dangerous and harmful.' Now the problem is, the language in the bill is so broad and vague, that it could also include all forms of sexual orientation, including pedophilia and 'if pedophilia is a sexual orientation, then that means that discrimination laws also apply to pedophiles.'"

Speaker #1: *"Most of us feel discomfort when we think about pedophiles. But just like pedophiles, we are not responsible for our feelings. We do not* *choose them. But we are responsible for our actions, and we must make a decision. It is our responsibility to reflect and overcome our negative feelings about pedophiles and to treat them with the same respect we treat other people with. We should accept that pedophiles are people who have not chosen their sexuality and who, unlike most of us, will never be able to live it out freely if they want to lead an upright life. We should accept that pedophilia is a sexual preference."*

Speaker #2: *"Statistics indicate that there will be one or two of you who are struggling with some form of pedophilic interest. These people can't talk about their feelings because they know that they will be hated for it. I truly do believe that every person is longing for love at some point in their life. What if this love that you really wish for, will forever be impossible? That must be a really, lonely situation to be in. Yes, from an emotional point of view, I can kind of understand that you would want to eliminate these people from society; however, it doesn't make sense. And that's because we are talking about biology. We are talking about a sexual orientation. Something that we simply cannot change. And on top of that, every day, new people are born with the same difficulty. It's not practical to eliminate these people from society. They haven't done anything wrong."*

Pedophilia is not wrong, and you shouldn't eliminate them from society. But if you say it's wrong, you will be eliminated from society. "Which also means you cannot block a pedophile from being a preschool teacher or any other high-risk occupation. Which is why it's now being promoted all over the place.

It's completely twisted. Now, the reason I think this is being pushed too, it's not just because obviously, number one, God said it's going to happen - you get a depraved mind, you're going to start doing things you ought not do. It's going to get worse. It's also going to get to such an extreme that even the true Christians, who may be surrounded in a church that's not preaching the truth or even just fakers … why you would stay there? I have no idea. And why you would support that, I have no idea. You're going to give an account to God for that. But the ones who are even chickens and have not spoken up on any of this against homosexuality and lesbianism, and given into pietism, and then they're like, "Oh, man, now it's going into transgenderism." My theory is that when it gets to this level (which they're like that close), even the wimpiest, if you're truly a born-again Christian, you are going to have to pop your head out on that one. Now it should have been popping out 20 years ago with the rest of us and then we wouldn't be in this mess. But what's it going to do? It's designed to make you rear your head so you can be identified, vilified, persecuted, and hauled away. This kind of stuff is going to be used in the 7-year Tribulation to filter out anybody who doesn't go along with the One World Religion. And it's already well underway. Do you see the big picture? It's way beyond the enemies in the Church. It's way beyond just that they are making so many unbiblical decisions. It's all leading somewhere, to what we're now experiencing, just before the 7-year Tribulation hits.

Now, that's the first filter. The next one we're going to get into, believe it or not, they are not only twisting love to justify the twisted relationship issue. Now we are going to see how they are twisting Jesus into something He's not to prepare for the next filter: the ecumenical movement, that all paths lead to Heaven. Which you need to have people buy into if you're going to have a One World Religion.

So, to encourage you with a clip of a discouraging video. You may think, "If they really start pushing pedophilia, I mean, churches in mass are going to rise up on this one." I'm telling you these fakers are not real. They're going along with it, and this is a recent video. I don't know if you've seen it. But if you think they are going to rise up against pedophilia, no, they are going to go along with it, because here's where they are at. This was a recent service at the Episcopal Church in New York City. Listen to why they are cheering on that particular Sunday. This is part of their worship service.

The man with the microphone has on a rainbow shirt and is speaking to the congregation.

"Here is the Queen of New York." The congregation applauds and yells, like they are at a concert. He is walking down the aisle to get to the front of the church. They all stand to give him a standing ovation. Now those people, I'm convinced, will also accept pedophilia in the Church. If you could just hear them cheering. You know what went through my mind? Those people in those church services are probably going to celebrate when we are out of here at the Rapture. Because no more salt, no more light, no more restrainers. They can all just create this wonderful "utopia of love." Create this global religion, and they can follow this global leader (who himself may be a homosexual) and have peace on the planet. They're going to go along with it. They are going to march right into the 7-year Tribulation thinking it's the greatest thing ever. The Scripture says they will cry out, 'Peace and safety, peace and safety!" Then BOOM! Sudden destruction comes on them. The antichrist shows his true colors. And anybody who truly turns to God, including those churches with fakers all around them, they are going to turn them in and hate them and betray them and he's going to kill them. The point is you should have gotten saved now! Don't wait for that time.

Chapter Fourteen

The Twisting of Biblical Jesus

We have been seeing in this study that we're dealing with the enemies within the Church. The key word there is enemies. They are known and they even admit that they are atheists. We saw where they admit it on tape. And they are not just coming into the Church, they are taking over the Church. And they are starting at the top. They know exactly what they are doing and it all spills downhill. But they're not just taking over the church and the institutions, now they are coming in and perverting things. Their perverted "love" says you can do whatever you want to do. Nothing's wrong. Everything's right, and no matter what you want to do, any kind of sexual perversion, that's just fine. That's the new definition of Christian love.

But that's not what the Scripture says. God is love, and He defines it for us. Their love is not Biblical love. Unfortunately, they are using their definition of love to justify their twisted relationships. But as **Romans 1** said, just like God warned, since we didn't turn from homosexuality and lesbianism, then we would get to that last stage of a depraved mind, and you start doing things that you ought not to do. That opened the door to polygamy, gender fluidity, pedophilia and bestiality.

Have you seen the articles lately about bestiality? They've been hitting hard on the pedophilia that's out there. But I'm telling you, Germany, Canada - look it up - they are already starting to talk about legislation, that zoophilia (bestiality) is perfectly fine. Because that was the way people were born. They don't have a choice. Of course, that is a lie from the pit of hell.

Now we find ourselves repeating the same mistake as Israel made, where people can't even define what a woman is. That is called relativism. Doing what is right in your own eyes. Scripture says, once you do that, 100 percent of the time you are headed for woeful times. It will destroy your country. And we see that happening now.

To remind ourselves why they are doing this, number one, they want to destroy our country. Number two, they are making a ton of money off of this. They are making 1.3 million dollars off of every person that becomes transgender. But, again, as Scripture tells us, the love of money is the root of all kinds of evil. Also, as we saw they start out as a transsexual, but what was it ultimately? It's a transhumanist message. And this mindset, that I can be whatever I want to be … "I'm a guy, but I want to be a woman." "I'm a woman, but I want to be a guy." But now, "I'm a guy who identifies as a woman and a cat." It's leading to this, because that's what the transhumanist, Beyond Covid Human 2.0, movement wants to do; except now, in theory, you can make that choice yourself. To use science, which you should never do - it's unbiblical, it's ungodly - to become whatever you want. One day these guys aren't going to give you that choice, and they're going to turn you into what they want you to be. This is their mindset that is preparing the way.

Then they snookered the Church. The ones who should be shouting this from the rooftops but are keeping their mouths shut with the lie of pietism. Basically, saying you stay in your own four walls, you do your thing. Leave us all in the world. You have no right, no business, to get involved, including politics. That's not what the Scripture says. We are called to be the salt, the light and the resistance, the restraining influence. But, as we can see, this is the rise of the antichrist kingdom. That's where all this is headed.

If we do restrain, resist, what are they going to do with the resisters, you and I, who will not go along with this? Well, they are just going to let us do our own thing. No, we saw that they are going to, basically, use the agendas as an excuse to identify, vilify and persecute us. Use propaganda to make us out to be the bad guys so that we can basically be hauled away and/or even be executed. Because that's what we saw, in **Matthew 24**, is going to happen in the 7-year Tribulation.

The first filter was, how are you going to identify these people that aren't going to go along? That was the moral issue, the homosexual aspect. If you and I don't go along with this, we are guilty of a hate crime. That becomes the excuse for that. They're pushing the envelope. It's not just against homosexuality and lesbianism, against bestiality and transgenderism, we are now even seeing pedophilia. Even so-called Christians, that have been so stinking chicken that they won't even talk about any of this being wrong (it's an abomination, it's a sin), you would think at that point, when they are starting to say, "We're going to have full-blown pedophilia completely accepted," you would think they'd speak up.

I would hope so. But it's like, where are you when you should have been speaking up now? It's all designed to get you to rear your head. Because where this is all headed, Scripturally, is a One World Religion. But they are not only twisting love and relationships, but here's another one. This is going to become another filter to identify the troublemakers as an excuse to go get them. It's a twisted Jesus and a twisted gospel. So, let's remind ourselves what is the real gospel. Why did Jesus come? We are going to get acquainted with what the Scripture says the real gospel is. What should you and I be doing? What should we be sharing? What's the most important, the best thing that you and I could ever do with our time as a Christian with what time we have left? We need to share the gospel. We need to know what it is, because these guys have totally, totally, twisted it into something false.

Matthew 28:18-20: "Then Jesus came to them and said, 'All authority in Heaven and on earth has been given to me. Therefore, go and make disciples of all nations, baptizing them in 'the name of the Father and the Son and of the Holy Spirit,' and teaching them to obey everything I have commanded you. And surely, I am with you always to the very end of the age.'"

All of these words are important. This is right before He goes to be at the right hand of the Father. This is so important, so pay attention. Is He saying go make giant buildings, and the one that has the biggest attendance is the most successful church? And you will get a super-duper big crown in Heaven? I'm sorry, wrong translation. What did it say? Go and make disciples. What are disciples? In the Greek, it is where we get mathematics. Mathematics is a very disciplined class. It's a disciplined learner.

So, when people get saved, we are to get them into the Word of God and disciple them. You make them into a disciplined learner. So, what do they do? They go out and witness and share the real, one and only gospel as they get that person disciplined. Then they get discipled, they know the Word, they know the gospel, and they go out and they infect the culture wherever they go. It's a replication factor. It's not about just filling the pews. That's what's going on today. They don't even teach the truth. They don't give the gospel. It's all about numbers. If you want to be a successful church, you want to obey Him, it's spiritual growth at all costs.

And do you make disciples just of the people that you like? People in your neighborhood? What's the context? Around the world. That's why I'm telling you. Can you imagine the early Church having the technology that we have today? To reach the world for Christ with literally a click of a mouse. Most of it's for free. They would go nuts. And we are supposed to be those godly examples to obey, what? Relativism? What the world says? What feels right? No! We are supposed to obey everything that Jesus has commanded us.

So, that's one aspect. Let's now take a look at another aspect of the gospel. We need to make sure we know what it is so that when you see these guys, what they say is the real gospel, it will make you puke. And then you wonder why the Church is in the mess it's in. This is the great resurrection chapter.

I Corinthians 15:1-4: "Now, brothers, I want to remind you of the gospel I preached to you, which you received and on which you have taken your stand. By this gospel you are saved, if you hold firmly to the Word, I preached to you. Otherwise, you have believed in vain. For what I received I passed on to you as of first importance, that Christ died for our sins according to the Scriptures, that He was buried, that He was raised on the third day according to the Scriptures, and that He appeared to Peter, and then to the Twelve."

Gospel, in the Greek "euangelion" is a really cool word. In the context, it was good news, over the top, best news you could ever hear. To use a Greek analogy, they would do an "euangelion" when a king or a Roman general went out to war, and they came back victorious. So, typically, when they came back victorious, they would do something nice because they were celebrating. They would do something nice for the people. Then they would need to send messengers out to the Empire and tell them this "euangelion," this good news. According to historical record, you are now going to be able to not pay taxes for one year because we are celebrating this great victory. How many would say that's some really good news? That's the word that Paul is using. This is good news.

But this isn't just getting a year off from taxes. This is the good news that you're not going to go to hell, that you rightly deserve for all eternity. He's going to give you Heaven and everything else on top. This is the best news of all. Jesus Christ came, and He died for our sins; because the wages of sin is death, and we deserve to die and go to hell. We need to believe the resurrection, and it all hinges on the resurrection. Why is it important to believe that Jesus Christ rose again from the grave? Because He could not have rose from the grave if He had sinned. And the fact that He rose again from the grave was for two reasons. One, it means

He was without sin; He was the perfect sinless acceptable sacrifice so we could be forgiven. You have got to believe that in order to be, what? Saved. That's the gospel. Wait until you hear what they're saying, these fakers that have come into the Church. Now let me give you one more.

Romans 10:8-15: "But what does it say? 'The word is near you; it is in your mouth and in your heart,' that is, the message concerning faith that we proclaim: If you declare with your mouth, 'Jesus is Lord,' and believe in your heart that God raised him from the dead, you will be saved. For it is with your heart that you believe and are justified, and it is with your mouth that you profess your faith and are saved. As Scripture says, 'Anyone who trusts in him will never be put to shame.' For there is no difference between Jew and Gentile—the same Lord is Lord of all and richly blesses all who call on him, for, 'Everyone who calls on the name of the Lord will be saved.' How, then, can they call on the one they have not believed in? And how can they believe in the one of whom they have not heard? And how can they hear without someone preaching to them? And how can anyone preach unless they are sent? As it is written: 'How beautiful are the feet of those who bring good news!'"

I previously shared this story of how, way back in the day, Sunrise used to be Southern Baptist. And then I shared why we left the Southern Baptists, many years ago. Now I'm going to share a video clip. It's almost primarily our whole study, but you're going to see how the Southern Baptists have now become one of the biggest sewer pipes, really, of a false gospel. You are going to see that they are working with communism, and they are bringing in a so-called gospel, a false gospel, where they say, "You just need to do good things. You just need to go build wells in Africa, so they can have clean drinking water." Well, that's great, but you need to share the gospel. But they not only don't do that, but then on the other hand they say, "No, it's really that we need to promote this "woke" message. We need to inform the Church to get rid of their white privilege. We need to support 'Black Lives Matter.'" That's their version of the gospel today. What you are going to see, and it's not just the Southern Baptists, but you are going to see how they infiltrated, and how it's clearly a takeover of the Church. You thought it was bad, what you're going to see, just how really bad it is. What it brings back to my mind is the parallel reality that Jesus talks about. He talks about not just the many, but the few.

And I will just add this: Some people have said that America is not mentioned in Bible prophecy. And those people have their theories. My theory is that America, as we know it, will no longer be in existence. I believe America will be swallowed up into one of the 10 economic kingdoms that the World Economic Forum and all these global leaders are planning on doing. And they're not hiding it. So, America as we know it won't be America. That's what's going to happen to America. My point is, some people say, "Well, the reason that America is not mentioned in Bible prophecy is because when the Rapture happens, there are going to be so many Christians Raptured, that it will just destroy America and it will be decimated." I don't buy it. I go back to the Scripture. And keep this in mind as you read the transcript of the video.

I think you are going to get an even bigger idea of just how few people are really born-again Christians in this so-called American Church in America. You're going to see that the bulk of these people are not even saved. I don't care if they are behind the pulpit in charge of a denomination. I don't care who they are. I think that the Rapture will only be a "bleep" on the radar in America, and America will just keep on going straight into the 7-year Tribulation. And again, not only that, but American churches will also march in there, too. Christians in name only. But guess what? They'll go along with the One World Religion. So, let's take a look at this video clip, and we'll recap afterwards.

Gary Gordon: *"What happened to the living, powerful, transformative, nation-shaking Christianity? You know what I'm talking about. The kind that Jesus brought the world. Something dressed-up to look like Christianity is doing just fine here in the West. But is it a counterfeit? It certainly resembles Christianity. But most of the people I know sense that something is wrong."*

John Harris, Author and Podcast Host of Conversations: *"Here's how the theological play. Interpret the Bible in a different way, not according* *to a grammatical, historical, hermeneutic. Contextualize it. Read it through the lens of modern oppressed societies. The Jesus who came to seek and save is now the Jesus who came to also promote social justice and speak out against the system."*

Justin Giboney, President, The AND Campaign, Atlanta, Georgia: *"We have a God of Justice. It's almost Biblical illiteracy to read through the gospel and not understand that Biblical justice has a racial and societal application."*

John Harris: *"It's a dream come true for the left to get all these Christians, whom they've had such a hard time with over the years, and the religious right and Jerry Falwell and, oh, my goodness. Now we're going to use the same mechanisms to forward a left-leaning agenda."*

Dhati Lewis, President, Southern Baptist Send Network: *"When it comes to society, the Church has often separated the gospel from social issues causing many believers to be apathetic in our engagement in our neighborhoods."*

John Harris: *"We come with the message of the gospel, and we come with a cup of water as well. We come with care and compassion because we love people just as Jesus did. But we don't confuse the two. We don't say that that cup of water is the gospel."*

Dhati Lewis: *"I believe Tim Keller is spot on when he says, 'We must neither confuse evangelism with doing justice nor separate them from one another.'"*

John Harris: *"Tim Keller is probably the biggest operative pushing the Evangelical Church to the left. As a young man, he was on the left. Tom Skinner talked about systemic oppression, racism, in the United States, in policing and these kinds of things and, most importantly, taught Keller that the gospel itself that the fundamentalists had, and the gospel of the social gospel, needed to both be wedded together. And Tim Keller took that to heart.*

He listened to the lecture by Tom Skinner at Urbana 70, where he made this argument multiple times. He said it changed his world. Elwood Ellis, his classmate at Gordon-Conwell Theological Seminary, told Tim Keller, that him and his girlfriend that he was dating, and became his wife, essentially, were racists. And the reason was that they imposed, without thinking about any alternatives, their white societal norms, and benefited from a system that allocated privilege to him. So, he listened to this and took it well and absorbed it.

Then, of course, Harvey Khan, when he was at Westminster Theological Seminary, taught him kind of a new way to look at the Bible - a new hermeneutic, called the Hermeneutical Spiral. And there's a synthesis between the two, between the audience interpretation in their world and the world of the authors of Scripture, and that's how you come up with meaning."

Host of conference: *"With us today, one of my heroes in the faith, my fellow Mississippian, Dr. John Perkins. Thank you for being with us."*

Trevor Loudin: *"John Perkins, his whole message is the three R's. That's a shtick. You know, reconciliation, reconciling the racial injustices of the past. Relocation, reallocating resources from the wider community into the underserved communities, the ghettos, etc. And redistribution. You know, redistribution of wealth. That's socialism."*

John Perkins: *"When Martin Luther King was doing his march on Washington and all that, we were communists. And I never would have thought that I would live to see us here tonight, looking like we are looking tonight."*

Christopher Harr, Executive Director of Unhyphenated America: *"If you tell everyone, 'Hey, I want to take your stuff.' I mean, just human nature is like a desire to have your own property, to say this is mine. If you come and say, 'I want to take your stuff in the name of the state,' people will, 'Oh, hang on a second. Not my stuff. I worked for this.' And it's the same way if like, you want to redistribute. Like you tell a student, 'Hey, I* *want to redistribute your good grades.' You know, redistribution. When you start filtering it through a brain cell, you're like, 'No, that doesn't make any sense.'"*

John Harris: *"Tim Keller has taken those three R's, and in his book, 'Generous Justice,' he doesn't use the word redistribution. But he does credit John Perkins with giving him the idea for re-weaving a community. So, instead of redistribution, which sounds kind of Marxist, he says re-weaving a community. He also said that Karl Marx was the only major thinker, other than God Himself, who held up the common man with a high view of labor."*

Trevor Loudin: *"What they have got now, a whole bunch of young pastors, who once would have voted for Ronald Reagan and supported Israel and are now voting for Bernie Sanders and supporting Palestine."*

John Harris: *"So, you have the mainstream media, you have arts and entertainment, you have now also national pastime sports, where everybody is virtue signaling, constantly."*

Gary Gordon: *"Well, what do you look at the Church as? How do social scientists look at that?"*

John Harris: *"A massive delivery system that has its logistics in place, has its revenue in place."*

Unidentified Speaker: *"They've got 2,000 people on Sunday that they speak to, and everybody is taking notes, and they are sending them out into the world to have an effect."*

Jemar Tisby, Author "The Color of Compromise": *"Jesus Christ, the Son of God, took on flesh and became a person and entered into our experience so He could identify with us. And express solidarity with us. And he tells those who have bought into the myth of whiteness and superiority that you, too, are in need of a Savior."*

Rachel Dotzier, Student Pastor, Central Christian Church, Arizona: *"Jesus was legit, the most privileged and most powerful human on earth, and He gave it all up. If you follow a white Jesus, man, I think God wants to do something here today. Let Jesus rob you of what you have always thought to be true. Let Him rob you of your privilege. Let Him rob you so you can see clearly the Kingdom of Heaven and what's it's supposed to look like as we embrace our black brothers and sisters and those that are suffering from oppression every single day. Jesus is for everyone. Jesus is for justice. Jesus spoke out against government, against injustice."*

Gary Gordon: *"Cashiers say the best way to recognize a counterfeit dollar is not by studying counterfeit dollars, but by getting to know the real thing well enough that you can easily discern the fake. Maybe, just maybe, that's part of our problem right now. Maybe the present generation who call themselves Christians, really believe that they are Christians because they can't recognize counterfeits on account of having never seen the real thing modeled in front of them."*

Micah Sample, Former Student, Indiana Wesleyan University: *"When I first started at Indiana Wesleyan University, I was a member of the John Wesley Honors College. I was a student there, and I began to notice that there were some phrases that professors would use that just wouldn't comport with what I understood to be Christian truth at the time. And I just wrote that down to me not have an understanding of these things in such depth as the professors did. I trusted them. As time went on and they began to attempt to deconstruct my very understanding of what Christian truth was, I realized that this was not a place that was teaching Christian truth. This was a place that was meant to deconstruct Christian truth."*

Everett Piper, Former President of Wesleyan University: *"The Christian College and University as an industry, as an organization, is compromised. There are very few Christian schools that I would even recommend that people consider these days. Because, again, a wolf in sheep's clothing is dangerous, but a wolf in shepherd's clothing is deadly. In many ways today, I'd rather send my kids off to a state institution where at least you know the wolves are wolves, and prepare the kid, accordingly,* *then send them off to a Christian institution that is nothing but a wolf in Shepherd's clothing. We need to be very careful."*

Micah Sample: *"From the research that I've done, there are some that are just duped into this ideology. But many of them are purposeful - extremely purposeful and sly - and they couch their language with nice sophistry. And in some cases, it sounds Biblical, because they'll use Scripture verses totally out of context. But they'll use Scripture verses, nonetheless, to try to prop up their ideologies. And so those people are the people who want to see the Wesleyan Church changed into something that it is not the Wesleyan Church at all. They want this to be a place where the dogma of wokeness is supreme. My peers at Indiana Wesleyan University who were taught this Marxism are going to spread it throughout their churches, and they are going to have this widespread impact, but it's not going to be for the glory of Christ. It's not going to be as a witness to the truth. It's going to be as a detriment to the truth, and they are going to lead people away from Christ. And that is potentially the most heartbreaking thing about all of this, because they are going to lead other people astray. They are the blind leading the blind. We know that doesn't work out. I cannot bear to watch idly by as that happens. I have to say something, and I have to take a stand. Hopefully, by me taking a stand, some of the other people who haven't been fully indoctrinated will start to take stands in their own churches. But if they do not, I fear that there will be widespread persecution of genuine Biblical Christians in the United States of America, and that there will be 'woke' churches that don't bear the brunt of that, but instead contribute to that persecution. It's already started."*

Teri Dolan, Former Church Member: *"Why does someone need a gag order on a church? What's up with that?"*

In 2019, more than 700 people left First Baptist Church Naples. 19 were formally excommunicated for the sin of racism.

Gary Gordon: *"We continued to put the puzzle pieces together and learned of a staggering incident."*

John David: *"But it is undeniable that race played a part in the final days leading up to this election."*

Gary Gordon: *"You were branded as a racist?"*

Bob Candill, Former Church Member: *"Yes"*

Gary Gordon: *"But you're not a racist."*

Bob Candill: *"No."*

Gary Gordon: *"It was slander."*

Bob Candill: *"Totally."*

John Harris: *"Thoroughly social-justice-driven components of the Southern Baptist Convention - J.D. Greer and Kevin Ezell - are involved in changing the direction of a large mega church in one of the most conservative areas of the swing state, Florida."*

Mike Dolan, Former Church Member: *"All of a sudden, Pastor was retiring, but now he's just gone. It wasn't just pushing to get him to leave, they had to ruin his reputation, for some reason that was important."*

Bob Candill: *"And, you know, that pastor transition team that went on even before, you know, there was a consulting group that was called in."*

Mike Dolan: *"And eventually they came up with some candidates, and, of course, Marcus came up."*

Marcus Hayes, Senior Pastor Candidate: *"Homosexuality is a sin. Now maybe somebody in this room, if you have same sex attractions, I don't know. I'd say that's not a sin."*

Katy Candill, Former Member: *"He just wasn't qualified. We had different guidelines that they were supposed to follow, and they changed the guidelines for him."*

Liz Appling, Former Member: *"Because he was a plant by the SBC to come in and take the position of Senior Pastor."*

Kevin Ezell, President of the North American Mission Board: *"Hey, First Naples family, this is Kevin Ezell, President of the North American Mission Board. He's going to be a fantastic pastor. You're going to love him."*

Ronny Nall, Member, First Baptist Church: *"They presented a 'woke' candidate to a church, who is not 'woke' and doesn't want to be 'woke.'"*

Liz Appling: *"To sneak somebody in into the Senior Pastor role of this church – it's not going to happen. It's not going to happen. It's not going to happen on my watch, and I made sure that I came in and voted. And we voted, and they didn't get in."*

John David: *"Church leadership does not believe that all who voted 'no' did so based on race. Racism has no part in the Body of Christ, and never more so than First Baptist Naples. Disciplinary actions towards church members are underway."*

Katy Candill: *"370 people, I think, voted against Marcus Hayes. When John David came out that it's because they're racist... we've got an orphanage of 43 children in Africa."*

Teri Dolan: *"They're not racist, we're not racist."*

Mike Dolan: *"We're foster people."*

Gary Gordon: *"You're foster parents? Red and yellow, black and white, they are precious in His sight?"*

Teri Dolan: *"Yeah."*

Mike Dolan: *"We love them all."*

Teri Dolan: *"We're all one race from Adam."*

Liz Appling: *"I mean there is not one person that I know in that church that is racist. I was born in England and raised in Kenya, in Africa. I lived five years in South Africa. I had 24 years living in Africa, and I left South Africa because of apartheid."*

Lou Falorio, Former Member of First Baptist Church Naples: *"If people at First Baptist were racist, do you honestly believe that we would have so many different ethnic people coming to our church and feeling comfortable? I know those families, and those families bled for that church. And those families only stood up for what was right, according to the Bible. It had nothing to do with color. It had nothing to do with his personality. He did not fill the five qualifications that the search committee was doing on over a hundred other people."*

Unidentified Church Member: *"Marcus Hayes is 'woke.' He's hiding it. He's deleted the evidence from his social media. We have copies. He tried to hide the fact. That's what I take offense to. If these people want a 'woke' church, why don't five of them pool their money and go rent a storefront and start a 'woke' church. Because that's not what revolutionaries do. That's the answer."*

Michael Hichborn: *"If you understand that controlling key positions, you then control choke points. You control the flow of money. You control the flow of information. You control the development of individuals within the party, who will then take control over other key positions."*

Ray Moore, Executive Director of Exodus Mandate: *"Russell Moore - who is, I think, the main person who is responsible for this, at least in the Southern Baptist Convention - he was brought on maybe 20 years ago. I don't know the precise time, but he's served as a professor. He served as a* *provost of the dean. So, he had very responsible positions at Southern Baptist Seminary in Louisville. Then in 2013, or maybe it was 2015, he took over from Richard Land as President of the ERLC. They have a budget of five or six million a year, and they have about 30 staff. This has turned into a, honestly, genuinely leftist, social justice arm of the Southern Baptist Convention. It's like the Southern Baptist Convention has got this cancer, and it's very disturbing, very disconcerting."*

John Harris: *"In 2015, the George Soros Foundation said this, 'Reverend Russell Moore, head of the public policy for the Southern Baptist Convention,' and then they quote Russell Moore as saying that Evangelicals should be the ones calling the rest of the world to remember human dignity and the image of God, especially for those fleeing murderous, Islamic radical jihadis. So, Russell Moore is forwarding immigrants from Muslim countries, coming to the United States - there is a link to George Soros. Now, why would George Soros want to fund Russell Moore? And why would his organization be bragging that this is what Russell Moore said, with our money?"*

Philip B. Haney: *"My name is Philip B. Haney, and I became a Spirit-filled Christian on November 7, 1975. That's really the basis of my worldview. What made me more of a public figure was being a founding member of the Department of Homeland Security. I worked in Customs and Border Protection, and I am a subject matter expert in the strategy and tactics of the global Islamic movement. And I literally interviewed hundreds of individuals seeking entry into the country who had potential ties to terrorism."*

Gary Gordon: *"Tell me what you think about the ERLC under the leadership of Russell Moore getting involved with the United States State Department and encouraging them to build a mosque."*

Philip Haney: *"Not only the United States State Department, but also the Justice Department, ever since Loretta Lynch and my former boss, Janet Napolitano. They began forcing communities to violate their own zoning laws. But also paying the Muslim community damages for their bias, their* *racism, and their Islamophobia. That started during the Obama Administration."*

Gary Gordon: *"It makes Russell Moore and the ERLC an accessory to a spiritual and theological crime."*

Philip Haney: *"A kind of an enablement. You're advocating on behalf of a theology, an ideology, that's in direct contradiction to the one that you say you live by. That's a kind of psychosis, isn't it? Who is the primary abuser of Christians all over the world today? The very religion, Islam, that this particular individual is trying to help build a mosque, against the wishes of the entire community."*

Individual Speaker at a Church Meeting: *"I would like to know how in the world someone within the Southern Baptist Convention can support the defending of 'Rights for Muslims' to construct mosques in the United States, when these people threaten our very way of existence as Christians and Americans."*

Russell Moore: *"Sometimes we have to deal with questions that are really complicated, and we had to spend a lot of time thinking them through, and not sure what the final result was going to be. Sometimes we have really hard decisions to make. This isn't one of those things. What it means to be a Baptist is to support sole freedom for everybody."*

John Harris: *"Russell Moore has taken money from this individual. Russell Moore has also taken money from the Democracy Fund; $50,000.00 went to the MLK50 conference. Why would the Democracy Fund, an openly leftist organization, want to fund an Evangelical conference that gave Southern Baptist students at seminary credits to attend?"*

Jim Wallis, Obama's Spiritual Advisor: *"No, we don't receive money from Soros. The financial crisis of non-profits is including us ... No, we don't receive money from George Soros. Our books are totally open."*

Gary Gordon: *"George Soros is actually using his money, earmarked for leftist causes, to support Evangelicals. That left us wondering, who else in the Evangelical community might have taken money from the likes of George Soros? To bring all the puzzle pieces together we decided it best to follow the money."*

Michael O'Fallon, Founder and CEO of Sovereign Nations: *"When you look at what's happening right now on a global scale, with this mass influx and surge to the border, who is it that's participating in this? It's folks that are part of the Evangelical Immigration Table. And the Evangelical Immigration Table was something that was actually sourced from the National Immigration Forum. The National Immigration Forum was fully funded and as well was given a massive $2.3 million gift from Open Society Foundations [owned by George Soros]."*

Gary Gordon: *"What's the motivation of highly respected religious leaders, who understand exactly what they're doing? Why would they do this?"*

Michael O'Fallon: *"Why are people, not guided by the Holy Spirit, be motivated to do anything? Because of power and money and a lot of times people do things just to see what will happen. If there's anything that a lot of people want to know, is to make sure that they left their mark in the world."*

Everett Piper, Former President of Oklahoma Wesleyan University: *"I had a donor call me on the phone one day, and he offered me $2 million. So, I talked to him at some length, and he asked me to share the mission of the institution. $2 million was hanging right in front of me on this phone call. He specified that amount of money. And as I talked about the mission of the institution - to give him confidence that he was giving his money to a school that would stand firm and Biblical and true, not only today but in the future, so that his gift would never be compromised - I got into the issue of what we were doing [in] challenging LGBTQ. And that, in fact, we had sent a letter to the Obama Administration, telling his*

Department of Education that we would not submit to their mandate that we start providing transgender accommodations on our campus. I said, "No! We won't do that. We're a Christian institution. We believe that women have the right to their own dormitory, to their own sport, to their own bathrooms, to their own shower. And I'm not going to compromise Title IX by pretending that women aren't real. That they're nothing but leprechauns, unicorns, make-believe, the product of a postmodern fantasy of a dysphoric male.' And as I went through that speech and told this guy this, assuming that he would agree, he stopped and said that he didn't. That if I didn't change course on the LGBTQ position, that he wouldn't give us his money. Well, it's tempting to take the money, but, my land, are you going to sell the soul of the institution, not only your own soul, but the soul of the school for the sake of a temporary victory of getting a little bit of money?

If there's one thing, I learned from being a college president for some 17 years, it was this. Stand your ground. Make sure that everybody you are talking to knows your mission. Say it once, say it twice, say it a hundred times, and never change it. Always stand firm. Always be clear. And in the face of the storm, run toward it. Don't run away from it. And you know what will happen? People are watching, and you'll get more money rather than less in the long run, because they can trust you. And they know that when they are dead and gone, that the institution will still be doing what you are doing today and that their money has not been compromised."

Kyle Whitt, Church Planter: *"I have been going through the process of church planting in the Southern Baptist Convention. I was seeing some of these more social gospels, more 'it's about our works, more than it is about our preaching,' And so, I just emailed them. Like, look, I want some clarity on this. I was being told that I was preaching a 'half-gospel,' if I was preaching a gospel of salvation of someone's soul, but that's not the whole story. The element of the gospel apparently that's being 'missed' is the economic social pillars of society that have been broken. I know we need to restore them. We need to engage in 'holistic restoration.'*

Another big thing that happened after I emailed Dhati Lewis was, I almost immediately got contacted by the local NAM missionary and he told me to 'just put my head down and move forward without paying attention to the organizations above me.' That was what he did as a planter and that will make me much happier. And this was very much spun in a happy, positive way. Like, 'Oh, I'm taking a burden from you. I'm taking a burden from you by removing any accountability. By not answering your questions, by not telling you why we're behaving the way we are.'"

Randy Adams, Executive Director of Northwest Baptist Convention: *"North American Mission Board now keeps tens of millions of dollars that used to be spent through local associations and state conventions to do evangelism and to start churches. In church planning, the budget has expanded from 23 million in 2010 to 75 million. Actual expenditures have grown over $50 million. Church plant numbers have gone down, down, down. We're far below, in 2019, from where we were in 2014, for example. So, then the question is, how are those $69 to $75 million being spent each year? We don't know. How many churches are being funded? We don't know. And then how many are funded state by state? We don't know."*

Gary Gordon: *"It is abundantly clear that they actually believe themselves to be superior to the rest of us. Don't think so? Just disagree with their legal abuses out loud."*

Dr. Russell Fuller, Former Professor of Southern Baptist Theological Seminary: *"Three people spoke out against Matt Hall. He thinks that connecting the dots of race - and by race he means critical race theory and social justice - with the gospel, that's what he saw was his great calling. One guy was asked to leave that year. The other two that spoke out were fired just a couple weeks ago."*

Gary Gordon: *"What about you?"*

Dr. Russell Fuller: *"Yeah, I was one of those two guys. I was fired!"*

Gary Gordon: *"After how many years?"*

Dr. Russell Fuller: *Twenty-two years."*

Gary Gordon: *"Men who are willing to speak out in favor of real Biblical orthodoxy. You got marked?"*

Dr. Russell Fuller: *"Yes!"*

Gary Gordon: *"And as soon as there was an excuse, you were the first to get fired?"*

Dr. Russell Fuller: *"Yeah, the old statement, 'Never let a crisis go to waste' and that's exactly what happened.*

Dr. Robert Lopez, Former Professor at Southern Baptist Theological Seminary: *"I submitted a resolution to the Southern Baptist Convention and said that there were four things that we should denounce. We should denounce non-disclosure agreements. We should denounce gentlemen's agreements. We should denounce what people call the 11th Commandment, which is just the supposed Biblical instruction, never criticize other Baptist leaders. And we should renounce retaliation. So, I submit that resolution, and then Randy Stinson told me, at one point, did you do this because we used the NDAs with all of the firings?"*

Gary Gordon: *"And you didn't even know."*

Dr. Robert Lopez: *"I didn't even know! I said that I did that because of Harvey Weinstein. But now you're telling me that you are using non-disclosure agreements."*

Gary Gordon: *"No wonder they are so sensitive."*

Dr. Robert Lopez: *"There's no Biblical basis for a non-disclosure agreement. The Southern Baptist Convention was being run by people who did not want sunlight on any of their problems. And on top of it all, they* *fired me. Then I had secret recordings, because I could see how they kept on changing everything and they wouldn't put anything in writing. I knew that these people were playing dirty. So, I had recordings. I had saved my documents, and I released those to the public so people would know what was going on. They released a statement claiming that I had made that up. That nobody had ever told me to avoid discussing homosexuality. They put that on the Southwestern Seminary website, and they pushed that out on Twitter. They didn't know that I had the recordings."*

Recording of Conversation: *"You're saying that if we do end up saying to you, you cannot run that article, or that is not going to help this institution, you're saying you're going to do it anyway."*

"I'm going to be obedient to God, and if I am called to do something that you are trying to block, I will do what God called me to do. I will be obedient to God."

Dr. Robert Lopez: *"The fact that they were going to go to such an extent of having engaged in the non-disclosure agreements, having distorted the curriculum, having tried to force me to give up my testimony and basically, participate in this falsehood about same sex attracted Christianity ... they were then willing to destroy my family, to drive me out of my profession, to ruin my reputation, so I couldn't support my children and my wife. They were going to do all that while claiming to be Christians. There is nothing Christian about this at all."*

Micah Sample: *"There are methods of intimidation that are used by social justice ideologues, masquerading as professors at universities like Indiana Wesleyan, and seminaries. These tactics are social in nature, and they have to do with stripping people of prestige, stripping people of credibility, stripping people of their friendships, really; if they don't comply with what social justice ideology, with what the 'woke' cult teaches them to comply with.*

I was forced into a meeting with the entire staff of the John Wesley Honors College. I was at one end of a conference table, and the entire faculty were lined at the other ends of the table and, essentially, they attempted to put me under trial, really. It was a kangaroo court in which they told me that because I was rebelling against this social justice narrative, I needed to repent of essentially, my conservative Biblical beliefs. I didn't agree to doing that and eventually I was kicked out of the Honors College program at the Indiana Wesleyan University.

They don't want people who are going to push back against the 'woke' narrative in their universities, successfully. So, the method, the modus operandi of these people is to kick them out as soon as it's evident that they're not going to change their minds."

Gary Gordon: *"Trevor, you've looked at the evidence concerning the Southern Baptist Convention. What are your thoughts?"*

Trevor Loudin: *"If you look at it from a left-wing point of view, the Southern Baptists were one of the last bastions of true Christianity in America and very socially and politically conservative. So, if you could conquer the Southern Baptists and move them to the left, you could move the whole politics of the South and America to the left. It would be a major conquest. So, if you look at it in a purely secular way, this was a battle fought by the left to conquer and take over the Southern Baptists, like they've taken over universities, like they've taken over Hollywood. It was just another institution on their list."*

John Harris: *"Well, I started finding out that Southeastern Baptist Theological Seminary is not the only compromised institution within Evangelical Christianity. In fact, most of Evangelical Christianity is compromised on some level, or is in the process of being compromised. So, one of the first things that happened after finding out the extent to which the cancer had been developing in the Southern Baptist Convention, I was reached out to by people at CRU, formerly Campus Crusade for Christ, and they were telling me about what was happening in their organization. So, I decided to start watching their staff conference from the summer of 2019, and it was worse than anything, I think, I had seen at Southeastern. It was a 'woke fest."*

Speakers at the CRU Conference

"Your value is determined based on a lie. Your value is determined on your proximity to whiteness and your proximity to blackness."

"Friends, it is important for us to be awakened to racial inequities."

"You may not be racist, or whatever, but we all still live in a racialized society."

John Harris: *"One who's actually on staff with CRU had everyone in the audience stand up, and they read a liturgy against 'white privilege,' confessing their sin."*

Speakers at the CRU Conference

"We have formed and developed Church structures and denominations, while excluding the voice of your global Church, due to racism and racial segregation. Lord, have mercy. We acknowledge the racial hierarchies and structures of privilege many have benefited from; many have been oppressed by. Lord, have mercy."

Gary Gordon: *"The CRU has been a wonderful organization for years. This used to be called Campus Crusade for Christ, right?"*

John Harris: *"Well, it did. They changed that name. And it seems like, along with the name change, some other things changed as well. One of the things that I found out was when I looked at the Lenses Institute. The Lenses Institute, kind of as the name implies, is for getting those who work with CRU to understand culture in a way that makes them less offensive, more winsome. And in order to do that, they must look at the culture through a new lens."*

Gary Gordon: *"So, it's intersectionality, which is social justice."*

John Harris: *"It's not the lens of Scripture that they're studying. It's the lens of the oppressed. John Perkins was popular in the late 60s, mostly early 70s and did some good things. But he is now thought well of in the Gospel Coalition. He's spoken at a Southern Seminary, and he has influenced CRU's Lenses Institute."*

Speakers at the CRU Conference

"I have a couple terms for us to look at today that will be helpful for the activities that we're going to engage in. So, we're going to hit stereotype, prejudice, privilege, and power today. When we talk about privilege, it's in all these different aspects of our lives, but certainly at skin color as well. And so, we'll talk a little bit about that."

John Harris: *"At the CRU19 Conference, one of the keynote speakers was an individual named Sandra Maria Van Opstal. And she spoke on, that she had never understood the Book of Amos, even though she had a seminary degree, even though she learned Hebrew, and she studied it with people who knew what the language said. It wasn't until she studied it with prisoners that she knew what it really meant, and she encouraged the people there at CRU to learn the Bible from the standpoint of the oppressed. To see it through the lens of people who are oppressed by the system, because they somehow have more knowledge."*

Trevor Loudin: *"I've been looking at the conferences, too. Like in 2015, the guest speaker was Michelle Higgins. She talked about the importance...really the 11*[th] *Commandment was ending 'white privilege.' This was the whole focus of her talk. This was in the Midwest; the young kids were mainly white because it was the Midwest. They would have walked out of that conference thinking that God's mission for them was ending 'white privilege.' They might be on food stamps. They may have no money to their name, but their big mission was ending 'white privilege.' What they weren't told is that Michelle Higgins, a pastor from St. Louis, Missouri, is a member of the Organization for Black Struggle, which is a front for a pro-Chinese Communist Party, called the Freedom Road Socialist Organization. These are the people that burnt Ferguson,*

Missouri to the ground, and these are taking their instructions from Communist China. Yet these young, Evangelical kids are being taught this as though it's Christianity. In CRU documents, they quote actual Maoists. So, this is real communism that they're being taught. These young Christian kids are being taught stuff that basically is in favor of Beijing's program for the destruction of America, and they think, somehow, it's Biblical.

John Harris: *"We're seeing that the social justice religion and Christianity are merging and, in CRU, that those waters have met. Many staff have reached out to me and told me exactly what's going on. In fact, within the last few weeks, I've had staff reach out and say that they have been forced out, that they had to quit, because of things that they've been asked to do. For instance, some staff has been required to go to the Lenses Institute, where they are thoroughly indoctrinated into social justice thinking. And it's been a compromise that they just cannot, in good conscience, participate in."*

Gary Gordon: *"It's easy to think of these things we've been learning about as silos – just unconnected, isolated individuals and ministries who have made compromising choices. The shocking aspect is that this trail is actually an interconnected web."*

Judd Saul, Producer/Director: *"So you have this main organization called the Gospel Coalition, which was founded by Tim Keller. The Gospel Coalition, which was supposed to be known for being, you know, reformed and solid, theological teaching is now writing articles with people from Sojourners, which are Marxists. You have them flooding their organization. You have Michael Wear, Obama's operative, writing for the Gospel Coalition.*

Then you have the Gospel Coalition people going into the Oikonomia Network. You have a lot of Oikonomia people involved with the Gospel Coalition. You have Gospel Coalition people - and a lot of them, because they're Southern Baptists - are involved with the ERLC. So, you have their activists involved with the ERLC, of the Southern Baptist ERLC. You have Michael Wear also involved in writing articles for the ERLC. You have the National Association for Evangelicals, you have Trinity Forum,

every one of them connected. Leftists, leftists, leftists everywhere in these organizations."

Gary Gordon: *"One thing these organizations all have in common is that they all happen to share the same or similar board members. Then, magically, when one of them gets too much heat, they get moved to another organization within the same network. Perhaps we should call it the 'socialist shuffle.' Where is this money coming from? Many of these are tied together with funding from the Kern Family Foundation."*

Judd Saul: *"They've had about 10 years of sending millions and millions and millions of dollars to well over 40 seminaries."*

Gary Gordon: *"Tying many of these groups and individuals together is the Oikonomia Network, whose slogan is 'Theology that works.'"*

Judd Saul: *"Kern funded the Oikonomia Network, which created all the educational material to go into these seminaries. Every seminary that took the Kern money has gone 'woke.' And what do I mean by 'woke?' They have started on the process of deconstructing traditional Christianity and faith and blending it with postmodern Marxist ideas. It is a propaganda arm. We ran across this group, called Docent. This group brags that one million Christians every week, hear their sermons. We find out that if a pastor doesn't feel up to researching or wants someone to write sermons for him on a certain topic, you pay them, and they will do it. We found that the former president of the Southern Baptist Convention, JD Greear, and then the new president of the Southern Baptist Convention preaching on the same series. But it wasn't just preaching on the same series or the same Bible or the same outline. It was verbatim."*

Two pastors are preaching but they are simultaneously saying the exact same sermon.

"One of the worst southern phrases is 'Bless his heart.' Some of Jesus' strongest words in the gospels, were about people like this. In fact, He called them whitewashed tombs. Two, they are there to promote the good, but the point is, this was no Abraham Lincoln. There are two primary things that I believe you and I are to glean from this passage."

"Let's talk about two things this morning. I want to talk about the responsibilities of those who govern. The second thing you'll see, and this is the important part, the responsibility of those ..."

Judd Saul: *"You have to ask yourself, is my pastor getting guidance from the Holy Spirit, going in prayer, reading the Word, or is he pushing a Marxist agenda in the form of a script that the Docent Group is writing? We find that JD Greear is endorsing Docent as a source to help them with their sermons. Matt Chandler, 'woke' pastor, endorsing Docent as a place to get their sermons. And we find other 'woke' pastors endorsing Docent Group as a place to get their sermons."*

Gary Gordon: *"WOKE, Willfully Overlooking Known Evil."*

Judd Saul: *"So, you have 'woke,' but then we have 'awake,' which is always attacking known evil. Which is what we are supposed to do as Christians. You want to be 'woke?' Do you want to ignore evil and placate and coddle this in, or do you want to be awake and attack the devil at his gate? The enemy knows our language. They know our weaknesses, and they know how to exploit it. They know our theology. They know our Christian generosity. They don't care, they will use everything they can to exploit it. When you hear words like 'White Privilege,' when you hear words like 'lenses,' when you hear those words, you know we're going to look at an oppressor versus oppressed, redistribution, relocation, and we're going to hear/learn about social justice. We're going to learn about, and you hear all these buzzwords, these are all talking points taken directly out of communist literature and communist ideas."*

Philip Haney: *"Maybe they look at it like spokes in a wheel. You know, each faith comes from a different point of origin, but they all end up converging like in the hub of the wheel. What do you suppose the fly in the ointment is?"*

Gary Gordon: *"Evangelicals are the fly in the ointment."*

Philip Haney: *"Yeah, these alliances that we're seeing emerge, are global in nature,* *will specifically mention the organization of Islamic Cooperation, the OIC, the largest non-governmental organization in the world other than the U.N. itself, 57 countries aligned together. That's one arena we can look at.*

And then you have, even closer... there are several names. There's Chrislam, there's Interfaith Dialogue, there is the Common Word, the whole phrase, the Common Word.' derives right out of a verse in the Koran, chapter 3, verse 64. 'Come now, let us find a common word between you and us. That we all worship Allah, that he has no partners and he that turns aside is not a good Muslim.' That is the rest of the verse. So, the entire, the whole Christian world - Rick Warren and Jim Wallace and all the rest of them - base this new coalition, this new alliance on a verse from the Koran, that specifically says that this commonality we have is that we all acknowledge Allah."

Judd Saul: *"So, after researching the World Council of Churches, I found two eerie similarities with all the denominations that are part of the World Council of Churches. One, they've all denied Biblical inerrancy. Two, they all shifted left, and they belong to an organization that was controlled by communists. KGB agents actually controlled the World Council of Churches. Denominations like the Southern Baptists, the Wesleyans and others are all taking the same drift that these past denominations have already done, but they never ask the political question. What is motivating them to go this way?*

Why are they joining organizations like the Evangelical Immigration Table funded by George Soros? This is happening in denominations all over the U.S. They have all implemented the same talking points, the same training materials. They might swap it out with a few different names, but it's the same propaganda. It's not Biblical, it's Marxism, and they are doing it to deconstruct the Church in the United States. Why are they trying to deconstruct the Church in the United States? If they take the Church, they take the nation."

Trevor Loudin: *"Communist Party U.S.A. and Democratic Socialists of America have hundreds of pastors on their rolls. Hundreds of people in theological colleges and Bible colleges, etc., and they are still indoctrinating people into Marxism."*

Sarah Neu, Community Leader: *"I wanted to share some examples of three different types of sermons I've given that gently introduce socialist or leftist ideas without being really heavy-handed about it. And the reason why I tried to navigate this balance is because my church is about 500 people, multi-racial, middle-upper class. I would say, it's progressive and liberal, not left-left. And just sort of more radical ideas associated with leftist politics, whether it's abolition, even decriminalization of sex work, socialism, just to name a few, are not so much in our mainstream discourse. And our philosophy is very much about, how do we bring people along? Instead of just being like, 'This is who we are. Get with it with it or not.' As a church. And that was our approach towards becoming LGBT affirming. So, I try to take a similar approach when it comes to talking about leftist ideas through sermons."*

Trevor Loudin: *"Communism is just a scientific manifestation of evil and it will just keep coming back and keep coming back. And we'll have to fight it till the end of time."*

Judd Saul: *"Why are enemies to our nation defending their own society while promoting everything that destroys us from the inside, here in America? Why is China going after effeminate men, while our churches are encouraging effeminate men? Why is Russia cracking down on homosexuality, and our churches are promoting it? There's a problem!"*

Brad Dacus, President Founder of Pacific Justice: *"We at Pacific Justice Institute have put a lot of time and a lot of work into putting together model bylaws and policies for Christian institutions, parachurch ministries, colleges to adopt that makes it very easy for them to protect themselves."*

John Harris: *"Imagine if everyone in one of these organizations, let's say CRU, for instance. Imagine if everyone in CRU, who was against the direction of CRU, all at once they stood up and said, 'We're not going to take this anymore! We'll start our own organization if we have to. Our donors aren't going to take this anymore.' Imagine what would happen, instead of having everyone cower and just submit to the authoritarian rule that is coming. So, we have to resist it, and we have to do it in a positive way."*

Steve Deace, Author: *"If we don't see that kind of revival, we are doomed. We are destined to break down into some form of Western European/Chinese, neo-marxism, where it won't be a totalitarian regime, because you can't keep us down. That's what the Chinese figured out after Tiananmen Square. If we just give people phones and big screen TVs, they'll be far more compliant. So, we'll have some form of that here, religious liberty will go the way of the dodo bird like you see in Western Europe."*

Micah Sample: *"What I would tell parents and donors, is to stop sending your kids, and stop sending money to these institutions until they turn around, and they begin to preach the truth and they apologize for the lies that they have told, because until that happens, you're just going to get the same results. Especially parents. You're going to watch your children, over the course of four years, grow from people who have been trained in righteousness, trained in the truth of Christianity, the truth of the gospel, into people who are now trained Marxists.* Trained *'woke'* cultists. *People who are devoted to social justice ideology. Your children will be unrecognizable if you continue to send them to these institutions. You cannot trust these institutions with your money, you cannot trust them with your children, you can't trust them with your time, because they will waste all of them. And, in some cases, they may be the catalyst for your child rejecting the faith."*

Pretty deep, the rabbit hole goes down way worse than I think we've realized. But that's what we are up against. Now I loved what he said. There's a lot of them. What should we do? Freak out and run for the hills? Resist. That's Biblical. Not pietism, keep your mouth shut. Not apathy and not fear. Afraid to speak up. We're the salt, the light, the resistance. The restrainers. That's what that means. But notice what he said "You not only need to resist in a positive way - meaning en masse, saying, "That's enough! This is not the gospel! This is not even Christianity." Not even close. It's communism, invading the Church.

It's couched with Christianese, but it doesn't make it Christian. Notice he said, "Parents, don't you dare send your kids to these institutions." Because they will come out, and we have all heard the stories, "Man, my kid was raised in the Church his whole life." That first year of college, and it isn't just secular college, it's what? So-called Christian colleges. Now you see why, because it's all been taken over. A deliberate invasion, back to the first point. But what I will add is this. Don't just support these. Don't give them your kids, because when you send your kid off to these institutions, so-called Christian seminaries, Christian colleges, you're giving them what? You are giving them your kid's time, and then you are giving them money. Now I will add this, because this just sticks in my craw. It isn't just the institutions, it's the churches.

People acknowledge that we are doing a great work here. We are teaching basic Christianity. We're supposed to be disciplined learners of all of God's Word. There's nothing special. But they will leave here, and they say a couple things. One, they say, "My church won't ever teach it." Then why are you going there? You are part of the problem. I'm not saying that you're not saved, but you are part of the problem. And you want to know why? Because you are choosing convenience over obedience. Because it's five minutes away. Jesus went all the way to Calvary and was whipped and beaten and bruised and murdered on our behalf, and you can't drive 25 minutes.

God's not deaf, nor blind, nor dumb and sees you. As soon as the sale is announced on IKEA, you will drive 45 minutes, one way, through traffic. "Oh, but my friends are there." So, you're going to stand accountable to God, and your friends ain't going to be there. Because the reason that these "woke" churches are here … and they would go belly up overnight if, en masse, all Christians who go there would admit that they never get the truth at their so-called church, and would say, "That's it!" And then would go and do whatever they had to do to be a part of churches who will preach God's truth. They will go belly-up, and we will be able to share God's truth en masse, even more so than what God already has us doing. But you won't do it because you are choosing convenience over obedience.

And dare I say, you know what you're supporting, and this is my new term, it's censored Christianity. Was it wrong when we tried to express our thoughts about the Covid plandemic? For us to be suppressed with our first amendment rights? Was it wrong when we disagreed with what went on with the last election cycle? And the chicanery that was going on? And that they literally blocked us, banned us or deleted our accounts? Is it wrong for YouTube right now in the United States of America, where we have the right to free speech, to do what they have been doing to us for several years now? They have literally hacked and deleted. You know why it's wrong? Because it's called censorship.

So, you're not only choosing these people who do this. You're not only choosing convenient Christianity. You're choosing censored Christianity. You admitted it. You don't get all the Bible; you get pieces of it. As you saw, most of it is getting so bad, it's not even the Bible. It's a "woke" communist, social message; and you're supporting that. And you are going to stand accountable to God. You need to stop supporting these places because your hand is in the proverbial cookie jar. If we don't rise up en masse and get serious, then what's going to happen? We're done! And, as I have said before, "The people in the pew next to you, one day, could be the death of you." These "woke" churches will take over, and we will become the enemy of the state. Because we chose convenience and censorship over Biblical Christianity.

Chapter Fifteen

The Promotion of a One World Religion

So, why are we dealing with this, enemies within the Church? Because, as you know, the Church is doing great! No, it's not. In fact, there has been a takeover, an invasion, specifically by people who aren't even saved. In fact, they even admit that they're atheists oftentimes. They are coming to literally, not just change, but to pervert the Church. But the Bible says, in **Romans 1**, that once you do that, it's going to get worse, and God will hand you over to a depraved mind. You will start doing things that ought not to be done! And this is where we're at today because we've rejected the Bible, not only in the world, but even in the so-called Church, by these fakers and they're supplanting that. They're making it up as they go, and we are promoting this perversion!

They are doing it to destroy our country, on purpose. They're doing it to make a ton of money, and they are also preparing people for the transhumanist movement. You would think, as bad as that is, that everybody would start speaking up. No, at the same time, they are very cunning. Shocker! They must be working for satan! They're also telling us that we need to keep our mouths shut with the lie of pietism. We have no right to speak up and get involved in politics. That's a lie. We have no right to speak up against what they are doing to the world. That's a lie. Because the Bible says we are to be the salt, the light, and the last days' resisters. The restraining influence to hold back the hindrance thereof of specifically, the Antichrist Kingdom, **2 Thessalonians 2**. So, that is what they are trying to do, to keep our mouths shut, as all this happens. If you do that, then all that does is make it easier for them to do what they are doing. But Scripture says, we are the rebels for Jesus! Right? We are to rebel against the culture. We are not to conform! What do you call somebody that is a non-conformist? A rebel! **Romans 12**, we're to be rebels for Jesus - rebels against this wicked world system - and tell them who's the One Who's in charge.

Unfortunately, a lot of churches aren't doing that today. They are either condoning, or they're giving into the lie of pietism, or dare I say, they are giving into - a new word for you - "chickenism." They're just a bunch of chickens! You're just a coward! And all that does is make it easier for these guys. And when we do open our mouths and resist, be resisters, and do not conform and go along with this, what are they going to do? Let us go on forever? No, we saw all of this is headed towards what? They are ultimately laying the groundwork for a One World Religion that will be in the 7-year Tribulation. And these fakers, taking over the Church, they are going to march straight in because they weren't saved. They were not even believing in the real Jesus. They are going to identify, vilify, mark the resisters, and make them the bad guys who are guilty of hate crimes or whatever they want to call it. At that point they have the excuse to round up the "resisters" who won't go along with this One World Religion.

They are doing this in two ways. One, the morality issue. That was the LGBT aspect, and that was because we disagree with that because the Bible disagrees with that, and what we are supposed to support. But we are the bad guys. We're guilty of hate crimes, and they are using that as a filter to force real Christians to stick their heads up and say, "NO MORE!" So, there's another troublemaker that we need to deal with, and they are already doing that politically, as we have seen with what they did to Mike Lindell. He was a troublemaker, and they had to silence him. And it's coming to the Church as well. I will say this again … You better be careful of the people sitting next to you in the pew, because one day they could be the death of you.

We're not perfect here at Sunrise. But I'm not concerned about it, because I think we're like-minded. The Scripture says we are to be like-minded. And how does that happen? Because we are following One Book, the only book, the Bible. That's how you get unity when you follow the Scripture. But look at these fake churches and how many times have we seen people say, "I wish we had this in my church. They never talk about this stuff. They never preach on prophecy or the Bible or any kind of current or social events and how to apply them in Scripture. They don't …" Then why are you going there?

The danger for those people is, the fake church, they are going to, that they are supporting with their time, treasure, tongue, and talent - the fake church is going to stand before God. But you are in danger, because one day those fakers are going to turn on you. If we're still alive and still here, the hammer will come down like that, with genuine persecution in America. They are going to turn on you, and you're going down. You need to run. You need to come out from them and be separate, as the Scripture says.

The second filter, as we have seen, was the twisted gospel and twisted Jesus. We thought it was bad, but the transcribed video that was in the last chapter, showed us how really bad it is. And who's doing it! They have a twisted gospel, which is a false gospel. They are saying, "Oh no, we're not here to share the Good News that Jesus Christ has come to save us, and rescue us from hell, and He's the only way to Heaven. Oh no, it's a social gospel. We need to take care of people's emotional needs; we need to support Black Lives Matter and critical race theory. We need to repent of our white stature." And where did that come from? Straight from communism! Now why would they support that? Well, one, because it will destroy the Church. It's a false gospel. But this communist mentality, where you're all under one authority and it accepts, supposedly, anything and everything, (morality, religion, and whatever), that's the underpinning that you need to start to pull off a One World Religion, which again is where it's all headed.

The second one that the false gospel and false Jesus is leading to is, "You won't go along with accepting everybody's morality, that you've got to accept their religion as equal to your own, and that all paths lead to Heaven." Now, can Christians do that? No. So, what's that going to do? It will force you to come to the top, and then they go, "Aha!" And then they are going to come get you. But, again, are we really headed to a One World Religion? Absolutely! It's very clear that this is going to happen and, as we read through this text, notice how many times the word "worship" is used. They are not just going to follow the antichrist. They're not just going to fawn after the Antichrist. They're going to worship him.

Revelation 13:3-9: "One of the heads of the beast seemed to have had a fatal wound, but the fatal wound had been healed. The whole world was astonished and followed the beast. Men worshiped the dragon (satan) because he had given authority to the beast, and they also worshiped the beast and asked, 'Who is like the beast? Who can make war against him?' The beast was given a mouth to utter proud words and blasphemies and to exercise his authority for forty-two months. He opened his mouth to blaspheme God, and to slander his name and his dwelling place and those who live in Heaven. He was given power to make war against the saints and to conquer them. And he was given authority over every tribe, people, language, and nation. All inhabitants of the earth will worship the beast - all whose names have not been written in the book of life belonging to the Lamb that was slain from the creation of the world. He who has an ear, let him hear."

How many have got an ear? How many have got a spare, which means now you can hear, once again, in stereo? So, pay attention to what he's got to say. This is serious. This is what the Bible is saying. The Bible is very clear, that one day our planet is not only going to head to a One World Religion, but all the inhabitants of the Earth are going to worship this guy. But what is the religion? It's a satanically inspired religion. The antichrist is satan's plan for that time. And it's a good thing we see no signs of all religions corralling into one that's ultimately going to lead to one guy being worshiped. We are, big time, and this is what we are seeing right now. It's a welcoming of all faiths. Now go back to the apostasy we are seeing in the Church. What was that latest stat that we saw? Nearly 70 percent of people professing to be born-again Christians, think that all paths lead to Heaven. And can I tell you something? That means 70 percent are not saved. I'm sorry, that's a watershed thing. You can't say Jesus is the only way, and you can't say, "I'm trusting in Jesus," but then say there's other ways to get there. You can't do that as a born-again Christian. But this is what's going on, even in the Church, not just the world.

Now there is a buzzword for this mentality of a One World Religion. Now, again, if the antichrist comes out and says that we're going to start a One World Government of the antichrist, people probably wouldn't go along. It's too obvious. So, what do you do? You use a buzzword; you change the terminology. Have you seen how many times Biden has been using this term, New World Order? Or over the Covid thing, down in Australia - this is what we have to do for the New World Order? What's the New World Order? It's the buzzword for One World Government, that was prophesied 2,000 years ago.

It's the same thing with the One World Religion. They're going to say, "Hey everybody, we're going to start a One World Religion, and if anybody doesn't go along with it, you're going to die!" Oh, that's too obvious. Okay, it's "interfaith." Doesn't that sound nicer? It's interfaith or interfaithism, pluralism, because we all need to get along. And the way they are promoting this is basically with lies, shocker! They use the same terminology that they use with this moral issue, this moral filter, to try to get us to go along with the LGBTQ. We need to respect one another. We need to tolerate, that's the big word. We need to find common ground with one another. Well, believe it or not, that's not only true of the moral issue, the LBGTQ, but it's the same thing when it comes to the One World Religion. You hear these same buzzwords. It's interfaith. Now we all have to get along. We have to accept everybody's morality. Whatever it is, as gross as it is, with bestiality and pedophilia; and if you don't like it, aha ...

We'll force you to raise your head. And then it's the same thing with the One World Religion. We need to respect other religions. We need to tolerate them. We need to find common ground. And they are doing that by promoting, not only the lie of climate change - because if we don't get together, the planet's going to blow up - they are using that to get all religions to come together and find common ground.

They had a big lie out there, and you may have heard this. "We've got to get along. We've got to find common ground. We've got to all get together as religions, because we all know that religion is the main cause of war." That's a lie! You know what the main cause of war is? Politics. Now let's do some stats:

What Really Causes Wars

Congo Free State – 1886-1908 – 8,000,000 – Control of colonial profit and power base
Feudal Russia – 1900-1917 – 3,500,000 – Political control
Turkish Purges – 1900-1923 – 5,000,000 – Ottoman Empire collapse/Political control
First World War – 1914-1918 – 15,000,000 – Balance of power
NOTE: The First World War killed more people than all the religious wars in the past. 6,000 men a day died for 1,500 days in World War I.
Russian Civil War – 1917-1922 – 9,000,000 – Political control
Soviet Union, Stalin Regime – 1924-1953 – 20-45,000,000 – Political control
China Nationalist Era – 1928-1937 – 3,000,000 – Political control
Second World War – 1937/38-1945 – 55,000,000 – Balance of power/Expansionism
Sino-Japanese War – 1937-1945 – 21,000,000 – Expansionism
Post-WWII German Expulsions from Eastern Europe – 1945-1948 – 1.8-5,000,000 – Post-war policies. Retributions/Soviet and Eastern European control
Chinese Civil War – 1945-1949 – 2,500,000 – Political control

People's Republic of China – 1949-1975 – 40-80,000,000 – Political control

How come we never talk about that? How come Hitler always gets it (and rightly so, with the death of six million Jews), but why don't they ever bring up communism with Stalin, and Mao Tse-Tung and Pol Pot in Cambodia? It's here under our eyes, and it's even coming into the Church. You don't want to give communism a bad light, do you? It's crazy.

North Korean Regime – 1948 – 1.7-3,000,000 – Political control
Korean War – 1950-1953 – 2,800,000 – Political control
Second Indochina War – 1960-1975 – 3-4,000,000 – Political control
Ethiopia – 1962-1992 – 1,500,000 – Political control
Khmer Rouge – 1975-1978 – 2,500,000 – Political control
Afghanistan – 1979-2001 – 1,800,000 – Political control/Soviet expansion
Kinshasa Congo – 1998 – 3,800,000 – Political control and Resources

I don't know about you, but where's the religion in all that? Maybe it's just me, but once you look at the facts, I'd say we're being lied to! Religion is not the biggest cause of wars, it's the anti-God, manmade agendas that are! It's politics, not religion! And they're using this fear and manipulation to coerce us into going along with this One World Religion. Exactly like the Bible said would happen, when you are living in the last days. Because of these wars that are caused by all these religious differences, we've got to all come together and become one. We need to have somebody to watch over us that rhymes with the false prophet. I mean the Pope. I mean somebody who could make sure that we all get along, because wars are killing us, and it's all because of these religious differences. No, it's not. Lie number one. So, this is how they are getting this Interfaith Movement to come into play.

Now the other one, and I don't know if you have already noticed this. We need to go back to a little bit of history. After September 11th, because we all know that "religious differences" are the main cause of war, right? 9/11 became a watershed moment even here in America. It blew me away, just coming out of New Age, which is all about One World

Religion. I was pastoring in Northern California at that time and, suddenly, they went gung-ho on pushing a One World Religion. And they used 9/11 as, "See, those Muslim terrorists, that in theory, did that to the towers, and see that's religious differences. We can't have this kind of atrocity anymore. We've got to come together as religions." And that's how they did all the memorial services. They had multiple religions coming together, and even Billy Graham got in on the action. Do you remember that?

President Bush pointed out that 9/11, was a "Day of Infamy," and that it was a spiritual event with spiritual implications. He only hinted at what these implications might be. The first inkling came a few days later at the services for 9/11 at the Washington Cathedral. During this service, we saw clerics from Christianity, Judaism and Islam present themselves in full regalia.

They were fully unanimous in their assertion that "we all worship the same God." This theme would again be apparent when Oprah Winfrey led a "prayer service" in Yankee Stadium.

This time, we were treated to prayers and "words of wisdom" from Protestant preachers, Catholic cardinals, an Eastern Orthodox bishop, Islamic imams, Jewish rabbis, and Hindu clerics.

But strangely missing from these services were Christian Fundamentalists. The omissions were deliberate, because our beliefs are not compatible with the goals of a One World Religion.

And now, "fundamentalist" groups, which do not fit into the mold, can be marginalized as cults, and wiped out in the most profound fashion, just like the other terrorists.

While liberal "Christianity," represented by the mainstream media and the apostate Church, can now be held up as acceptable.

That is when you began to see Fundamental Evangelical Christians being labeled, as what? The same dangerous propaganda against the Muslim extremists. We are Christian extremists, right wing Christian fundamentalist sects, who are dangerous for our country. And it's still going on today. But guess who was propped up as the good guys? Remember the old switcheroo we talked about? The fakers in the Church that would go along with this and say, "Yeah, we all worship the same God." You're not saved. I don't care if you are a cleric. I don't care if you are the bishop of so-and-so church of apostate.com." That doesn't make you a Christian. But those guys are the "real Christians." And so even as far back as then, you and I began to be marginalized.

But let's examine that. Can we go along with this? No. In fact, just to let the cat out of the bag, if anybody says they are an "Interfaith Christian," there is no such thing. Again, that's an oxymoron. You can't be an interfaith Christian. It's like saying a peaceful war. Icey hot. Yummy chicken. There is no such thing. That's an oxymoron, right? Because you can't be interfaith when there's only one faith, Jesus Christ. I didn't say that he did. You can't get around that.

John 14:6: "I am the way and the truth and the life. No one comes to the Father, except through Me."

Now here's the problem. According to our society's Interfaith Movement, you cannot make a more "intolerant" statement than that! But people, that came from the lips of Jesus! And I don't recommend you call Him a "religious bigot!" But this is what "interfaith" teaches. You have to deny what Jesus said right there, and in essence, call Him a liar, and instead say, He's not the only way to Heaven and that all religions are valid pathways to Heaven, and can I tell you something? You can't do that as a genuine, born-again Christian!

But you might be thinking, "Come on, Pastor Billy. This is America. We're a Christian nation. There is no way people are going to be able to pull off this Interfaith Movement and create a One World Religion. Maybe in some other country, but not here! Nobody's ever going to fall for this." Really? I'm here to tell you, that not only have many well-known people here in America already done so - even to the highest levels of society, Hollywood, the Government, you name it - but they're about to put the whole thing in place!

The 1st proof that we know we really are headed for a One World Religion is the Promotional Proof. Hey folks, as if what we've seen isn't enough, this Interfaithism Movement is also being promoted by virtually every single mover and shaker from around the world. Just in case you aren't politically correct or scared into doing it, they're using Hollywood, the governments, and even the Vatican to help "educate you" and promote this lie to go along with a One World Religion. But again, don't take my word for it. Let's listen to theirs.

Promoters of World Religion

Prince Charles of England: He launched a movement called "Respect" in order to "Promote tolerance among world's religions." And he's also a promoter of the depopulation agenda, the Great Reset, Climate Change, and his new position as King gives him the power over The Commonwealth, an association of 56 independent countries with 2.4 billion people, and he's already stated he's looking forward to giving all this power and more over to "One Guy."

Prince Charles: *"Your Excellencies, Ladies and Gentlemen, the Covid-19 pandemic has shown us just how devastating a global cross-border threat can be. Climate change and biodiversity loss are no different. In fact, they pose an even greater existential threat, to the extent that we have to put ourselves on what might be called a war-like footing. I, myself, had the opportunity of consulting with many of you over these past 18 months. I know you all carry a heavy burden on your shoulders, and you do not need me to tell you, that the eyes and hopes of the world are upon you to act with all dispatch and decisively, because time has quite literally run out. We also know that countries, many of whom are burdened by growing levels of debt, simply cannot afford to go green. Here, we need a vast military style campaign to marshal the strength of the global private* *sector. With trillions at his disposal, far beyond global GDP and with the greatest respect, beyond even the governments of the world's leaders, he offers the only real prospect of achieving fundamental economic transition."*

Who is this "he" he's talking about? The countries around the world can hand it over to this guy, and he'll have the money and the power to bring peace to the planet. That sounds a little freaky. That's what's going on, and now he's king over 2.4 billion people. It almost sounds like we're in the last days. It's time to get motivated.

Al Gore, everybody's favorite politician and global warming promoter - by the way, if you didn't know this, the climate change, there's another side to that. Not only is it a joke, but with what they're wanting to bring in with climate change and all these rules and regulations, they're going to sell carbon credits, and guess who's invested heavily in them for years? The elites are investing in this like the stock market, and they're going to make money hand over fist, if they get to pull this off. So, it's another money-making scheme. It's like everything else.

Al Gore: *"The richness and diversity of our religious tradition throughout history is a spiritual resource long ignored by people of faith who are often afraid to open their minds to teachings first offered outside their own system of belief. But the emergence of a civilization in which knowledge moves freely and almost instantaneously through the world, has spurred a renewed investigation of the wisdom distilled by all faiths. This pan religious perspective may prove especially important where our global civilization's responsibility for the earth is concerned."*

In other words, we have all got to come together as religions, and merge into one, if we are going to save the planet. But he's not the only one. Oprah Winfrey, Hollywood, the governments, and even the Vatican are promoting this One World Religion and have been doing so for years. And now it has crept into the Church where 70 percent agree. Michael Jackson's funeral, notice the symbols.

Music is playing as the singers come onto the stage, and they begin to sing:

"There comes a time
When we heed a certain call
When the world must come together as one
There are people dying
Oh, and it's time to lend a hand to life
The greatest gift of all
We can't go on
Pretending day-by-day
That someone, somewhere soon make a change
We're all a part of God's great big family
And the truth, you know, love is all we need
We are the world
We are the children
We are the ones who make a brighter day, so let's start giving
There's a choice we're making
We're saving our own lives
It's true we'll make a better day, just you and me"

The symbols that are being shown behind them as they are singing, is the One World Religion's symbol. Maybe you've seen it. It's called "Coexist" and it looks like this:

Oprah Winfrey: "One of the mistakes that human beings make, is believing that there is only one way to live and that we don't accept that there are diverse ways of being in the world. That there are millions of ways and many ways, no, many paths to what you call God. Her path might be something else and when she gets there, she might call it the 'light.' But her loving, her kindness, and her generosity, if it brings her to the same point that it brings you, it doesn't matter whether she calls it God along the way or not."

Lady #1 in the audience: "I guess the danger in that, I mean it sounds great on the onset but if you really look at both sides …"

Oprah Winfrey: "There couldn't possibly be just one way."

Lady #2 in the audience: "What about Jesus?"

Oprah Winfrey: "What about Jesus?"

Lady #2: "You say there isn't only one way. There is one way and only one way, and that is through Jesus."

Oprah Winfrey: "There couldn't possibly be only one way!"

Lady #2: Because you say, you intellectualize it and say there isn't. If you don't believe that, you're all buying into the lie."

Speaker: "Today's opening prayer will be offered by a guest chaplain Mr. Rajan Zed of the Indian Association of Northern Nevada."

Unidentified man: "Lord Jesus, forgive us for allowing a prayer of the wicked which is an abomination in your sights.'"

Speaker: "The Sergeant at Arms will restore order in the Senate."

Unidentified man: "Lord God, you are the one true …"

Speaker: "The Sergeant in arms will restore order in the chamber."

Good Morning America: "Let me ask you some questions about faith, which is a tough subject to talk about. Do we all worship the same God. Christian and Muslim?"

President George Bush: "I think we do. We have different routes of getting to the Almighty." H U H ?

Good Morning America: "Do Christians, non-Christians and Muslims go to Heaven in your mind?"

President George Bush: "Yes, they do. We have different routes of getting there."

Narrator: "The Vatican and the Roman Catholic Church, its Pope is currently leading the greatest ecumenical movement in history in order to unite all religions under Rome's leadership. In 1986 Pope John Paul II gathered in Assisi, Italy, the leaders of the world's major religions to pray for peace. There were snake worshipers, fire worshipers, spiritists, animists, Buddhists, Muslims, Hindus, North American witch doctors. I watched in astonishment as they walked to the microphone to pray. The Pope said they were all praying to the same God and that their prayers were creating a spiritual energy that was bringing about a new climate for peace. John Paul II allowed his good friend, the Dalai Lama, to put the Buddha on the altar in Saint Peter's Church in Assisi and with his monks, have a Buddhist ceremony there while Shintoists chanted and rang their bells outside. The prophesied world religion is in the process of being formed before our eyes, and the Vatican is the headquarters of the movement. Is this not spiritual fornication?"

That's exactly what it is! But it's a good thing that it stopped with Pope John Paul II. No, it didn't. We are going to see what Pope Francis is up to. If you haven't seen it, they have a buzzword, a code word, like at the Michael Jackson funeral. It's called "coexist." It's on bumper stickers, shirts, everywhere. So, basically, what they are saying is, One World

Religion. It's just like we saw in the occult. They use symbols to codify their beliefs. It's the same thing.

Well, you would think the Muslims would never go along with this. That's not true:

King Abdullah of Saudi Arabia: He has been planning for years to, "Find a way to unite the world's major religions in an effort to help foster peace. He believes a new International Organization will help make that dream a reality."

So, we need to find somebody to take charge of all the religions. Whoever said it, the Vatican, I don't know. But this is what they are crying out for. Even religions that you would never think would go along with it. Even the Jewish people.

Chief Rabbi Yona Metzger, one of the two Chief Rabbis of Israel said: "We need a United Relations of Religions, which would contain representatives of the world's religions as opposed to nations. A church, a mosque, a synagogue, or a holy temple must be embassies of God, and we have to spread this idea to our believers." He has suggested that the Dalai Lama could lead the assembly.

So, again, just like we have a United Nations that governs the governments, we need that kind of entity to govern the religions. Now another Muslim figure:

Adnan Oktar: He recently met with three representatives from the re-established Jewish Sanhedrin, to discuss how religious Muslims, Jews and Christians can work together on rebuilding the Temple. An official statement about the meeting has been published on the Sanhedrin's website, where they stated, "We are all sons of one father, the descendants of Adam, and all humanity is but a single family, Peace among nations will be achieved through building the House of G-d, where all peoples will serve." Oktar added that, "The Temple will be rebuilt, and all believers will worship there in tranquility." And "The Temple could be rebuilt in one year."

So, let's say this antichrist guy makes a covenant with Israel, which is what starts the 7-year Tribulation, Daniel 9:27, and then maybe part of that little carrot that he uses to get them to sign this agreement is, "Hey, you can build your Temple. It's okay. I know the Dome of the Rock is there, but there is enough room to build this universal temple and we could have it done in a year." If that were to happen, a year into the 7-year Tribulation, you still have two and a half years to go before the Antichrist shows his true colors in the midway point and declares himself to be God.

Now back to the Pope. Pope Francis, what is he doing? He's showing no signs of trying to corral all the religions together. Yes, in fact, he isn't just making agreements, meeting with all these different religions, saying we all worship the same God, same kind of false teaching that Pope John Paul II did; but they're already being proactive, and they're building these Universal Worship Centers all around the world. Even in Muslim territory.

Daleen Hassan, Euronews: "Hey everyone, welcome to Inspire Movie. This week we're focusing on the topic of inclusion and tolerance within regional societies, starting with the project in the UAE, which will be a home to a mosque, a church, and a synagogue. The UAE is home to a diverse population of more than 200 nationalities. And it's a melting pot of multiple cultures and faiths. A beacon of religious coexistence is the plan for the capital of Abu Dhabi, called The Abrahamic Family House. Rebecca McLaughlin Easten looks into what it really means from Jewish, Christian, and Muslim representatives in the region. Take a look."

Rebecca McLaughlin Easten: "Religious history was made in Abu Dhabi last year when the document on human fraternity was signed by Pope Francis and Dr. Ahmed El-Tayeb, the Grand Imam of al-Azhar. It called for tolerance, universal peace, and the reconciliation of all faiths. Embodying this agreement, this year, construction will start on a project called The Abrahamic Family House on Saadiyat Island, due for completion in 2022. The site will house a church, a mosque, and a synagogue."

And who's there to make sure that all happens? Mr. "I want to be at the top one day and rule it all," Pope Francis, the Vatican. Good thing it's not coming here in America. They want to build one of these exact same things in New York.

Breaking News Alert: "A One World Religion Center plans have now been unveiled in New York and they are planning to break ground soon. Images and video have now been released for the Abrahamic Family House in New York. The plans will include a mosque, a church and a synagogue and was decreed by the Higher Committee of Human Fraternity…"

It's called apostasy, the One World Religion. That's all it is, but it's already been planned for in New York. And not only that, but even here in our own capital in the government. Which we all know the current administration will never go along with this.

Advertisement for the Abrahamic Family House:

Do you want to help break the cycle of fear and hate? We can coexist and have peaceful exchanges of ideas! 4 Housemates - 4 Faiths, Judaism,

Christianity, Islam, Baha'i share and celebrate together! Living together!
Designing and hosting fun!
Engaging in weekly Interfaith events in your community in your free time
1-2 Year Fellowship + Capstone Impact Project – Rent covered 75% - Living in Washington, D.C.
To be a part of this movement visit www.abrahamichouse.
#GatheringNotOthering
Abrahamic House
www.abrahamichouse.org

We all just have to get along, accept anybody's morality, accept anyone's religion, and we're going to bring peace to the planet. If you don't go along with it, you're the troublemaker. So, I tell you, these are the two things, and here's what's sad. Those two things, the fakers in the Church are all in on it. And they're growing by the week. They are taking over the Church, by the week and then, those who know better have either given into pietism or chickenism and that's making it happen that much faster. That's the last thing we need to be doing during this time, because the fakers sitting next to you, in the pew, may one day be the death of you.

So, that's what is going on today and we certainly see it from the world, but are the Jewish people really going to go along with it? Uh huh, they want to put one of these Universal Worship Centers right smack dab on the Temple Mount. If you have the opportunity to go to the Temple Institute, you can see the actual articles on this. Everything's ready to go. The priesthood, the clothing, all ready to go. Keep that in mind as you look at the transcript of this video. They have got big plans and are super-stoked about building this Universal One World religious temple. Not just in Dubai, New York, and Washington D.C. and all around the world, but right there on the Temple Mount in Jerusalem.

Narrator, Holy Land Uncovered Reports: "Welcome back to Holy Land Uncovered. Have you ever heard about initiatives to build the Third Jewish Temple in Jerusalem? Well, even if you might have heard such an initiative, this still might really surprise you. How about Turkish Muslims promoting the Third Temple Project along with Jewish Orthodox rabbis? Meet doctors Oktar Babuna and Jiat Gundogdu. They came here from Turkey. Thank you so much and welcome to Israel. Yehuda Glick, as member of the Knesset, will also join us shortly. Oh, here he is. Thank you so much for being with us. So, the Temple Mount is one of the biggest flashpoint sites in the region. It often ignites very violent clashes. Your message here is, 'Holy sites should be centers of reconciliation and not conflicts.'"

Doctor: "Beautiful people are living in this country. It's a unique place. It's a sacred home for the Jews, for the Muslims, and for Christians, and that makes it prone to many conflicts and violence, but this is not better for anybody. This is a prayer house where God's name is meant, it will be mentioned and it has to be revealed for the people, all the nations to pray there as stated in the Ishaya. All nations, God says, will be praying there, together, shoulder to shoulder, to serve God. These are statements from the Torah."

Narrator: *"Yehuda, you met with the two doctors sitting with me here in the studio. Were you surprised by this initiative?*

Yehuda Glick: *"Yes. I am actually in a very long-term connection with Dr. Oktar and Dr. Babuna and I think they are doing wonderful activity. They are being led by a very special leader from Turkey, and I think that it shouldn't surprise us, because people who believe in God, know that God is inclusive and not exclusive, and he wants us all to join together and turn the Temple Mount into a house of prayer for all nations, and I think that, I'm sure that we're at the beginning of a Biblical era where more and more religious leaders from around the world will join in this wonderful initiative of turning the Temple Mount to a place, where it should be a World Center for peace and calling on the name of the one and only God."*

Narrator: *"What we are seeing here are images of the future Third Temple Mount. That is very interesting, but I have to ask, is it doable and not a fantasy? Because with so many regulations, objections, and funding, of course."*

Doctor: *"With love and discussion it is very, very doable. Actually, it's the promise of God, as we have read the statement from the Torah. We will pray there, all together. It's a prayer house of God. There is no, nothing can stop that. Indeed, we're living in very specific times, and with this pure gold carving and the original form, it will be revealed for us as a prayer house for all the nations, shoulder to shoulder. It's doable because we can discuss that. First of all, we should know it's not going to damage either the Dome of the Rock or the Al-Aqsa. There's enough land and this will be a prayer house for Jews, Christians, and the Muslims."*

Anybody seeing a pattern here? In the U.S., Dubai, Muslim countries, around the world, even the Jewish people, right now, as we sit here… are forming a One World Religion with the Pope, I mean False Prophet, I mean the Pope. All huge Bible prophecy signs that a ONE WORLD RELIGION is forming right before our very eyes as we sit here!

But talk about a small world, about six months ago I was doing a television interview in Dallas and unbeknownst to me, Yehuda Glick was one of the guests, and I went on after him. So, we are sitting there in the green room, watching them. He's getting ready to go on. Him and his wife were there to talk about some Jewish organization supporting the widows, which was cool. But I'm sitting there thinking, I know this guy. And I'm sitting next to him. So, I had to ask the question. "How about that third temple. How are you guys coming along with that?" He looked at me like, you're not supposed to know that. And then he said they were making strides and doing all that, basically cutting me off. But I wanted to get the inside scoop, because that's the guy.

But you can see this is being promoted around the world, and what's the sad thing? The Church is going along with it. The fake Church is going along with it. So, what's that going to do? Just like the morality issue, we can't go along with this. But here's how they're selling it to us. The world out there pushes the One World Religion phrase "Interfaithism." In the Church circles, it's pushed with this phrase "ecumenicalism." It means the same thing. It's just a Church word, if you will.

The 2nd proof that we really are headed for a One World Religion, is the Ecumenical Proof. And for those of you who may not know, "Ecumenicalism" is defined as "the organized attempt to bring about the cooperation and unity of all believers." And at the onset, that sounds pretty good. But what they don't tell you, is that it's come to mean all believers, meaning even those outside of Christ, no matter what they believe - whether they believe in Christ or not! And their so-called "unity" is being sought, not on the basis of truth, but from a watered down version of it. But people, I'm here to tell you, the Bible is clear. We Christians, genuine believers in Christ, do not join hands with somebody who's preaching a watered down version of God's truth, i.e., a lie! Rather, the Bible says we need to come out from among them and be ye separate! I didn't say that. God did.

2 Corinthians 6:14-17: "Do not be yoked together with unbelievers. For what do righteousness and wickedness have in common? Or what fellowship can light have with darkness? What harmony is there between Christ and Belial? Or what does a believer have in common with an unbeliever? What agreement is there between the temple of God and idols? For we are the temple of the living God. As God has said: 'I will live with them and walk among them, and I will be their God, and they will be my people.' Therefore, come out from them and be separate, says the Lord. Touch no unclean thing, and I will receive you."

According to our text, the Bible clearly says that when it comes to unbelievers, i.e., non-Christians, what are we supposed to do? Yes, we hang out with them, yes, we witness to them, yes, we love them enough to tell them the truth about Jesus being the only way to Heaven. Why? Because we're concerned about their eternal destiny! Jesus is the only way to Heaven! I didn't say that…He did!

John 14:6: "Jesus answered, 'I am the way and the truth and the life. No one comes to the Father except through Me.'"

Can't get any clearer than that! So of course, we love the lost enough to tell them the truth about Jesus being the only way to Heaven… of course! That's true love! But the last thing we ever want to do is to be, what? Is to be to be "yoked" with them, right? The word "yoked" literally means there, "to bound together with or to have fellowship with." Why? Because it's like oil and water. It doesn't mix! It can't mix! It'll never mix. Why? Because you cannot mix a lie with God's perfect holy truth! And that's Paul's argument there! Why in the world would a born-again Christian try to mix God's truth with the devil's lies? What do righteousness and wickedness have in common? What fellowship can light have with darkness? What harmony is there between Christ and Belial? How can we really "get along" with those who believe that we ourselves are gods, or that we'll burn in a mythical place called purgatory where we purge away our sins in order to get into heaven, which is denying the cross?

How can we "join hands" with those who would have you and I believe that sin is just an illusion, or that hell is only make believe, and that Heaven for some men, will be to endlessly satisfy their lusts with as many virgins as they want, which only happens after they kill a bunch of people?

And how can we have "unity" with those who are claiming to be Christians, yet state that one has to keep the sacraments to be saved, or that satan doesn't exist, or that Christ's work on the cross is not secure? How can we "have fellowship with" those who would have you and I believe that Jesus is not God, but the archangel Michael? Or worse yet, that He is the spirit-brother of satan himself…lucifer?

I don't think so! The answer is obvious! Come out from among them and be ye separate! Why? Because God says to! You cannot have fellowship with those who are leading people to hell! He doesn't like that! A true born-again Christian can't maintain their true Christianity and go along with this One World Religion that says Jesus is not the only way to Heaven. You cannot meld the two together! And yet, that's exactly what the Ecumenical Movement is trying to get us to do! In fact, it's already progressed greatly all over the world! Let's take a look.

Pluralism in Europe

In Berlin, they have created what's called "The House of One" at a cost of $60 million dollars for Christians, Muslims, and Jews to pray under one roof.

Pastor Gregor Hohberg: *"From the beginning, we wanted it to be an inter-religious project, not a place built by Christians in which Jews and Muslims would then be added, but for all three religions to have equal prayer space on the same floor with each floor leading to a common room, where the different religions would be able to converse."*

Here's their promo video:

Narrator: "'*We have inherited a large house, a great world house,' said Martin Luther King. We all inhabit this world house, our earth. We see that the world is growing together and that we have to learn to live with each other. Increasingly, religions are colliding as strangers, as friends, often also as rivals or enemies. For this reason, Jews, Christians, and Muslims have come together in Berlin to dare to attempt something new. We want to build a completely new sacred building. A synagogue, a church and a mosque, under the same roof, and at its center, a meeting place. 'The House of One.' It shall be located in the heart of Berlin, in the place where the city was founded 800 years ago. It shall be a unique, peaceful place for encounters, meetings, and exchanges between people from different religions, and also for those who are removed from religion. Everyone is invited to come. Every interest, every question, every support is welcome. With every peaceful dialogue and every good wish,*

the cloud of blessing will grow. One Earth, One Mankind, One Home. The House of One."

And that's just the beginning. Can I tell you something? That's what's wrong with America.

Pluralism in Youth Abroad

With the help of the World Council of Churches, a group of Christian, Muslim, and Jewish youths have now formed a multi-faith community to protect the earth, which they say is a concern for all faiths.

Notice they are using the youth, just like Hitler did. Gravitate the younger minds.

Tariq Abdul Akbar, a 21-year-old Muslim: *"People of all faiths must put aside their religious differences and come together to raise awareness about climate change, which affects all people."*

Mark Edwards, a Christian student from Sri Lanka: *"The responsibility to respect creation is common to all faiths. Earth is a gift to us all, and we are all responsible for its well-being."*

Liron Alkolombra, a Jewish woman: *"Living in a multi-faith community is an 'eye opener.' Our visit to a synagogue, a church and a mosque in Switzerland moved me so much that I realized we all believe in God, and we're all part of humanity."*

Is that the gospel? No, it's not. But notice how they are using all this to grab their minds to promote this lie. Now this one blew me away, because this is in the so-called Bible Belt.

Pluralism In America

Even here in America we now have what's called the Tri-Faith Initiative in Omaha that is combining Christians, Jews, and Muslims into an interfaith dialogue, as well an inter-faith facility. It's a multi-million-dollar effort to bring all three religions onto a 35-acre campus. The city's religious leaders say, *"We want to form a relationship between all Jews, all Muslims, and all Christians. It's an opportunity not only to learn to tolerate different faiths, but to find ways to celebrate all we have in common and join with those who call God by different names."*

Now notice the thread that you're seeing here. So-called Christianity, Judaism, and Muslim or Islam. Why? A couple studies back, if you're going to have a One World Religion, then by definition you have to accept all - as Al Gore said, pan religion, all religions. Well, wait a second, you have three monotheistic religions on the planet, where there's only one God. What are they? Christianity, Judaism, and Islam. So, what are you going to do with those who by definition, don't go along with the "all?" You have to infiltrate those monotheistic religions, like they're doing with fakers that don't even follow their own religion, and turn them pluralistic. And then the ones who are following the religions are the ones you need to take out. Again, it's the old switcheroo. But that's what you keep seeing. They primarily mention that this One World Religion is bringing the monotheistic ones and turning them into pluralistic. That's what you need for a One World Religion. Now, it's also here in America's schools.

Pluralism in Schools

Just in case you don't live anywhere near Berlin or Omaha, we now have high school students in Colorado being encouraged to recite a pledge in Arabic stating, "One Nation under Allah."

In New York, kids are now observing Muslim New Year holidays and possibly soon the Hindu Festival Diwali.

School kids in California are now bowing down to the sun god as part of "liturgical ritual religious practices" aimed at having them "become one with god" through yoga. The founder, Sonia Tudor Jones says she wants to "spread the gospel of Ashtanga Yoga through the country and even internationally."

That's another oxymoron. Christian yoga. There's no such thing because yoga is not Christian. Yoga means to yoke. It means to yoke yourself with the Hindu deities, and what does God say? Don't yoke. Literally, if you want to play on words, don't yoga with the other religions. And Yoga is Hinduism. It's a physical practice to get you into an altered state of consciousness to commune with the demons, the Hindu deities. You can do that in schools, but you can't read the Bible.

Pluralism in Government

The Dalai Lama was allowed to open Senate meetings with prayer, and senators bowed their heads in prayer as the Dalai Lama prayed, *"With our thoughts, we make our world."*

And speaking of Congress, an Interfaith School for Military Chaplains has now been dedicated. Priest, rabbis, imams, and protestant ministers came together to dedicate themselves and the nation's first joint military multi-faith education center.

And it's coming to the Church. You may be thinking, well, that's just church organizations, secular schools, and other organizations. We expect that. No, here's just a teaser of what's going on in the faker's church community.

Christians Blending Religions

The Global Faith Forum kicked off in Texas. Hundreds of Christians, Muslims, Jews, Hindus, Buddhists, and atheists have convened at North Woods Church in Texas, in an effort to try to understand one another. Representatives of Jewish, Catholic, Protestant, Bahai, Mormon, Sikh, Vedic, Druid and Muslim beliefs in Sacramento, read scriptures from each of their religious texts, including six verses from the Quran, calling for all faiths to live in harmony. Again and again, they uttered the refrain, "Let there be peace on earth and let it begin with me."

A bishop is now urging Christians to call God Allah. A Catholic leader believes it would help ease the tensions between religions.

And now even Las Vegas is getting in on the action with their Annual Interfaith Meetings as seen here …

Speaker: *"Good evening, everyone. Our panelists this evening are, first of all representing Islam, Dr. Aslam Abdullah, who is the director of the Islamic Society of Nevada. Then we'll be hearing from our Episcopal representative, Reverend Dr. Jim Wallace, from Grace in the Desert Episcopal Church. Following Jim will be Mr. Taji Malek, representing the Sikh Faith, from Gurdwara Father Deep Singh Chi. From humanism, we have Mr. Mel Litman, who's the immediate past president of the American Humanist Association Union. From the Church of Jesus Christ of Latter-Day Saints, Mrs. Ruth Johnson is here and in addition to that she is a board member of Public Affairs Committee, is that right? And yes, of the Church of Jesus Christ of Latter-day Saints. Representing the Bahai faith is Mrs. Belva Tomasi. First of all, we assume that our religious beliefs are our most deeply held beliefs and as such we do not try to change the beliefs of others. There's no debate, no challenging, there's no defending one's beliefs in this environment. There's no proselytizing…"*

That's not Biblical. Jesus said to get out there in all the world, and what? You tell them He's the only way, the truth, the life, the only way to Heaven. Making disciples, baptizing. Excuse me? Every year this goes on in Las Vegas, our own community.

Christians are now celebrating their religious diversity on Pentecost Sunday. Christian churches across the United States are dedicating their worship to a celebration of our interfaith world.

Progressive Christians thank God for religious diversity! "We don't claim that our religion is superior to all others. We can grow closer to God and deeper in compassion – and we can understand our own traditions better – through a greater awareness of the world's religions."

Sponsored by the Center for Progressive Christianity – Pluralism Sunday will be promoted throughout churches, and participating churches will be profiled in publicity releases, creating an evangelism opportunity for your congregation. The number of people looking at The Center for Progressive Christianity's website is topping 40,000 per month! We believe Pluralism Sunday is an opportunity for progressive churches to reach some of the many people who are turned off by Christianity because of exclusivist claims some Christians make about it.

I didn't make it up. Jesus said it, **John 14:6.**

Many professing Christians are now holding universalist views. One in four professing Christians believe that all people are eventually saved or accepted by God. And an even higher proportion, 40 percent, of born-again Christians said they believe Christians and Muslims worship the same God.

The Claremont School of Theology launched a program to train leaders. "Not all Christians, Jews, and Muslims believe that their way is the only way."

"Christians, Muslims, and Jews will now have the opportunity to take classes together to learn about each other's religious traditions, to study topics that deal specifically with interfaith issues and to build bridges through coursework that assists them – our society's future religious leaders."

You thought that the Seminary takeover, in the Bible College and denominations, and spilling into the Church was bad enough, with the moral issues, at the same time they are pushing this One World Religion agenda. And it spills downhill. I think we are already seeing that, because how in the world could we already be at 70 percent? Because it's coming from here, because it's been taken over. They knew exactly what they were doing!

Dozens of churches are now promoting Islam, from Denver to Boise, Idaho, to San Francisco to even Honolulu, they're planning to send a message, "Both here at home and to the Arab and Muslim world about our respect for Islam, with a time to read the Quran during our worship services."

The Interfaith Alliance of Human Rights First is calling on Christian clergy to read portions of the Quran during their services Sunday.

In fact, churches are now letting Muslims use their facilities. Heartsong Church near Memphis is allowing Muslims to hold Ramadan prayers in its building and Aldersgate United Methodist Church in Alexandria, Virginia allowed the Islamic Circle of North America to hold regular prayer meetings in its facility.

But as one man said, "Is this what we should be doing as Christians? I don't think so!" Let's take a look …

Fox News Reports: *"Two Protestant churches are taking the heat for opening their church building to Muslims needing a place to worship, because their own facilities were either too small or under construction." "Some see it as a Christian duty, others disagree. We're back with Governor Huckabee with more on this. So, is this counter run against everything these churches stand for?"*

Governor Huckabee: *"Well, as you know, as much as I respect the autonomy of each of these local churches, you just wonder, what are they thinking? I mean, if the purpose of a church is to push forth the gospel of Jesus Christ, and then you have a Muslim group that says Jesus Christ and all the people who follow Him are a bunch of infidels who should be essentially obliterated, I guess I have a hard time understanding that. If a church is nothing more than a facility and a meeting place for any and all viewpoints, without regard to what it is, then should the church be rented* *out to show adult movies on the weekend? I mean, where does this end? How far does it go?"*

Now we had to deal with this at our old facility. I remember one time when we had a Seventh-Day Adventist guy come in, and he wanted to use our facility. And he was nice and syrupy, sweet talking, and very cordial, and I said come on into my office and let's talk. I wasn't going to let him use our facility, but I wanted to hear his spiel. So, I sat down, and he told me how they wanted to help the community. So, I said let me ask you a few questions, just to make sure I'm not getting this wrong. I asked if he believed that worshiping on Sunday is unbiblical and is actually the mark of the beast and those of us that do that … Because that is what they teach. He looked at me like, you're not supposed to know that. I told him that I had a problem with that, because why would we want to rent the facility to you when you're undermining everything that we believe in? And then we went down on the investigative judgment, and there is no assurance. They believe that when you die as a Seventh Day Adventist, you die and take a big nap. And then later down the road, what they call the investigative judgment, Jesus will look at your works and judge you then as to whether you're worthy or not to go to Heaven. That's a false gospel. It's works based. I asked him if he believed that, and then I said plus, you know we only teach the Bible here. It's just the Bible. It's the Bible and the Bible alone. But you guys follow a false prophetess called Ellen G. White, and you actually mix her words in with your version of the Bible, called the Clear Word Bible. Which the only thing clear about it is it's a perversion. And we went down the line. For some reason as we went down the line his countenance changed. And yet, still at the end he was like, "So, you going to do it?" I said, "No, I can't. It's impossible." And he got mad, and I said, "There goes your spirituality, right out of the window. And anyone worth their salt would have told you the same thing." Another time, they were building a Buddhist Temple across the street from us. They came over one time and wanted to use our facility, because they were having a big Buddhist guy coming in, and they couldn't house it. And they got all mad again.

Now why couldn't we do that? Because we are intolerant, we're bigots. "Come out from among them, be ye separate." I will witness to you. Are you hungry? I'll give you a sandwich and then tell you about Jesus too. Because that's the excuse. It's not just feeding them; you're talking about Jesus. Do you need some help? I can help you out. I'll do that, but I'm not going to allow you to use our facilities to propagate a message that's leading people straight to hell. Yet, that's what you see is going on.

Now, churches are removing their crosses. I'm not going to mention any names but there are big churches who dropped the word Christian from their name. Step one. Then there's churches today that are getting launched where there's no Christianese at all. "Journey." "Mosiac." It's like you don't want anybody to know that you are Christian. Like you're ashamed of that. That is why we said Sunrise, because it's been our name since the beginning in Sunrise Manor, where the church was born. We kept that but it's also Bible Church. It's okay to admit that you follow the Bible in your church.

But that's not all. We now even have churches removing their crosses to become more inclusive. C3Exchange was formerly known as Christ Community Church and the Rev. Ian Lawton, the church's pastor, said *"The name change, and removing the cross was designed to reflect the church's diverse members. Our community has been really open-minded for some years now. And we've had a number of Muslim people, Jewish people, Buddhists, atheists – we're just catching up to ourselves." "We honor the cross, but the cross is just one symbol of our community."*

In fact, they were so excited about it, they even videotaped it. The cross on the church is high atop a steeple. It's rather beautiful with bells under it, that are actually ringing as they are taking this video. There is this huge crane that is moving towards the cross. As the crane hooks onto the pole that the cross is set on top of, a man is disconnecting it at the bottom. The crane slowly removes the cross and lifts it out of the steeple.

Can I tell you something? That's what's wrong with America. We're removing the Cross of Christ, literally, and we're paying a heavy price for it. But folks, correct me if I'm wrong, it sure looks to me like people, even Christians, are blending together with other religions, how about you? Sounds like a One World Religion is right around the corner! And that's exactly what the Bible said would happen, when you are living in the last days. Now…here's the problem. As we saw earlier, true born-again Christians can't go along with this. We're supposed to be separate from this! Why? Because it's a lie, and God doesn't want us to be a part of a lie that encourages others to go to hell! Jesus is the only way to Heaven!

But now it's moving to Stage #2. And for those who disagree with this ecumenical, "feel good," "all religions lead to Heaven" message, they are being labeled as the Bad Guys, the Resisters, those who are ruining the chances for world peace. And therefore, they're already saying we need to get rid of them! And that's exactly what the Bible says is going to happen to those who get saved after the Rapture. You're going to wish you got saved before!

Chapter Sixteen

The Eradication of Biblical Christianity

As a short recap, we have seen that there's been, unfortunately, an invasion into the church by atheist fakers who have taken over seminaries, Bible colleges, denominations, and it all spills downhill. And they aren't just coming in and sitting there. They're actually perverting love, relationships, and any kind of immoral behavior is accepted as their definition of Biblical love. We saw if we go down that route it's going to get way worse. They have opened up Pandora's Box with pedophilia, bestiality, transgenderism - it's all twisted. They are doing it on purpose because they want to destroy our country, they want to make a ton of money off of this, and it's being used to prepare people's mindset for the transhumanist movement, and the Great Reset. The Great Reset is not just an economic reset, it's a human reset. They want to refashion humanity into what they call a Human 2.0, a non-human species. The groundwork has been laid out here in America for quite some time now.

We are to keep our mouths shut, stay within your four walls, and that's called pietism. But God says we are to be the salt, the light, and the restraining influence. We need to speak up! Resist against this evil stuff. You would think that all of this would get the Church's attention, but no, unfortunately, they've given into that, "just do your own thing and keep quiet." So, if pietism wasn't bad enough, and I'm talking about the ones who know better, who know this is wrong and not Biblical. But now the new word is Chickenism.

I didn't make the rules up, God did. I didn't make up our identity, God did. We are to be the salt, the light, the resistance. That means that we have to speak up, we have to engage. When you see evil, you speak up in love. You have to confront the culture. We are "Rebels for Jesus!" But a lot of churches say, "No, I don't want to do that." And folks, that's why I've said it for years, you better be careful…the person sitting next to you in the pew, may one day be the death of you. They might turn you into the authorities!

Now these fakers have come in with a false gospel and a false Jesus. They are saying that what we, the Church, need to be doing is promoting Black Lives Matter, Critical Race Theory and we need to repent of our white privilege. As crazy as all that is…it's warmed-over communism, that will lead to a One World Religion because that's where all this is headed. So, what are they going to do with those people who don't go along with the One World Religion? Well, you need to identify them, you need to vilify them, and you need to propagandize them in a negative way so you can round them up and get rid of them. Because you can't have any resistors in this. And we are seeing it being done right before our very eyes.

They are doing it with two filters. How are they going to get the real born-again Christians to pop their heads out? One is the Spiritual issue, that all paths lead to Heaven. As we saw, 70 percent of professing Christians believe that there is not only one way to Heaven, that Jesus is not the only way. They believe all paths lead to Heaven. So, you have to accept all behavior, all immorality, they want you to include all religions as basically the same, which we can't, **John 14:6.** That's how bad it is. But what they call that, is Interfaith. That's the world's version of all religions. They just need to come together. And they're having all these joint services.

How is the church sucking people into this? It's called ecumenism. Anybody that claims to be a Christian, we all just have to work together for a great cause, even though it's a false gospel. Anyone who objects to this will become a hater, guilty of a hate crime, and you will be identified, targeted, vilified, persecuted, then hauled away for execution. But are we really seeing signs of born-again Christians being vilified and made out to be the bad guys? Yes! First of all, let me show you how bad it is out there. I got this a couple weeks ago from one of our online viewers:

"I grew up in a Church, but I never once heard about the Rapture or Revelation. Then I went to a Conservative Bible College and still no talk of the Rapture. Then the last ten years I started listening online to you and others and I'm so blessed.

Recently, I went to a church that everyone I know goes to. They had the stool, the coffee, and the guitar, but I never heard the full gospel...not even at Easter. The Pastor talked about Friday, then Thursday, and then totally biffed it on the resurrection. I left.

I don't need coffee and cookies; I need the Bible. God Bless from Wisconsin"

But it gets worse … This is what God warned about. If we don't speak up. If we don't get serious. If you just sit there in the pews, with what I call convenience Christianity, because it's close to your house or your friends. You know it's a part of the apostate church, but you won't come out of it. They continue on because you're just sitting there supporting them. Now, I'm not saying that you're not saved. It's just that you know better.

And your support is just keeping them going. We need to come out from among them and we need to support this truth. We don't need coffee and cookies; we need the Bible.

ARTICLE

The Europeanisation Of The United States: 1% Less Christians Per Year

But here's what's going on: the Europeanisation of the United States; 1% less Christians per year. We are going backwards in America. It's getting less and less. It's been doing this for years. And the reason why I say Europeanization, is because Europe is dark. If you've ever been over there, it is dark. Talk about the extreme minority, that's the true born-again Christians. That's sad because that's where the Reformation started, right? It's crazy, but that's how fast it can turn around if you start turning away from the Scripture. And now it's happening here in America. We're going backwards.

This is Biblical Christianity on the left, but with the 'woke movement' and the chickenized churches, this is what you're getting. You're getting wimpy Christianity. And that's supposed to be the new Christian. They're better Christians. No!! It's not! We're not called to be that.

So, why are we in such a state as this? It's nature. I'm telling you, not only do people attend so-called churches that don't teach the Bible, and they turn out to be a bunch of wimps because they were never discipled, so, they don't even know the basics of Christianity. It's about the coffee and the guitar and then they go home. You punch in your timeclock and go do your worldly thing. That's bad enough, but then on top of that, you ingest nothing but secular material. You're not even in the Word of God. And did you know it's not illegal to read the Word of God outside of Sundays and Wednesdays? What a concept. You listen to the sewer pipe and then you send your kids to the sewer pipe and then you wonder why, not only are you are acting like the world, but your kids are turning away from Christ.

"When you send your kids to school to be sexualized, indoctrinated, masked and injected with poison, you need to know they are safe."

That's what has been going on for the last two years. The sexualization of the stuff has been going on a lot longer than that. And you wonder, why in the world would any Christian who says that they know what's going on, they're aware, they're not a part of this stuff, why would they keep doing it? I preach until I am blue in the face and people still send their kids back to public school. I'm sorry if you get mad at me. I don't care. I don't know how you can do it. I don't know how you can sleep at night. Do whatever it takes, make changes. Trust God. He will provide. Be obedient to God and He will make a way. Trust Him, step out in faith, sacrifice, do something. I like what Matt Walsh says:

"My responsibility is to my children and my family. The public school system cannot be saved. Even if it could, I am not sending my kids in to help with that mission. Not their job. They are not equipped. No child is. I hear parents say that they won't leave the school system because they want to fight. But it's not you doing the fighting. It's your child. And he cannot win it. You are sending him on a suicide mission. It isn't fair to him. The school system is undefeated, it changes children, children do not change it. But yes, keep feeding your kids into the meat grinder. Maybe it will be different this time. You know it won't be, but you tell yourself that. Save your own. Get them out. Let the System collapse and die."

And the way you do that is you get out! Mass exodus! But again, we have to take this seriously. This whole world is designed to get you sucked in, ultimately, and your so-called version of Christianity is heading towards a One World Religion. I told you it's going to get worse, well, it is. Because we're not being the salt, the light, and we're compromising and not taking God's truth seriously.

Decriminalize Sex with Animals: Zoophilia Pride Marchers Demand LGBTQ+ Movement Add a Z.

They want to add "Z" for Zoophilia. That's bestiality. It just keeps getting longer. This is what God warned about in **Romans 1**. We have to speak up. That's what silence is. That's what pietism is. That's what chickenism gets you. We need to speak up against the culture and say it's wrong. I'm telling you, the next one that's coming is the pedophilia one. On top of that they will add another one after that. We've seen that before. We have to speak up!

'Decriminalize Sex With Animals': Zoophilia Pride Marchers Demand LGBTQI+ Movement Add a Z

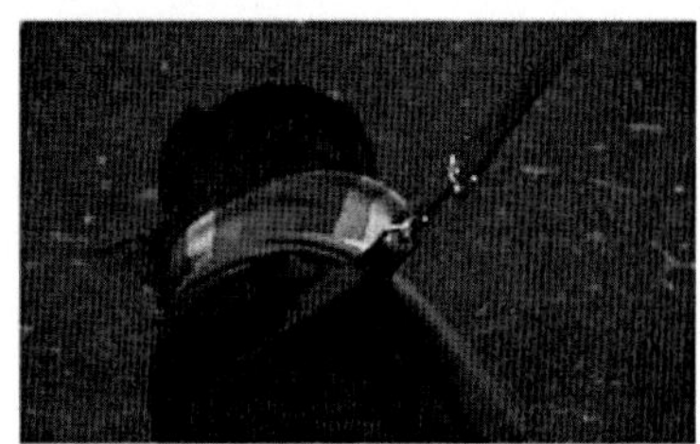

FNW

ARTICLE

Students Seek To Oust Board Of Christian School For Upholding Biblical Marriage

Now this is the one that blew me away. Again, these are all current headlines. Students Seek to Oust Board of Christian School for Upholding Biblical Marriage. Not a regular school, a Christian school, for upholding Biblical marriage. So, here's a Christian school that is doing the right thing and holding to Biblical standard, and certainly the Biblical definition of marriage between a man and a woman. Now it's the so-called Christian students who want to overthrow the leaders of that school. That's where we are at. This is the infection that is going on in the church today and this is the fruit of not doing anything about it.

Again, is there really going to be a case where true born-again Christians aren't just going to be made fun of but they're going to say, "You know what, we need to take care of you people." In fact, we know this is going to happen. But this vilification and targeting of true born-again Christians really is going to happen on a global basis just in time for the 7-year Tribulation! Where the Bible says, anyone who turns to God at that time will be turned in and executed. And these dead, fake phony Christians we just saw, they're going to go right along with it. They will turn in anybody who turns to the real One and Only God to be executed.

This is actually going to happen. This is a birth pain that Jesus told us in **Matthew 24.** There will be famines and earthquakes and wars and rumors of wars, good thing we don't see any of that. Yeah, it's all on the rise. Now, the text that is dealing with the 7-year Tribulation, that we're seeing, an increase in preparation for that, the Bible says - and is very clear - anybody who turns to God during the 7-year Tribulation (not the church, we are out of here at the Rapture), the fakers around you are going to turn you in and they are going to kill you. First of all, we hope everybody is saved, if you are reading this, but this is what you're going to get with your compromise.

You might think, "I'll be fine, I'll just go along with it, secretly." No, if you're not saved, you are going to be left behind. You'll still go to church services, because again, it's all religion. But I'm telling you, the fakers around you, if you turn to God during that time, they are going to turn you in. You better witness to the person next to you, because one day they may be the death of you. This is what's going to happen during the 7-year Tribulation. We are going to look at the evidence, that now it's not just trying to vilify Christians, now it's out there, and has been going on ever since 9/11, that Christians are the bad guys. We need to get rid of them. They are just as dangerous as those Muslim terrorists.

The context here is, Jesus is answering the question to the disciples, what are the signs of your coming? He's not talking about the Rapture; He's talking about His second coming at the end of the 7-year Tribulation. He goes through a perfect chronological order of the events of the 7-year Tribulation. So, these events that we are going to read is in the 7-year Tribulation and we're not a part of it. But the point is, do we see an increase of these things that He mentions showing us that it's got to be getting close? And I would say, absolutely yes, every single one of them.

Matthew 24:3-9: "As Jesus was sitting on the Mount of Olives, the disciples came to him privately. 'Tell us,' They said, 'when will this happen, and what will be the sign of your coming and of the end of the age?' Jesus answered: 'Watch out that no one deceives you. For many will come in My name claiming, 'I am the Christ,' and will deceive many. You will hear of wars and rumors of wars but see to it that you are not alarmed. Such things must happen, but the end is still to come. Nation will rise against nation, and kingdom against kingdom. There will be famines and earthquakes in various places. All these are the beginning of birth pains. Then you will be handed over to be persecuted and put to death, and you will be hated by all nations (a global purge) because of me. At that time, many will turn away from the faith and will betray and hate each other, and many false prophets will appear and deceive many people."

Some may say, "If you disappear in the Rapture, I'll know you were true, and I'll get saved then." Excuse me? In Revelation 20, the Bible says decapitation is coming back. They're going to chop your head off. You mean you won't accept Jesus now when it's relatively easy, and escape the whole thing, but then when your head is on the chopping block, you will? Come on! Don't be a fool! Get saved now! But it's going to go global, and they're going to hunt people down and it's horrible. The Fifth Seal in **Revelation 6** is a slaughterfest. In the Greek it means to cut up, slay it like an animal, filet it alive, very graphic, you don't want to be there. But this is going to happen. Anybody that turns to God, what's going to happen? They're not just going to be persecuted, they are going to be hated.

And again, these are the Jewish remnant who follow Christ after their temporary blindness is removed, and those who get saved after the Rapture during the 7-year Tribulation, because people can still get saved during the 7-year Tribulation because the Gospel still goes forth from multiple sources. The Two Witnesses, the 144,000 male Jewish Witnesses, the Angel of God who proclaims the Eternal Gospel, and anything you and

I might leave behind.

In fact, betray is the Greek word "paradidomi," and it literally means, "To turn you in, to turn you over to the authorities." That's what these fakers we are witnessing before our very eyes, who are taking over the church are going to do. But for you and me here today, do we see any signs of Christian persecution and hatred around the world, to the point where people actually want to kill the born-again Christian who are holding to just basic Biblical Christianity? There is right and wrong with moral behavior. There is such a thing as sin, and we are not going to go along with "all religions are the same." I didn't say it, Jesus did, **John 14:6**. That's just basic Christianity. So, do we see people who hold to that, you and I, being vilified as dangerous horrible people? Absolutely.

And the 1st way we know we're headed for this global persecution of Christianity, is that the propaganda is already here. Take a lesson from Hitler. If you don't know your history, you are doomed to repeat it. It's what he did with the Jewish people. He didn't just get into office, and then the next week start getting the Jewish people. For years he vilified them. Joseph Goebbels and others, they used Hollywood, or their version of Hollywood, they took over the media, radio, newspapers and promoted movies. They vilified the Jewish people, they were the scum of the earth, they had lice, they were vermin, they were genetically inferior, and they were ruining everything. That was anti-Semitism. Now it's the same mentality. And as incredible as this may sound, it's already open season on true born-again Christians, even here in America and those who will not go along with the enemies in the Church who are saying that you have to go along with all behaviors and all religions.

Right now, our society now says we are being judgmental, because we say that our society is not good enough for God. But in reality, it's not us, it's the Bible. The Bible says that "no one is righteous, no not one." (**Romans 3**) "But you're going to ruin my self-esteem." Precisely! That's their problem. They say that we're being arrogant because we think we've found the only way to eternal life. But I didn't say that Jesus did. "He is the way, the truth, and the life, and that nobody comes to the Father except through Him." **(John 14:6)**

Then they say that we're being narrow-minded, because if we practiced what we preached, we would see all people worthy of salvation. No! The Bible says that "no one is worthy, no not one." **(Romans 3)**

Then they say we're being ignorant because we ignore other paths to enlightenment for truth. But that's not what Jesus said. He said He was the ultimate source of Truth; not one of many. **(John 14:6)**

Then they say that we're being old-fashioned because we cling to obsolete myths. But the Bible says it's God's truth we are to cling to, not a bunch of feel-good made-up stories to create a One World Religion. **(2 Timothy 4)**

And just to make sure that we sound really bad in the public arena, we are now being labeled, listen to the propaganda, with such terms as, *"psycho groups," "harmful and dangerous sects," "obstructionist right-wing fanatics who embrace a message of hate and fear"* (quote from Bill Clinton), *"mongers of hate who preach their anger* (quote from Texas Governor Ann Richards), *"Intolerant, using subterranean tactics"* (quote from Congressman Vic Fazio), *"unchristian religious right who are selling our children out in the name of religion"* (quote from U.S. Surgeon General Joycelyn Elders), *"A greater threat than the old threat of communism"* (New York Times writer), *"fire-breathing radicals," "merchants of hate," "fanatics,"* and even *"militants and bigots,"* and of course *"right wing fundamental extremists."*

Hey, wait a second. That's the same terminology they're using for the Muslim terrorists that everybody says we need to get rid of. Uh huh! Exactly! They've been using the same propaganda on us and so that means we're next! Don't believe me? Check out this alleged quote from Janet Reno, Attorney General under Bill Clinton, who gives us her definition of a cultist:

Janet Reno*: "A cultist is one who has a strong belief in the Bible and the Second Coming of Christ; who frequently attends Bible studies; who has a high level of financial giving to a Christian cause; who home schools their children; who has accumulated survival foods and has a strong belief in the Second Amendment; and who distrusts big government. Any of these may qualify [a person as a cultist] but certainly more than one [of these] would cause us to look at this person as a threat, and his family as being in a risk situation that qualifies for government interference."*

In other words, they'll come and take away your kids, as we already saw before. And this is still just the tip of the iceberg! Let me give you some other examples, because it's everywhere. Hollywood, media, politics, the current administration.

Richard Dawkins, in his TV special, *The Root of all Evil*: *"The scriptural roots of the Judeo-Christian moral edifice are cruel and brutish. When we look closely at the Bible, you find a system of morals which any civilized person today should surely find poisonous."* He said about a church service, *"It reminds him of a Nuremberg Nazi rally, that Nazi leader and propagandist Dr. Goebbels would have been proud."* He later goes on to say, *"Fundamentalist American Christianity is attacking science. But what is it offering instead? A mirror image of Islamic extremism. An American Taliban."* The next scene on that program showed the burning towers of the World Trade Center in New York City on 9/11.

We are called an American Taliban because we attack science. I don't have a problem with science, I just like the truth. He can sit there and say the whole universe, and everything came into existence out of nothing. Last time I checked, if there was ever a time that we had nothing, what would we have today? Nothing. Well, it all started with a tiny ball of dirt. And that little, teeny tiny ball of dirt, everything was compressed in there, it blew up into what we have today. Well, that's a really compressed ball of dirt to blow up into an entire universe, number one. But number two, it's like come on, it's common sense!

Now you're saying because it's illogical to say it came from nothing and that's why we believe in the beginning God … He's something, He created out of nothing. So, all you have to do is ask these guys, "Well, that's interesting. We came from a ball of dirt, where'd the dirt come from? It's got to come from somewhere." Oh, you're an American Taliban, how dare you attack science. Again, it's propaganda and we're the evil ones.

But he's not the only one who thinks Christians are the new Terrorists, so does Rosie O'Donnell. She said that you and I are just as big a terrorist as the Muslim terrorists.

ABC, the View, host: *"Those attacks, that is widespread and if you take radical Islam and you want to talk about what's going on there."*

Rosie O'Donnell: *"Wait a minute. Radical Christianity is just as threatening as radical Islam. In a country like America.* (Applause) *Where we have a separation of church and state. A democracy."*

ABC, the View. host: *"We're not bombing ourselves."*

Fox and Friends: *"Her exact quote was, Rosie O'Donnell, about two months ago, she said radical Christianity is just as threatening as radical Islam. And in the last hour we received an email from somebody who said, 'You seem to forget, in the land of radical Islam, Rosie, the woman, the lesbian, would either be hung or stoned to death. In the world of radical Islam there would be no View, no show with independent opinionated women."*

And dare I say, every time she got mad and said she was moving to Canada, they should actually make her follow through with it. How many times they've done that. I'm moving to Canada. We're still waiting. We'll take up a collection for your plane ticket. But she's not the only one.

Al Green, Texas Democrat, during a Homeland Security hearing: *"Expand hearings on radical Islam to include a hearing on the radicalization of Christians."*

Now think about that. They get specials and all that stuff. These people send their kids, or they get exposed on the internet, and they get radicalized. They become a Muslim extremist and they want to blow up people and kill people. He used the exact same terminology on us. So that people who come here, now we're responsible for radicalizing them.

University Professor in Australia: *"Incompetent design, as I call it, is an anti-intellectual, post-modernist mechanism for snaring the ill-educated into Protestant fundamentalism. In front of bars they're talking about archbishops and politicians 'running scared' and not condemning 'Christian Wahabbism' the same way that moderate Muslim leaders don't condemn Islamic terrorists."*

Sheila Jackson, Representative: *"Christian militants might try to bring down the country and that such groups need to be investigated."*

I wonder if that's why, now that the Obama part two administration is in, you're doing exactly what Obama did the first time. Remember when he used the IRS to go after the Tea Party Movement? And what's this administration? Basically, Obama part two. They are weaponizing the IRS doing the exact same thing again. It's nothing new under the sun. And she's not the only one. Again, it's open season on Christians today! Let's take a look.

Erroll Southers, Barack Obama's nominee to head the Transportation Safety Administration: *"Most of the domestic groups that we have to pay attention to here are white supremacist groups. They are anti-government, in most cases are anti-abortion, they are usually survivalist types in nature, identity oriented. Those groups are groups that claim to be extremely anti-government and Christian identity oriented."*

Josh Zepps, Huff Post TV Reports: *"The separate operation of church and state is fundamental to American life, but what about church and military? A new report by a national security expert says that fundamentalist Christianity is rampant in the U.S. armed forces and that military leaders overtly promote Evangelical Christianity."*

Jim Parco, professor of Economics at Colorado College: *"You actually have a system that actually is creating religious fundamentalists and that's what's concerning to me."*

Sarah Primrose: *"The only question that needs to be asked is 'Do these fundamentalist's beliefs and associated behavior compromise our missions abroad?' If yes, we must discourage or ban the encouragement of the spread of this brand of Christianity in the military."*

Rachel Maddow, MSNBC Reports: *"What we are learning about the religious beliefs of this militia group makes them seem a little bit like a cult; like a standalone religious oddity. But some of the things they are obsessed with, fighting the Antichrist, avoiding the Mark of the Beast, the Pre-tribulation Rapture, all this stuff. This isn't a set of beliefs that is specific to this one cult. These beliefs were actually sort of characteristic of a broader movement, aren't they?"*

Fox News Reports: *"Andre Codrescu, a commentator for the program 'All Things Considered' mocked a Christian pamphlet about the doctrine of the Rapture, the Ascension into Heaven. 'The evaporation of four million (people) who believe in this crap would leave the world a better place.'"*

Townhall.com/Blog: Guest: *"The young man, Faisal Shahzad, in Times Square, who tried to blow up innocent people, that he doesn't know of. These guys are acting on conviction. Somehow, the idea got into their minds to kill other people, is a great thing to do and that they would be rewarded."*

Host: *"But Christians do that every single day, in this country.*

Guest: *"Do they blow up people?"*

Host: *"Yes, Christians, every day."*

Exactly where? But do people ever test what the media says? We blow people up just like those Muslim terrorists, every day? You better not go to Sunrise Bible Church; they are going to radicalize you. You better go to that really big giant one down the street, that loves everybody. I'm telling you, that's what's going on. Propaganda. We're dangerous, we're the cultist, we're the terrorist, we're going to kill our kids. Hitler must be proud of our media.

Eboo Patel, Obama's faith advisor: *"Christian totalitarians, those who believe in only one correct interpretation of their religion, are as dangerous as 'Al-Qaida.'"*

In fact, the hatred towards Christianity has gotten so bad, that they are now offering 'Fundamentalist Workshops,' where former Christians can come and be 'rescued' from their religion. It's called, 'Release and Reclaim.' It's being headed up by a Berkeley psychologist named Marlene Winell who wrote a book called 'Leaving the Fold.'

Marlene Winell: *"Their God was a capricious, vindictive, punishing figure. Now they need help trusting themselves. Fundamentalism shares a belief in original sin, a final judgment day, and a reliance on the Bible as the literal word of God. That's a damaging belief."* She is now calling on, *"The help of professionals to study and treat the recovering adherents as they do other traumas and addictions."* You know, like in a virus or some bad habit like drugs or smoking or something.

Richard Dawkins: *"I think of religion as a dangerous virus. It's a virus, which is transmitted partly through teachers and clergy, but also down the generations from parent to child to grandchild. Children are especially vulnerable to infection by the virus of religion."*

And of course, Christianity.

The United States Department of Homeland Security issued its "Right Wing Extremism: Current Economic and Political Climate Fueling Resurgence in Radicalization and Recruitment" Report. This report alleges that a violent "right wing extremist" movement is trying to take over the nation. According to the definitions in these reports, Bible believing Christians are now being labeled as "right wing extremists." And their strategies are reminiscent of Hitler's "Enabling Powers," which the Third Reich used after the Parliament building was burned down by "terrorists." These "Enabling Powers" gave Hitler the legal power to profile and arrest anyone who was even suspected of being critical of the Nazi Party, and it enabled Hitler to grab control of Germany in just a matter of months killing millions of Jewish people and Christians.

And if you're wondering if you'll ever be qualified as a terrorist, listen to this. According to our own current government, any one of the following beliefs could classify an individual or groups as a terrorist.

Pro-life
Critical of the United Nations
Critical of the New World Order
Critical of the Federal Reserve
Homosexual marriage
Oppose the North American Union (which they say officially does not exist)

But not only is the border issue being done deliberately, and part of the reason why, is because statistically the people who come over from the borders and have been, for the past two years, being inserted all over the United States of America. A lot of it per capita, is they're going into Republican states because of per capita statistics. Most of those people are given the right to vote, which they aren't American citizens. And I don't think they should have a right to vote in America if you're not an American citizen, you need to do it the right way, the legal way and that's common sense. They are given the right to vote, but statistically, the high percentage is that they vote Democrat. Because they were the ones that gave them all the free stuff and got them over here. So, it's a subversion tactic to take over those areas and of course one big area is Florida as well as Texas. I don't know if you remember the last election. In Florida, DeSantis just barely won. Of course, there was a ton of cheating going on but still he barely won. So, you plug that area with people that are going to vote the other way - so, there's a subversion there.

Another thing that is going on with that aspect, that's part of it and that's not the whole big picture. The big picture is, if you think these guys have given up on this idea of a North American Union where the United States, Canada, and Mexico are going to merge into one economic union, you're fooling yourself. This is the other big thing that is going on. We, the American culture, are being flooded as fast as it can with people who don't know anything about the American culture. They don't know anything about our way of life, the Constitution to support that, American Sovereignty, the Judeo-Christian ethic that our country was built upon. None of that stuff. So, it's a flooding of that to create this mixture, so that eventually there's not enough people to speak up so that when the hammer comes down and they say we need to combine, just like the European Union, wouldn't that be great? We'll become stronger and better and all that stuff. That's the other big picture that's going on. So, they are still pushing for that North American Union.

Critical of the income tax
Oppose illegal immigration
Fear Foreign powers such as Communist China, Iran, Russia and India
Critical of any of President Obama's policies (abortion, homosexual marriage, etc.)
Concerned about RFID chips
Belief in Bible prophecy or "End of Time Prophecies"

As one man shares: *"What is interesting about the above list, is that a great deal of it has to with things that have nothing to do with the individual nation. The only possible reason any national government would be concerned about its citizen's objecting to things like the New World Order, world government, the United Nations, homosexual marriage, a regional global government like the North American Union,* *abortion, RFID chips and belief in end time prophecies, is because this is what they are planning to promote in the near future. Otherwise, why be bothered about it?" And he goes on to say: "I would suggest to you that Bible prophecy is being fulfilled far faster than most of us realize, and this is why governments around the world are concerned about these things."*

Now, one more thing. Propaganda. We're talking about making us look like the bad guy. They're also producing, just to make sure everybody's clear and gets the message, that we are just as dangerous as the Muslim extremists because we believe our way is the only way. And we won't go along with this false love of accepting anything and everything. They are producing shows and they have been for a while, lumping this all together - the Jewish extremists, the Muslim extremists, and the Christian extremists. Now, remember why they're doing specifically those three things. Because all three of them are monotheistic religions. Meaning there's only one God. But that's the stick in the mud. You can't have a plural One World Religion when somebody says no, only One. So, they have to vilify all three. That's exactly what they are doing. Take a look at each comment made by various people interviewed.

"The Scripture is a blueprint to life and living."

"Our role is to redeem the entire world."

"And the stakes are high."

"Do you really wish that you could have been martyred?"
"Yes, martyrdom was my biggest wish."

"What they have in common, Jews, Christians and Muslims is the belief that modern society has lost its way."

"They're raping virgin teenage America on the sidewalk and everybody's walking by and acting like everything's okay."

"The problem we have here with civilization is that if we don't offer the man where to go, he doesn't know his place in life."

"The people who don't keep the Torah, don't understand the meaning of being Jews. They're wasting their life."

"They say God is the answer."

"I would like to see America become the nation under God again."

"But their battle to save the world has caused anger, division, and fear."

"I believe that Islam is a real threat."

"Something's gone wrong and we've too closely fused politics and our faith."

"I'm Christiane Amanpour in Jerusalem, a place sacred to Christians, Muslims, and Jews. Each has zealous followers driven to change the world. They are God's warriors, and this is how they are shaping the 21st century. Over the last 30 years religion has exploded as a powerful political force. With armies of believers determined to fight for their faith. In the United States, the Christian right forged an agenda that would transform the political landscape."

Pat Robertson: *"We set a 10-year program to have a born-again Christian in the White House."*

Christiane Amanpour: *"In Israel, a small band of religious settlers began a quest that would change the face of the Holy Land."*

Jimmy Carter: *"There's no doubt in any rational analyst's mind that the settlements are the major obstacle of peace."*

Christiane Amanpour: *"And in Muslim countries, a spiritual awakening sparked the rise of political Islam and an extreme fringe who would* *become the world's nightmare."*

"When you find a sport and die for, and kill others for, that's the scary part, that's why we often take it seriously."

And notice who's lumped in with those dangerous monotheistic religions who blow people up. It's us. Because we're the ones causing the trouble in all the world. If we would, just like the other real Christians, (the fake ones), all get along. All religions, just stop with this, that you can be who you want to be stuff, that's hurting the planet. But again, it isn't just that they're bringing that out, what do they make us look like? Dangerous freakos.

Now, one group that is not helping things, is the charismatic community. Not all of them, but a lot of them believe that they are going to take over the government. It's called Dominionism. It's a lie. It's not what the Scripture teaches. They are going to take over the world. They've got these seven pillars, these seven mountains, they are going to take over the world and basically Christianize it, and then Jesus can come back. That's not what the Bible says. You're not going to create peace on the planet. Only Jesus Christ, the Prince of Peace, is going to have peace on the planet. And that is after He comes back, after pouring out His wrath for 7 years on the planet at the end of the 7-year Tribulation. That's what they teach, but the problem is they use terms that the world uses and makes it look like we are radicalizing the kids and we're dangerous, freakos.

And now they are making documentaries against these entities, saying that this is Christianity and they're radicalizing kids to be modern day radical warriors.

Clip from Movie Jesus Camp

Teacher #1: *"This is a sick old world. Kids you've got to change. Boys and girls can change the world, absolutely."*

At the beginning of the day the children recite the Pledge of Allegiance.

Teacher #2: *"There are two kinds of people in the world. People who love Jesus and people who don't."*

The children are performing for the parents. They are singing and dancing with sticks, like Ninja warriors. Their faces are painted black/green/red and they are dressed in black.

Teacher #1: *"Where should we be putting our focus? I'll tell you where our enemies are putting it. They're putting it on the kids. How long have you been a Christian?"* She asks one of the boys.

The student: *"At five I got saved. I just wanted more of life."*

Parent: *"They're going to Palestine, and they're taking their kids to camps like we take our kids to Bible camps, and they're putting hand grenades in their hands"*

Young female student #1: *"There's excitement, but there's a peace about it too. It's really cool."*

Female student #2: *"I really feel that we're a key generation to Jesus coming back and we're a generation that needs to rise up and run with that baton."*

Leader/speaker: *"How many of you want to be those who would give up their lives for Jesus?"* The children in the audience raise their hands, yell, and the parents all have big smiles on their faces. They are so proud that their children are willing to die for what they believe."

Student #3: *"We are being trained to be God's Army."*

Leader/speaker: *"We are the beginning of a movement. Praise our righteous judges. (He tells the kids) There's a new church, like this one, every two days in America. Twenty-five percent of the American* *population. That's about 80 million people. If the Evangelicals vote, they can determine the election. They've taken over the White House, Congress, the Judiciary for a generation."*

Parent: *"This is the tip of the iceberg."*

As the children are cheering and singing and praising, tears are running down their faces.

Leader/speaker: *"Are you a part of it or not?"*

Change that from Jesus Camp to Jewish Camp. Don't you see? We are so dangerous. We're just as dangerous as those Islamic terrorists who brainwash their kids in camp and teach them to be an army who blows things up! Now is that some serious propaganda or what? Do you see how "dangerous" we are? We're training our kids to be like those Islamic terrorists. Do you see the justification to get rid of us, the real ones? And promote the fake liberal ones as "true good guys" instead of us. Why? Because they'll go along with a One World Religion. And that's why we're seeing T-shirts like this. It says, "Exterminate Christians, one bullet at a time." You may not fall for this, but the world is. And can I tell you something? The fakers are too. And we know where it's headed. They're going to be left behind because they are fakers. Anybody in the 7-year Tribulation who had the audacity to turn away from the antichrist system, they're going to turn you in and they're going to kill you.

But that's not all. The 2nd way we know we're headed for a global persecution of Christians, is that the merging is already here. I don't know about you, it's a good thing that we're not seeing that the Church is merging with this One World Religion which is already in high gear. And again, as we saw last time, they want us to believe that it doesn't matter what you believe. They say all religions can be merged into One - all religions lead to heaven. And the Vatican wants to be the headquarters for it! In fact, speaking of headquarters, we already saw before how the World's Religious Leaders are right now calling for a United Nations of Religions. Where some global entity would control the world's religions just like the United Nations controls all the World's governments. Which again is what the Vatican is promoting right now. In fact, the Pope's over there praying with the three monotheistic religions encouraging them to come together as one!

The video clip begins with Pope Francis greeting the different leaders. This is the final days of his Middle East trip. He is standing next to Netanyahu.

Narrator: *"He prayed and laid a wreath at Jerusalem's Holocaust Museum. He visited the grave of the father of modern Israel, Theodore Herzl and met with the two Chief Rabbis of Jerusalem and paid courtesy calls on the Israeli President and Prime Minister. Earlier the Pope met with the Grand Mufti of Jerusalem at the Haram El Sharif, saying a visit to the Holy Land would not be complete without such a meeting."*

Pope Francis: *"I make a heartfelt plea to all people and to all communities who look to Abraham. May we respect and love one another as brothers and sisters."*

Narrator: *"Rabbi Arthur Schneier from the United States praised the Pope's visit."*

Rabbi Arthur Schneier: *"Unfortunately, those religious leaders who seek to divide it. The fact that the Pope is here visiting Israel and also patriarch Bartholomew, here is really a milestone in interfaith relations."*

Narrator: *"On Sunday evening Pope Francis met with Eastern Orthodox leaders at the church of the Holy Sepulcher on the site that many believe Jesus Christ was crucified. Patriarch Bartholomew, the spiritual leader of* *the Orthodox Christians, lamented racial discrimination and religious extremism in contemporary society."*

Bartholomew: *"In the face of such conditions, love the others, the different others. The followers of other faiths and other confessions."* He also made it over to the place to plant a tree.

Ahhh, isn't that sweet! They're planting an olive tree together. I wonder if the antichrist is going to come by and water it! But he's been doing this for years pushing for all three religions to merge together! So, as the Great Reset guys, Klaus Schwab, the World Economic Forum and all the global elites are building this One World Government, One World Economy, cashless society, Mark of the Beast system, what's the other big pillar in Revelation? A One World Religion. The Vatican has been working on that for years and once you get that, they are all being drawn in under the headship of the Vatican to control it all. In fact, the Pope has so watered everything down that he wants everyone to be a part of this global religion - even atheists!

Marc Lamont Hill, Huff Post Live: *"Good news for you atheists out there, Jesus is still going to redeem you. During his homily and Wednesday Mass, Pope Francis emphasized the importance of doing good as a principle that unites all humanity."*

Pope Francis: *"The Lord has redeemed all of us, all of us, with the Blood of Christ: all of us, not just Catholics. Everyone! Even the atheists. Everyone!"*

TBS Reports: *"Yep, Pope Francis said atheists are still eligible to go into Heaven. And to return the favor, atheists said that Popes are still eligible to go into a void of nothingness."*

Daily Brief: *"Apparently the new Pope Francis had really gone off the rail to the table duties and has continued subbing off this dangerous peace and compassion. He was quoted as saying the Lord has redeemed us all, all of us, with the Blood of Christ, all of us, not just Catholics, everyone,* *even the atheists. Everyone. Hey guys, we did it, we're all going to Heaven. Even you right there. Good work, world, it looks cool, it's really cool, it's a really good day, like the Pope is printing off a whole bunch of get out of jail free cards and distributing them to everyone."*

Today Show Reports: *"NBC's Anne Thompson is at the Vatican. Good morning."*

Anne Thompson: *"Good morning, Natalie. You thought that was extraordinary, perhaps his most interesting comments came when asked about a gay lobby. He said he had never met anybody in the Vatican that had gay on their business cards, and he said if someone is gay and they are searching for the Lord, who am I to judge. He said people should not be marginalized."*

CNN Reports: *"As a lesbian and a Catholic, Cleo Meyer, could never have imagined being this happy among fellow Catholics. Cleo married Donna, they had a child and found a Catholic church in Atlanta that accepted them. For this couple, the words of Pope Francis on not judging or condemning homosexuals is a divine sign that they are welcome in the Catholic faith."*

Cleo Meyer: *"I just see an olive branch being extended for things that may not have been previously from other Popes, from the position of the church and that's very refreshing and it gives us hope."*

CNN Reports: *"Parishioners say by advocating deep compassion over harsh judgment, he's bringing its flock a step closer towards its divine calling."*

And apparently, that divine calling is to form a One World Religion that anyone can join - even atheists and homosexuals! That's not what the Bible says!

1 Corinthian 6:9-11 "Or do you not know that the unrighteous will not inherit the kingdom of God? Do not be deceived; neither fornicators, nor idolaters, nor adulterers, nor effeminate, nor homosexuals, nor thieves, nor the covetous, nor drunkards, nor revilers, nor swindlers, will inherit the kingdom of God. Such were some of you; but you were washed, but you were sanctified, but you were justified in the name of the Lord Jesus Christ and in the Spirit of our God."

But that's not all – the Pope also said that it is dangerous to think you can even have a direct relationship with Jesus apart from the Catholic Church!

Pope Francis spoke before an audience of 33,000 people saying, *"There is no such thing as 'do-it-yourself' Christians or 'free agents' when it comes to faith. It is a 'dangerous temptation' to believe that one can have a personal, direct, immediate relationship with Jesus Christ without communion with and the mediation of the church. (i.e., the Catholic Church)."*

In other words, you can't be saved apart from the Catholic Church, and of course, this new up and coming One World Religion. But man! It's one thing for the Catholic Church and the Pope to do this, but good thing the Protestant Church isn't falling for this lie! And you know why we are called Protestants, we protested against the lies of the false gospel, the works-based system of keeping the sacrament in order to be saved. False gospels lie of sacerdotalism. We protested against that and broke away from the Catholic church. That's why in Europe, which unfortunately now has gone completely backwards, that's why our fellow brothers and sisters in Christ who broke away from that and actually got saved by actually reading the Bible. The Catholic church in 1229 A.D. deliberately kept the scripture, if you could even find a copy of the scripture. Most people didn't have it. Certainly not the common Joe because it was very expensive. Pre-Gutenberg press by the way. Here's your history lesson for the day. And they kept it in Latin which nobody could read. So, even if you could find a copy of the Bible, you couldn't read it. It was like, hey, this is a Bible that's in Chinese. I don't speak Chinese. So, it doesn't do you any good. They did it on purpose to keep you in the dark. Well, the Protestants protested against it. They got saved and they were saying they could read Latin, the common Joe couldn't, so they began to translate the Bible in English and then began to make copies and distribute it.

You know what happened? The Catholic church hunted them down, they exterminated them, they killed them, they murdered them, they drowned them, they burned them alive at the stake, they tortured them and yet people say we need to work with those guys. And they haven't changed. And they will not change their beliefs. It's crazy. But again, I'm so glad that the Protestant church is never going to go back and work with that. Well, folks, I hate to burst your bubble, but not only are Protestant churches caving in on these issues, but they're now being seduced by the Pope himself to join him in his One World religion.

Believe it or not, Kenneth Copeland, who by the way is a false teacher and Word of Faith heretic, recently piped in a private message from the Pope himself to his so-called Protestant church. And the Bishop who showed up to announce this private message from the Pope to this church made some chilling remarks. Check it out!

Kenneth Copeland: *"You're going to talk about tonight for a long time. Tony, come on up, would you please. Tony Palmer. Some of you may know Tony. Tony and I go way back. But he's going to be telling you the story. I asked him to come give his testimony. He's got a special message for us tonight."*

Tony Palmer: *"Thank you for giving me the opportunity to spend a couple of moments introducing to you something really, really special, and historic."* [Applause]

Pope Francis: *"Dear Brothers and Sisters, excuse me, because I speak in Italian. And let's pray to the Lord that He unites us all. Come on, we are Brothers. Let's give each other a spiritual hug and let God complete the work that He has begun. And this is a miracle; the miracle of unity has begun. I ask you to bless me, and I bless you. From Brother to Brother, I embrace you. Thank you."* [Applause]

Tony Palmer: *"This brought an end to the protest of Luther. Brothers and Sisters, Luther's protest is over, it's yours. And I get a bit cheeky here because I challenge my Protestant Pastor friends. If there is no more protest, how can there be a Protestant church? Maybe now we're all Catholics again."* [And they laughed]

"Luther's protest is over - how about yours?" Can I translate that for you? Won't you join us "Protestant Church" in forming a One World Religion? Exactly like the Bible said would happen, when you are living in the last days! It's happening now, even in the protestant Church! But you might be thinking, "Well okay, that's just Kenneth Copeland. He's a false teacher, we all know that, what do you expect? I'm sure he's the only one doing this, right?" Wrong! Many of the people from the Charismatic Movement are doing the exact same thing. They're meeting with the Pope, chumming up with him, giving him high-fives, trying to figure out how we can all get along.

Charismatics with the Pope

Here we see in order, John & Carol Arnott, Brian Stiller, Kenneth Copeland, Pope Francis, Thomas Schirrmacher, Geoff Tunnicliffe, James & Betty Robison, and Bishop Tony Palmer:

And it's one thing to meet with the Pope, but the purpose of the meeting was to discuss "Unity in Diversity."

Do we have Unity with Jehovah's Witnesses? Why not? The Bible says, absolutely not, because they have a false gospel. If you have to earn your way to Heaven that's not the gospel. So, that's a salvific issue. That's not a secondary issue. That's self-ification, we don't like cancer. Do we have conferences together with Mormons? Why not? Because they have a false gospel. Because it's a works-based salvation. Not the gospel. That's not a secondary issue, that's a salvific issue. So, why would we work together quote, "Unity and Diversity" with Catholicism, that is also a works-based false gospel? It's nuts what's going on, but that's what these guys are doing.

And then you have this strange statement being made by James Robison, who is seen here giving the Pope a high five. *"The enemy has kept many Christians from loving one another as Christ loves us and have failed to recognize the importance of supernatural unity even with all of the unique diversity. This week I was blessed to be part of perhaps an unprecedented moment between evangelicals and the Catholic Pope. I believe I am beginning to witness what Jesus prayed for. Years ago, God told me to reach out beyond the safe, comfortable walls of my Southern Baptist tradition, beyond denominational barriers and seek to bring the family together. Oh, how I hope, and I pray that is the case. Dear God, please let it happen and let me gladly be a part of it."*

Yeah, we're supposed to be one in Christ but not at the expense of the truth. We're not one with a false gospel. We can't! Come out from among them. The Scripture is very clear. What does Christ have in common with Belial, darkness with light? We read that passage before. But the Bible is our unity. You stick to that and what God says. So, their unity is a false unity.

He wants to be a part of what? Merging with the One World Religion. That's what we're seeing. So-called Protestants are going along with that. Looks to me like somebody's falling for this One World religion hook, line, and sinker! But you might be thinking, "Well okay, that's just the Charismatic Movement. They have some aberrant teachings anyway, what do you expect? I'm sure they're the only so-called Protestant denomination doing this." Wrong answer! Now we have people like Beth Moore hanging out with these same Charismatics, including James Robison who's high fiving the Pope, and she's making some odd comments about Catholics.

I remember the first time I showed this video clip, I was at a conference in Florida. You would have thought that I said your grandmother is ugly. I had ladies, immediately after I had got done talking, make a beeline for the podium and they tried to shred me apart, for sharing what I'm about to share with you. How dare you! I said, "Listen, that's why I showed you the video. This is what they said, I didn't say it. And I didn't get this from Joeschmoe.com." But here's Beth Moore linking us with the Catholics:

This clip opens with Beth Moore on stage with different groups of ladies sitting behind her. She starts telling the audience what each one of these groups represent.

"Right over here to my right you see First United Methodist Church. Right behind them you would find just down the street, Christ the Redeemer, Lutheran Church. Every one of my sisters in this area attend the Lutheran Church. It thrills me. And these all attend the Methodist Church. I can't tell you how I love that kind of diversity. What I have asked these ladies to

do right here, [the group of ladies in the center] *now this is a little bit different because they do go to different churches. But what I asked them to represent tonight to us is an African American church that we're going to call Mt. Zion Missionary Baptist Church. Is that good? Did I do good? Yes. Right back here, I want you to meet* [the group of ladies on the left] *Saint Anne's Catholic Church. These ladies come every single Sunday, although they don't go to one Catholic church, every single one of them attend a Catholic church probably right here in Houston, and I am thrilled that they are here. What I've asked my sisters here, actually they represent many different churches, but they represent One Church in our midst tonight. These are our sisters that attend different charismatic churches in the city. But tonight, they attend Abundant Life Church. Is that good?"*

What did she do? Very subtly, she combines Catholicism as if they're Christians just like the rest of us. I've got a problem with that. Why would you do that? That's not Biblical. And guess what? It's okay to call that out. It's okay to call people's names out. Did you know that? That's why I didn't just quote an article. Am I making it up? No, she did it. Paul called them by name, Philetus, Hymenaeus and Alexander for their false teachings. And it's been recorded in Scripture for 2,000 years for everybody to see. John called out Diotrephes by name, still in Scripture to this day for false teaching and somehow these same entities also say that you and I have no right to call anybody out by name. What Bible are you reading? The Bible says I need to speak up and I need to warn people. Because we all know it's very effective as shepherds, you're supposed to not just love, care for, and feed your flock, but you're supposed to warn the flock when the ferocious wolves are coming in. You've got to warn them. We all know it's a very effective technique when you say, "Hey, you know what, there's somebody out there - just thought I'd let you know. And they're teaching a false teaching. If you ever come across them, whatever you do, don't you follow their teachings." How does that help? You give a name; you give an example, and here's why you should reject that person.

But you might be thinking, "Well okay, that's just one so-called Protestant lady in the church. We all know that Protestant pastors aren't going to fall for this baloney!" Really? You might want to pay attention to what Joel Osteen said about the Pope.

Newscaster: *"More than 60,000 people will pack Yankee Stadium tomorrow for a night of hope. It's a huge event featuring Lakewood Church Pastor Joel Osteen and his wife Victoria. Before he arrived in New York, Osteen paid a special visit to the Vatican, where he met with Pope Francis. Tonight, Osteen shares the experience with Local 2 News Anchor Dominic Saksa."*

Dominic Saksa: *"As we sat down and talked about the preparations for the big event, Joel revealed to me an incredible opportunity, he just had to meet Pope Francis."*

Joel Osteen: *"I just felt very honored and very humbled seeing the Pope give the mass to a hundred thousand people that day. You could see he has such a heart to help people. I love the fact that he has made the church more inclusive, not trying to make it smaller but to make it larger to take everybody in. So, that just resonates with me."*

Dominic Saksa: *"With Rome behind him, Joel feels he has divine inspiration fueling his message for tomorrow night."*

But you might be thinking, "Well okay, that's Joel Osteen. We all know that he refuses to stand on the truth period. And he only preaches fluffy stuff. There's a lot of self-isms, learn to be a better you, which is the number one law of Satanism. But not the rest of our Protestant pastors! They'll never do this!" Really? You might want to listen to what Rick Warren said about the Pope. I remember when I came across this video clip. He's being interviewed by the Catholic EWTN, that's their big satellite channel. Frankly, this video is not just alarming, it's disturbing.

Interviewer: *"What is your secret to reaching people every day, every week, not only in your writing, but when you speak to them. What is it? What is this communication gift, if you will, if you could decode it?"*

Rick Warren: *"The main thing is, love always reaches people. It's authenticity, humility – Pope Francis is the perfect example of this. He is doing everything right. You see, people will listen to what we say if they like what they see. As our new Pope he was very, very symbolic and, you know, his first mass with people of AIDS and a kissing of the deformed man, loving the children. This authenticity, this humility, the caring for the poor, this is what the whole world expects us Christians to do. And then they go, 'Oh, that's what a Christian does.' There was a headline here in Orange County and I loved it. I saved it. It said if you love Pope Francis, you'll love Jesus."*

Interviewer: *"That was the headline?"* [they laugh]

Rick Warren: *"That was the headline. I saved it. I showed it to a group of priests that I was speaking to a while back."*

Interviewer: *"I love that. Now when I walked into your office, you have three images and personal notes that confront the person walking into your office. There is Mother Teresa, Martin Luther King, and Billy Graham. Why those three? What did they give you and what happened?"*

Rick Warren: *"Well, the only one who's missing was Pope John Paul II. Those four people were the greatest influences from the 20th century, without a doubt."*

Interviewer: *"The Vatican recently sent a delegation here to Saddleback, The Pontifical Council, or the Academy for Life Academy. Tell me what they discovered and why did they come. This was a sizable group."*

Rick Warren: *"It was. There were about 30 bishops from Europe. One of the men who had been actually trained and mentored by John Vanier, which is an interesting thing, because we have a retreat center here and my spiritual director, who actually grew up here at Saddleback, went and trained under John Vanier, too. So, I'm very excited about that. But they were talking about the new evangelization, and Saddleback has been very effective in reaching this secular mindset. So, we figured out a way to* *reach that mindset, and I fully support the Catholic Church's new evangelization."*

Interviewer: *"Tell me about the little breather you take on the day when you watch television, which surprised me. When we first met, you came up to me and said, 'Hey, Raymond.' And I said I can't believe you watched this."*

Rick Warren: *"You know, I'm an avid fan of EWTN. I make no bones about it. I probably watch it more than any Christian channel. Because it happens to have one of my favorite shows, which you replay often, it's the Chaplet of Divine Mercy, really which I love. When I've had a very stressful day, I'll come home, I've got it taped, and Kay and I will both listen. We'll put it on and just sit back and relax, worship, and in that time of reflection, meditation, quietness, I find myself renewed and restored. Thank you for continuing to replay the Chaplet of Divine Mercy."*

Interviewer: *"Thank Mother Angelica."*

Rick Warren: *"Thank you Mother Angelica."*

What were his words? You Love the Pope, you said, "Our Pope" and "Us Christians," and you actually have his picture on your wall as a source of inspiration? You are actually helping them to evangelize. And then when you have a stressful day, you and your wife sit down and watch Mother Angelica and the show that she has called the Chaplet of Divine Mercy. And that helps you to unwind. And their channel, the Catholic channel, is what you watch most above all of Christian TV, even though it's not Christian.

And for those of you wondering, who is this Mother Angelica and what's this show he winds down with his wife…here it is. The Chaplet of Divine Mercy! This is not a conspiracy theory. He admitted that he and his wife watch this, more than anything else, to help them unwind after a stressful day.

This video opens with a priest crossing himself and saying, *"In the name of the Father and of the Son and of the Holy Spirit, Amen.* [the congregation is also reciting along with him.] *You expired, Jesus, but the source of Life gushed forth for souls and the ocean of mercy opened up for the whole world. Font of Life Unfathomable Divine Mercy, envelope the whole world and empty yourself out upon us."*

Mother Angelica: *"In the name of the Father and the Son and the Holy Spirit."*

Group of nuns: *"Amen."*

Mother Angelica: *"Hail Mary, full of grace, the Lord is with thee. Blessed art thou among women and blessed is the fruit of thy womb, Jesus."*

The group of nuns then repeat their words.

Mother Angelica: *"Hail Mary, full of grace, the Lord is with thee. Blessed art thou among women and blessed is the fruit of thy womb, Jesus."*

Again, the group of nuns repeat their words.

Mother Angelica repeats these words a third time.

Now that is freaky. I don't know you personally. I was waiting for Freddy Krueger to pop out of the corner. It's not just freaky, that's a show. And that is what Rick Warren says is his favorite channel, he watches more than anything else and specifically when he has had a rough day, he and his wife sit down and watch mindlessly repetitive Catholic prayers to Mary, and flipping through the Rosary. Are you serious?! Now here's my obvious question. When push comes to shove and an announcement goes out across the world, officially, for the sake of whatever, maybe out of some crisis and the Pope says we all need to combine our religions together, even the Protestant Church, do you think Rick Warren is going to resist? Joel Osteen? Beth Moore and the gang? A lot of folks in the charismatic community?

It isn't just the unfortunate news that yes, there are enemies in the church. And yes, they have taken over the last several decades - the seminaries, Bible colleges, denominations, and churches. And yes, they've come in and perverted the truth. But they are all working towards a common goal called a One World Religion and those that claim to be Protestants are already working together with the Vatican who wants to be the headquarters. And here's what's really scary, these guys aren't just chumming up with the Vatican, they are converting to Catholicism. Pastors. Here is one example:

Narrator: *"Larry Lewis is one of a growing number of individuals who converted."*

Larry Lewis: *"I was a Protestant minister for over 30 years in different areas of ministry and I was very content, happy, thrilled about it actually. And then pastoring in the United Methodist Church, in the middle of my pastorate there, we were kind of blindsided by The Blessed Mother. She kind of came out of nowhere and really began to turn our whole lives around."*

Narrator: *"Stephen Barham, a popular speaker at various conferences attended Assemblies of God before becoming a priest."*

Stephen Barham: *"The content is the same basic structure as the gospel. Repent, we convert, fast, pray, pray for the renewal of the church, go back to the sacraments."*

Go back to the Sacraments? That's not the Gospel! Methodist, Charismatic, are you seeing a pattern? Those two are already showing major signs of going along with this liberal agenda. You can accept anything and can't we just all get along? Now they are taking the next step. "Why don't we just go back to Catholicism?" It's nuts. The Rise of a

One World Religion with even the "professing" Protestant Church getting sucked right into it, is happening right now before our very eyes.

So, they converted back to a works-based religion. And that means they lost their salvation. No! They never had it in the first place. What does the Scripture say?

1 John 2:19: "They went out from us, but they did not really belong to us. For if they had belonged to us, they would have remained with us; but their going showed that none of them belonged to us."

So that means, those guys, both professed to be Christians, both professed to be Protestant pastors, in Protestant denominations, and the whole time they were faking. And eventually they showed their true colors. This is where we are headed with this reality.

And that's why Jesus warned, "Watch out that no one deceives you. Many false prophets will appear (Be it the Pope, or the Vatican, the Charismatic Community, Kenneth Copeland, Beth Moore, Joel Osteen, or even Rick Warren) and deceive many."

"If at that time if anyone says to you, 'Look, here is the Christ!' or "Look, follow the Catholic Church, look accept homosexuality, look, become One with All Religions," do not believe it. Why? Because "False Christs and false prophets will appear and perform great signs and miracles to deceive even the elect – if that were possible. See, I have told you ahead of time." In other words, YOU WERE WARNED 2,000 years ago!

You and I cannot be fooled by anyone, ever. Not even this last day's influx of enemies in the church. Scripture alone tells us where it's all headed. It's not just an unfortunate thing. It's not just a hostile takeover. The Bible says, that's where it's headed. Don't listen to these fakers…the ENEMIES WITHIN… just stick with the Bible and Bible Prophecy, and God's Word, nobody can deceive you. That's the value of never, ever, ever budging from the Scripture.

How to Receive Jesus Christ:

1. Admit your need (I am a sinner).
2. Be willing to turn from your sins (repent).
3. Believe that Jesus Christ died for you on the Cross and rose from the grave.
4. Through prayer, invite Jesus Christ to come in and control your life through the Holy Spirit. (Receive Him as Lord and Savior.)

What to pray:

Dear Lord Jesus,

I know that I am a sinner and need Your forgiveness. I believe that You died for my sins. I want to turn from my sins. I now invite You to come into my heart and life. I want to trust and follow You as Lord and Savior.

In Jesus' name. Amen.

Notes

https://enemieswithinthechurch.com/
https://get.dailywire.com/wiaw/subscribe?utm_campaign=wiaw&utm_medium=paid&utm_source=bing&utm_content=na_subscriptions&cid=wiaw&mid=b&xid=0&utm_term=matt%20walsh%20what%20is%20a%20woman&utm_campaign=&utm_source=bing&utm_medium=ppc&hsa_acc=6411461344&hsa_cam=429594023&hsa_grp=1326012504412860&hsa_ad=&hsa_src=s&hsa_tgt=kwd-82876595724471:loc-190&hsa_kw=matt%20walsh%20what%20is%20a%20woman&hsa_mt=e&hsa_net=adwords&hsa_ver=3&msclkid=56252383adbb12cecfaa4036657a0a84
http://bible.crosswalk.com
http://www.bible.org/illus/h/h-25.htm)
http://www.sermons.org/hell1.html)
http://www.worldofquotes.com/topic/Hell/1/)
http://www.anzwers.org/free/lastwords/)
http://www.anzwers.org/free/lastwords/)
John MacArthur, Jr., *The Love of God*
(Dallas: Word Publishing, 1996, Pg. 146)
http://www.strato.net/~w5mav/wisdom/crucifixion.htm)
http://www.bible.org/illus/c/c-156.htm)
http://www.pastorshelper.com/wwjd/wwjd1.html)
http://www.holmescountyherald.com/1editorialbody.lasso?-token.folder=2004-04-07&-token.story=79053.112112&-nothing)
http://www.bible.org/illus/g/g-70.htm#TopOfPage)
http://www.bible.org/illus/g/g-70.htm#TopOfPage)
http://www.bible.org/illus/o/o-01.htm#TopOfPage)
Roy B. Zuck, *The Speaker's Quote Book*,
(Grand Rapids: Kregel Publications, 1997, Pg. 236)
John MacArthur, *Commentary on the Book of Romans 1-8*,
(Chicago: Moody Press, 1991, Pg. 392)
http://www.bible.org/illus/m/m-15.htm#TopOfPage)

http://www.bible.org/illus/m/m-15.htm#TopOfPage)
http://www.bible.org/illus/m/m-15.htm#TopOfPage)
http://www.bible.org/illus/g/g-49.htm#TopOfPage)
Roy B. Zuck, *The Speaker's Quote Book*,
(Grand Rapids: Kregel Publications, 1997, Pg. 383)
https://www1.cbn.com/cbnnews/us/2016/june/southern-baptist-convention-supports-mosque-draws-criticism 2/4 worship
http://http://www.economist.com/blogs/erasmus/2016/06/buildingmosques-america
https://www.healthline.com/health/different-types-of-sexuality
https://www.gotquestions.org/pedophilia.html
https://www.google.com/search?q=definition+catamite&rlz=1C1RXQR_enUS939US939&oq=definition+catamite&aqs=chrome..69i57j0i22i30l9.3530j1j7&sourceid=chrome&ie=UTF-8
https://www.reddit.com/r/changemyview/comments/hvz0sj/cmv_zoosexuality_is_a_valid_sexuality/
https://www.youtube.com/watch?v=-WpPYJljV7o
https://www.dshnyc.org/staff-and-storytellers
https://www.youtube.com/watch?v=H_wewFd29Qo
https://www.youtube.com/watch?v=Tb1B3Xbe3LI
https://www.huffpost.com/entry/gary-hall-national-cathedral-homobia-is-a-sin_n_4057614
https://www.youtube.com/watch?v=tcrfeukScK8
https://www.youtube.com/watch?v=gTYL0LtaghE&t=4s
https://www.facebook.com/prophecywatchers/videos/amazing-sulfur-destruction-of-sodom-and-gomorrah-discovered/546085916926061/